PRAISE FOR SAM HORN'S *ConZentrate*

"*ConZentrate* helps you fast-focus your infinite energies to get extraordinary results—right here, right now."
—Mark Victor Hansen, cocreator of
Chicken Soup for the Soul

"Does your train of thought ever go off-track? Then you need *ConZentrate*! A remarkably readable book with simple and sustainable solutions to get your mind going in the right direction again."
—Allen Klein, author of *The Healing
Power of Humor*

"*ConZentrate* is perfect for people who multitask all day long. This book teaches us how to focus on what's most important—even when we've got a two-page To Do List and three projects that were due yesterday. Now that's progress."
—Daniel Burrus, author of *Technotrends*

"Finally...a book with *practical* suggestions on how to stay focused when we are juggling different projects."
—Martin Edelston, President,
Boardroom Inc.

"For the sake of your health, your work, your family, and your love, read this insightful, informative, and funny book about the art and science of being fully alive before you die."
—Paul Pearsall, Ph.D., author of *The
Pleasure Principle* and *Wishing Well*

"At the very center of proactive and happy lives is the cultivation and control of thought. Sam Horn provides very fun, practical, and helpful suggestions to help cultivate productive thoughts."
—A. Roger Merrill, coauthor of *First
Things First* and *The Nature of
Leadership*

"Employing an accessible, succinct format, Horn successfully shows readers how to sharpen their minds."
—*Publishers Weekly*

"Strikes the right balance between practicality and spirituality...Easy to read with a lively style and literally jammed with common sense and usable insights. Get it for all your over-scheduled friends, but only after you give it to yourself!"
>—David Kundtz, author of *Stopping* and
Everyday Serenity

"Sam Horn has written a gem of a book. Full of imagination and energy, this book will help all who read it and entertain and enrich them as well. The Zen of concentration—such an important skill to master in these disconnected, fast-paced times—'ConZentrates' the mind of anyone who reads this terrific new book."
>—Edward M. Hallowell, M.D., author of
Connect, Worry, and *Driven to Distraction*

"*ConZentrate* is a light at the end of the tunnel of the chronic confusion, distractions, and conflicting priorities so many struggle with daily. Sam Horn breaks down the complexities and offers practical solutions."
>—Victoria Moran, author of *Creating a
Charmed Life*

"Sam's wise, wonderful, and insightful book is an anchor for those of us adrift in life's undertow. I cannot think of anyone who would not find it useful in every day life."
>—Jonathon Lazear, author of *Meditations
For Men Who Do Too Much* and
*Remembrance of Father: Words to Heal
the Heart*

"Packed with innovative ideas you can use and see results immediately. Do you want to learn how to pay attention to the important things in life while you laugh out loud? Read this book."
>—Mary LoVerde author of *Stop Screaming
at the Microwave*

"Certainly 'ConZentration' is a major key to getting organized, and Sam's book offers practical tips and techniques."
>—Barbara Hemphill, author of *Taming the
Paper Tiger*

ConZentrate

Also by Sam Horn

Tongue Fu!®

What's Holding You Back?

ConZentrate

Get Focused and Pay Attention—
When Life Is Filled with Pressures,
Distractions, and Multiple Priorities

Sam Horn

ST. MARTIN'S GRIFFIN   NEW YORK

CONZENTRATE. Copyright © 2000 by Sam Horn. All rights reserved. Printed in the United States of America. No part of this book may be used or reproduced in any manner whatsoever without written permission except in the case of brief quotations embodied in critical articles or reviews. For information, address St. Martin's Press, 175 Fifth Avenue, New York, N.Y. 10010.

www.stmartins.com

Design by Maureen Troy

ISBN 0-312-19847-7 (hc)
ISBN 0-312-27010-0 (pbk)

First St. Martin's Griffin Edition: February 2001

10 9 8 7 6 5 4 3 2 1

CONTENTS

◉

Acknowledgments

◉

When you drink the water, remember the well.

—Chinese proverb

Anyone who has written a book understands why authors often thank a long list of benefactors. Friends, family, and associates sustain us during the couple of up-and-down years it takes to finish a manuscript. We are so full of gratitude when our project is finally finished, we want to make sure they know how much their efforts on our behalf are appreciated.

So, a heartfelt *mahalo* (Hawaiian for "thank you") to the following individuals for being a wellspring of strength, support, and humor.

Cheri Grimm, my sister and business partner, for her wisdom, initiative, and balancing perspective, and for continuing to be there for me in more ways than I could possibly express.

Jennifer Enderlin, a dream editor, whose patience, insights, compassion, and expertise continue to exceed my expectations and fondest hopes.

Laurie Liss, my "I can't believe I'm so lucky to have her represent me" agent, who brings so much to the table and helps me realize my professional goals.

Diane Gerard and Gerald Tomory, Shannon and John Tullius, Denise Moreland, Sara Harvey, Mary Loverde, Karen Waggoner, Gar DuBois, Ann Petrus, Maryellen Lipinski, Leslie Charles, Maggie Bedrosian, Sue Murray, Rebecca Morgan, Dorothy Douthit, Leslie Duvall, copy editor extraordinaire Nancy Inglis, and my sons, Tom and Andrew Horn. Thank you all for keeping me smiling, reminding me to practice what I preach, and for helping me ConZentrate on what's most important—enduring friendships.

Introduction

Would you like to be able to keep your mind on what you're doing—even while phones are ringing, people are walking back and forth, and you've got seven other projects competing for your attention? Would you like to know how to set up the state of flow so you can perform your best? Would you like to learn how to be "here and now," instead of "here, there, and everywhere"?

You're in the right place, then, because that's what this book covers. I know you're busy, so I promise not to waste your time on theories. Theories don't help much when we're trying to ConZentrate on something and our mind is a million miles away. You'll learn how to focus on *what* you want, *when* you want, for *as long as* you want. You'll also discover how to:

- Lengthen your attention span and keep your mind from wandering
- ConZentrate in a chaotic office—despite DNI (distractions, noise, interruptions)
- Stay on task even if you have ADD or ADHD
- Switch from project to project (without losing your mind or sense of humor)
- Motivate yourself to pay attention when you're tired, bored, or overwhelmed
- Have peace of mind anywhere, anytime
- Access and sustain the exquisite state of ConZonetration
- Block out bothersome thoughts
- Improve your ability to remember names, data, and daily details

I've had fun writing this book, and I hope you have fun reading it. I've divided it into "read bites"—short chunks of *self-contained* information—so you can dip into it and derive value even if you only have a few minutes to spare. I've also packed the pages with laugh-out-loud anecdotes, thought-provoking quotes, and inspiring success stories so you can see how other people have already applied these ideas and benefited from them.

In L. Frank Baum's classic *Wizard of Oz*, the Scarecrow desperately wants to be given a brain. The false Wizard promises him, "If you will come to me tomorrow morning, I will stuff your head with brains. I cannot tell you how to use them, however; you must find that out for yourself." If you're ready to learn how to use your brain (what Woody Allen called his "second most favorite organ"); if you're ready to learn how to pay attention to what's really important at work, home, and school, in relationships, sports, and life; turn the page and let's grow.

PART 1

Want to Get a Head?

Life consists of what a man is
thinking all day.

—Ralph Waldo Emerson

WAY 1

◉

What Is ConZentration, Anyway?

Every time I ask what time it is, I get a different answer.

—Henny Youngman

I know how Youngman feels. Every time I ask people what concentration is, I get a different answer. Former New York Mets manager Wes Westrum said, "Baseball is like church. Many attend, but few understand." Concentration is like that. We do it every day, but up until now, few of us have understood exactly what it means or appreciated the pivotal role it plays in almost everything we do. The following five definitions incorporate both the traditional interpretation of the word and my new approach to this all-important skill.

As you read these definitions, please think back to a specific time you experienced that type of ConZentration. Remember where you were and what you were doing. Re-experience how good it felt to focus so clearly and comprehensively.

1. ConZentration is the ability to be single-minded. Charles Dickens described a character in one of his books this way: "He did each single thing as if he did nothing else." Focusing on one task can be a challenge because we often have many different things to do. That's why it's important to understand that ConZentration means *temporarily* ignoring less important obligations. Deferring other projects doesn't mean they're not important, just not as important as the priority we've selected right now.

2. ConZentration is interest in action. What did the Zen practitioner say to the hot dog vendor? "Make me one with everything." Can you think of a time you were so engrossed in what you were doing, you became one with it? Perhaps you were reading a good novel, playing chess, or gardening. Remember what an exquisite experience it was to lose yourself in that activity? Athletes call this the zone, that blissful state in which we're not even thinking about what we're doing, we're just doing it. When we're enthralled, captivated, or spellbound, we are in a state of flow, or as the poet Virgil observed, "all aglow in the work."

3. ConZentration is mental obedience. Do you sometimes suffer from "mind mutiny"? One student laughed upon hearing this definition and said, "Sometimes my mind acts like a rebellious teenager. I tell it what to do, and it ignores me." ConZentration is the power to make our mind do what *we* want, rather than letting it do what *it* wants.

4. ConZentration is cerebral staying power. Noel Coward commented, "Thousands of people have talent. I might as well congratulate you for having eyes in your head. The one and only thing that counts is: 'Do you have staying power?' "

Bryce Courtenay, author of the best-selling novel *The Power of One*, was asked by a Maui Writers Conference attendee, "What's the secret to being a great writer?" Courtenay replied in his dramatic, gravelly voice, "*Bum glue.* Nothing beats sitting at your desk and writing until it comes out right."

Famous philosophers throughout time have arrived at the same conclusion: mental tenacity—the ability to persist in a "state, enterprise, or undertaking in spite of counterinfluences, opposition, or discouragement"—is the key to attaining what we want in life. As Seneca said, "There is nothing which persevering effort and unceasing and diligent care cannot accomplish."

5. ConZentration is mindfully managing our T.I.M.E. (Thoughts, Interest, Moments, Emotions). Please note the new definition of T.I.M.E. Traditionally, we've measured time in days, months, and years. Wouldn't you agree, though, that when we think back over our life, we don't remember days, months, or years; we remember *moments*. Specifically, those moments in which our thoughts, interest, and emotions were fully engaged in a person, place, or process.

While developing the concept of ConZentration, I reached an interesting conclusion. If we reframe our concept of time, we can remove our compulsion to race through life. Instead of thinking there's never enough time, we realize we have all the time we're going to get . . . right now. We come to understand the best way to make the most of our time, is to make the most of this moment.

American psychologist and philosopher William James said, "Our experience is what we attend to." In other words, our life consists of what we pay attention to. If we focus on meaningful, positive things, we'll have a meaningful, positive life. If we focus on meaningless, negative things, we'll have a meaningless, negative life. Yes, this is simplistic. It is also enduringly profound and one of life's great truths. As Buddha said, "We are what we think. All that we are arises with our thoughts."

In the final analysis, the quality of our life depends on our ability to consciously choose who and what we give our Thoughts, Interest, Moments, and Emotions to.

Examples of ConZentration

For one who has conquered the mind, the mind is the best of friends. But for one who has failed to do so, his very mind will be the greatest enemy.
—Bhagavad Gita

Seminar participants often ask for a good example of ConZentration. One of the best demonstrations of ConZentration I ever witnessed was years ago in New York's Grand Central Station on a busy Easter weekend. For some reason, only one person was manning the octagonal information booth in the center of the concourse. Travelers were running up from all sides, pounding on the glass windowpanes, waving their arms, and yelling, "Where's Track 19?" "How do I catch the train to Connecticut?" "Can I purchase my ticket on the train?"

By all rights, the employee should have been a nervous wreck. Instead, he was the picture of ConZentration. Why? He was calmly giving his complete attention to the individuals who had waited in line, instead of chaotically trying to serve everyone at once. He was the personification of all five definitions of ConZentration. He was *single-minded*, putting his *interest in action* and making his *mind obey*. He was courteously *controlling* these very stressful circumstances and *mindfully managing his T.I.M.E.* He persisted in giving unceasing and diligent attention despite a confusing environment that was doing its best to tear him to mental pieces.

Focus and Flow

At times I think and at times I am.
—Paul Valéry

ConZentration is a *focus* we facilitate and a *flow* we fall into. One is a thinking "doing" state, the other is a nonthinking "being" state. One requires exertion (we ConZentrate on studying for a test) and the other is effortless (we get caught up in a movie and lose track of time). You'll learn how to do both in this book.

When was the last time you experienced the congruent state of focus and flow when everything was right with the world? Perhaps you were sharing a holiday meal at the dinner table with your family. Everyone was in good spirits and good health, and you were flooded with a sense of gratitude. Maybe you were skiing through fresh powder snow on a beautiful blue-sky day. Your knees were pumping on the turns and bouncing over moguls, and you were in a state of pure exhilaration. Perhaps you got caught up in reading a romantic novel; hours went by and you weren't even aware of it.

What those experiences had in common was ConZentration. You were completely immersed in and connected with what you were doing. Alan Watts said, "This—the immediate, everyday, and present experience—is IT, the entire and ultimate point for the existence of a universe." ConZentration helps us focus on and in the moment, instead of frantically rushing from moment to moment.

Action Plan 1. What Is ConZentration, Anyway?

I used to think the human brain was the most fascinating part of the body, and then I realized, "What is telling me that?"

—comedian Emo Phillips

I still think the human brain is the most fascinating part of the body, and you will too as soon as you start noticing how exquisite experiences can be and how effective you are when you give things your full attention.

Today's assignment is to increase your awareness of the many different ways you focus during the day. Consciously catch yourself ConZentrating. Put your interest in action by savoring every tangy bite of a crunchy apple. Discipline your mind to stick with an unpleasant chore and experience the satisfaction that comes from a job well done. Turn on your answering machine when you get home and control your T.I.M.E. by enjoying an evening at home without interruptions.

When an interviewer asked TV newscaster Diane Sawyer the secret to her success, she said, "I think the one lesson I have learned is that there is no substitute for paying attention." Promise yourself you'll accept no substitutes. Resolve today to "give notice," and you will reap the rewards of a day lived mindfully versus mindlessly.

Confusion	ConZentration
We pay attention to everything "Look at this to-do list. I don't know where to start."	*We pay attention to one thing* "I'm going to get this letter written and mailed."
We're apathetic about what we're doing "This is the most boring book. It's a total waste of time."	*We're interested in what we're doing* "I'm going to learn one new thing from this book."
We have mind mutiny "I don't feel like working on this project."	*We have mind mastery* "I'll work on this project for one hour."

Confusion	**ConZentration**
Other people control our T.I.M.E. "Uh, yeah, I guess I'll chair that committee, since you can't get anyone else."	*We control our T.I.M.E.* "I won't be able to take that job, but I'd like to recommend Bob."
We give up when the going gets tough "I'm tired. I'll complete that budget report Monday. What's an extra day?"	*We persevere when the going gets tough* "I'm tired, but I'm going to finish that report and turn it in on time."

WAY 2

◉

If You Don't Mind

We are the hurdles we leap to be ourselves.

—Michael McClure

Some participants attend my workshops out of self-proclaimed desperation. "I'm losing my mind," they say half seriously. "I can't ConZentrate," they claim.

I share the good news that in almost every instance, an inability to ConZentrate isn't caused by a mechanical failure of the brain. It's not that they *can't* ConZentrate; either they're doing something that's undermining their ability to focus or they're *not* doing something that would enable them to focus. If they identify and fix that fault, they'll be able to fix their attention on what they want, when they want.

Blockheads

Do not look where you fell, but where you slipped.
—African proverb

The following twelve ConZentration no-nos are the obstacles that keep us from paying attention as perfectly as we'd like. As you read through them, ask yourself which have been compromising your ConZentration. In the future, instead of getting frustrated if you can't ConZentrate, stop and notice where you slipped up. Once you've identified what's wrong, figure out how to go around that block and you'll free up your ability to focus.

Block 1. No privacy. Science fiction author Isaac Asimov said, "Nothing interferes with my concentration. You could put on an orgy in my office and I wouldn't look up. Well, maybe once." Many of us have the exact opposite situation. *Everything* interferes with our concentration. Our workplace is such an orgy of distractions and interruptions, we look up every other minute to see what's happening. Do your surroundings support or sabotage your efforts to stay focused?

Block 2. No instruction. I've asked thousands of people if anyone ever taught them how to ConZentrate. Only a handful have said yes. Most of us had the mental equivalent of being thrown into deep water and told to "think or swim." ConZentration is a *skill*, much like playing a musical instrument or using a computer. We can't expect to do it well if we've never been instructed how.

Block 3. No discipline or patience. Helen Keller said, "We can do anything we want if we stick to it long enough." Unfortunately, some people don't stick to much of anything. They've adopted Carrie Fisher's tongue-in-cheek philosophy that "instant gratification takes too long." They've developed what's called a low frustration tolerance, the unhealthy habit of abandoning activities as soon as they become uninteresting or unpleasant. As Robert Byrne describes it, "there are two kinds of people; those who finish what they start, and those who . . . "

Block 4. No clear order or plan. Robert Frost quipped, "I'm not confused, I'm well mixed." If your mind is confused about what it's supposed to do, it usually doesn't do anything. It can't ConZentrate if it is given:

- no order ("I really need to work through that in-basket" isn't an order, it's wishful thinking.)
- a negatively stated order ("I don't want to forget that appointment.")

- an impossible-to-achieve order ("I'm going to study all night so I can ace that test.")
- too many orders ("I'm going to listen to these language tapes while fixing lunch, monitoring the kids in the pool, and cleaning the kitchen.")
- contrary orders ("I'm going to stop smoking today, but it's okay to have a few cigarettes while I'm playing poker with my friends.")

Block 5. No energy. F. Scott Fitzgerald once said, "Suffice it to say that after about an hour of solitary pillow-hugging, I began to realize that for two years of my life I had been drawing on resources I did not possess, that I had been mortgaging myself physically and spiritually up to the hilt." Do you sometimes feel you've been mortgaging yourself to the hilt? Are you running on empty? ConZentration is directed mental energy. It's hard to direct mental energy if we're exhausted and don't have any.

Block 6. No one-track mind. "Who do they think I am?" Leonard Bernstein once exclaimed. "Everybody?" People with a peripatetic ("movement hither and thither") schedule find it almost impossible to focus on one think at a time. Type A people and those with ADD (attention deficit disorder) have hyperactive minds that go, go, go all the time. As one woman described it, "I have one speed—all-out." Such people find it hard to stay focused because their butterfly brains constantly flit from one thing to the next.

Block 7. Nobody home. Other people have a brain that ruminates more than it races. When asked what she thought of the city of Oakland, California, Gertrude Stein said, "There's no there, there." Daydreamers can relate to this: they are physically present, but their minds are often elsewhere (hence the word "absent-minded"). Part 8 of this book suggests specific steps people can take to stay O.N. T.A.S.K. despite spaciness or a mind that's going a mile a minute.

Block 8. No interest. "If you only care enough for a result," thought William James, "you will almost certainly attain it." A fundamental rule of human behavior is that action requires incentive. The mind needs stimulus to start. In other words, if our heart's not in it, our head won't be in it. You may be thinking, "I'm in trouble, then, because I've got to ConZentrate on things I don't care about." Rest assured. Part 3 covers a variety of ways to *arbitrarily* provide interest so you can focus when you don't feel like it.

Block 9. No belief. When Yoda levitates a spaceship in *The Empire Strikes Back,* Luke says, "I don't believe it." Yoda replies, "That is why you fail." The reason some of us can't ConZentrate is because we *believe we can't.* When skeptics walk into my seminars and claim, "I've *never* been able to focus," I ask them to think of a time they concentrated well. It could be the time they stayed up all night to finish a term paper . . . and only became aware of the time when the morning paper plunked against their front door. One women said she ConZentrated *very* intensely . . . while giving birth!

Maybe they were in a survival situation and had to ConZentrate or else. I'll always remember the scary story a cave diver told the class about the time he switched over to his second oxygen tank, only to find it almost empty. He realized he had less than five minutes to find his way back out of the cave and up to the surface before he ran out of air. He related how, instead of panicking (which would have scrambled his brain and used even more of his precious little oxygen), he had the presence of mind to first take a few seconds to mentally retrace the route he had taken in. He knew he had only one chance, so he ConZentrated with all his power at every junction to make sure he took the right turn. He realized his ability to face up fully in that frightening situation saved his life.

In the twenty years I have been asking this question, *everyone* has been able to think of at least one occasion in which they focused completely on someone or something. It doesn't have to be a situation as dire as the one the cave diver found himself in. It can be something as simple as becoming engrossed in a video game. Identifying an occasion where they've ConZentrated well helps people drop their self-limiting label so they can approach ConZentration with an open mind. The truth is, *everyone* can

ConZentrate—maybe not every time we want, maybe not as long as we want, but we can do it.

Block 10. No frequent practice. Just as a couch potato wouldn't be able to jump out of his La-Z-Boy lounger and run a half-marathon, a couch potato head can't expect to ConZentrate on command if he's been mentally lazy. If we want to be in good physical condition, we need to exercise our body frequently. If we want to be in good psychological condition, we need to exercise our brain frequently. Many retirees tell me they're afraid of losing mental acumen as they get older. I tell them studies on aging show senior citizens can stay sharp if they *regularly* involve themselves in cerebrally challenging activities that require complex thinking. In other words, a decreased ability to ConZentrate is more often a result of the brain rusting out, not wearing out.

Block 11. No right. "Sometimes when you look in his eyes," noted David Letterman, "you get the feeling someone else is driving." Are you ConZentrating on *your* priorities? Or are you a people pleaser who lets other people drive your life? Some people know they're focusing on the wrong things, but they don't want to disappoint friends, hurt family members, or alienate customers and coworkers, so they "go along to get along" and end up saying yes to T.I.M.E.-consuming commitments when they would rather say no. The result of all this? A life that is not their own.

Block 12. No commitment. "To affect the quality of the day," observed Henry David Thoreau, "that is the art of life." Unfortunately, many people entertain any and every thought that comes to mind, even those that adversely affect the quality of their day. Either they don't realize they're thinking by default, not design, or they are not disciplined enough to focus on thoughts that serve, rather than sabotage, them. Perhaps it's simply never occurred to them they need to learn how to think proactively—that this just doesn't happen by itself.

You're different. Robert Louis Stevenson said, "To become what we are capable of becoming is the only end of life." By reading this book and making a commitment to improve your ConZentration, you are taking steps to become more of what you're capable of being.

◉

Action Plan 2. If You Don't Mind

I know of no more encouraging fact than the unquestionable ability of man to elevate his life by a conscious endeavor.

—Henry David Thoreau

A clever student once quipped, "It seems like I'm a blockhead because I do all these ConZentration no-nos. Is there hope for me?" His question gave me a perfect opportunity to share Martin Luther's encouraging quote: "Everything in the world is done by hope." I reassured him by saying that people who hope to elevate their ability to ConZentrate can—if they make a conscious endeavor to leap these hurdles instead of crash into them.

It's time to determine which of these culprits have been blocking your attempts to ConZentrate. Review the twelve obstacles and identify which have been undermining your mental efforts. Understand, once and for all, that you can rule your mind . . . if you knock these blocks off.

Confusion	ConZentration
Distracting, chaotic space "I can't get anything done with all this noise."	*Private, uncluttered place* "I'm going to the library so I can work without interruption."
Think or swim "I know I'm supposed to ConZentrate, but I don't know how."	*Training in ConZentration* "I'm going to read ten minutes of this book every night."
Instant gratification "This is taking too much time. I'm so frustrated, I'm quitting."	*Delayed gratification* "I know it won't happen immediately, but I'm going to persevere."

Confusion	ConZentration
Confused purpose or no plan "I'm just going to jump in and figure it out as I go along."	*Clear purpose and plan* "I'm going to think things through so I know how to proceed."
Exhausted and ill "I can't focus on this. I am too tired."	*Energetic and fit* "I'm raring to go."
ADD and/or hyperactivity "I'm bouncing off the walls. I have the attention span of a hummingbird."	*One think at a time* "I will tackle that later. For now, this has my full focus."
Absent-minded "I love to daydream. What would it be like to be married to Brad Pitt?"	*Attentive* "Yes, I heard your question. The answer to that is 1949."
Bored and unmotivated "I don't feel like studying right now. Calculus is a waste of time anyway."	*Incentive and interest* "I'm going to study now so I can score well on that test tomorrow."
Limiting labels "It's hopeless. I've always been a space cadet, and I'm always going to be a space cadet."	*Limitless labels* "I know I can change my mind—for good—if I apply myself."
Mental couch potato "Now that I'm retired, I'm going to take it easy and relax."	*Mentally active* "I'll keep my mind sharp by doing the daily crossword puzzle."
Otherhood "I really don't have time to help you with that budget report. Well, okay, if you insist."	*Appropriately assertive* "Sorry, I can't help you, Sue. I've got a budget report due, too, and I need to input this data."
Lack of commitment "What's the big deal about ConZentration? It can't be all that important."	*Make a commitment* "My mind is my future, and I'm going to make the most of it."

PART 2

Train Your Brain

If I look confused, it's because
I'm thinking.

—Samuel Goldwyn

WAY 3

◉

ConZentrate on Command

There is nothing so disobedient as an undisciplined mind,
and there is nothing so obedient as a disciplined mind.

—Buddha

Does your mind have a mind of its own? This chapter explains how to train our brain to obey orders so that it does what *we* want instead of what *it* wants.

While writing this book, I surprised my sons with the puppy they'd been wanting for years. Within days of getting our joyful, energetic Jack Russell, we realized he needed to be trained quickly or we were going to have a . . . *Reign of Terrier.* As long as we were playing with JR, our house was not at risk. If we weren't, everything was fair game. Shoes, socks, couch corners, table legs—nothing was safe. JR was constantly in motion, seeking the next, newest play toy.

This was a metaphor begging to happen. JR's distractibility was similar to that of our mind's. Our thoughts are also perpetually in motion, jumping from here to there, seeking mental playthings. As with JR, if we want control rather than chaos, we need to manage that mental energy.

Knowing this was one thing, accomplishing it was another. Jack Russells are known for being bullheaded. They're smart and friendly, but also willful and stubborn. We did the smart thing and signed him (and us) up for obedience school. That first night, we kept trying to get JR to do what *we* wanted (i.e., lie down, stay). Predictably, he kept doing what *he* wanted. (Hmm—just like our mind, eh?) We wanted him to sit; he wanted to play with the golden lab next to him. We ordered him to heel; he rolled over to get his tummy scratched.

If we had given up in those first few frustrating sessions, we'd still have a wild and crazy dog wreaking havoc wherever he went. His lovable traits wouldn't have been so lovable the third time he ruined a good pair of sandals or the umpteenth time we had to retrieve him from a neighbor's yard. We persisted with his training, though, because we knew the better he behaved, the more freedom we could give him. I'll say this another way because it's such a crucial point. The more disciplined JR became, the more independence he could have.

How so? If JR obeys our commands, he can run loose on the beach because we're confident he'll come when he's called. If we can trust him not to wander out on the street, he doesn't have to be kept on a chain. The better trained JR is, the happier he is and the happier we are. The same is true with our mind.

Mind Mastery or Mind Mutiny?

A reporter asked Brigadier General Wilma Vaught,
"What did you want to be when you grew up?"
Her quick response was "In charge."

Don't we all want to be in charge—of our mind? Yet, like JR, left to its own devices, free to wander *at* will instead of obeying *our* will, the mind can become our worst enemy. We need to be able to trust our mind to do what we tell it. If we're in a staff meeting and our mind is thinking about everything but the agenda, we need to be able to retrieve our thoughts so we can speak in complete sentences when it's our turn to talk.

One seminar attendee didn't quite grasp this concept. She asked, "Why do you talk about the mind as if it were a separate entity? My mind and I are one and the same, aren't they?" Well, technically speaking, yes. Practically speaking, no. There are dozens of books explaining the difference between our conscious mind and our subconscious/unconscious mind. What I've found in years of speaking on this topic is that most people know exactly what I mean when I talk about our mind having a mind of its own.

The mind (i.e., the reactive, child voice) is usually egotistical and indulgent. It thinks only of what it wants without regard to whether the action is fair, timely, or appropriate. Our self (the proactive, adult voice) considers the consequences of our behavior and strives to think wisely and act rationally.

For example, if you think, "I need to sit down and pay those bills tonight," that is your higher self speaking. That is the voice of reason reminding you to do the responsible thing. A funny thing happens, though, when you head toward the desk to extract your checkbook. Your mind (that little self-centered voice in your head) says, "The bills can wait. I'd rather watch TV." The mental gauntlet has been thrown down. What do you *do*? What *do* you do?

Our objective is to train our brain to obey the proactive voice—to do *what* we're supposed to, *when* we're supposed to, the *way* we're supposed to. Instead of giving in to the urge to indulge in and/or dwell on hedonistic or destructive impulses, we want to take the mental high road and ConZentrate on constructive thoughts, images, and actions. The next question, of course, is "How do we manage that?"

Fundamentals of ConZentration

What is called sustained voluntary attention is a repetition of successive efforts which brings back the topic to this mind.
—**William James**

We learn to sustain attention just like we learn to tie our shoes: by repeating the multistep process from beginning to end until we can do it *without thinking*. We give our mind an assignment, hold our mind on following that assignment, and bring our mind back to that assignment if it wanders. We do this over and over, until our mind obeys *without rebelling*.

The following **Five-Minute F.O.C.U.S.** exercise teaches our mind to behave. Doing this F.O.C.U.S. exercise every night for the next two weeks will train your mind to come when it's called.

F = Find a private place.   Isolate yourself and remove distractions. Sit in a comfortable chair; close your door; turn off the radio, TV, cell phone, or whatever distracts you. It works best to do this at the end of the day so you're not preoccupied with other obligations. If you're really tired, go ahead and get in bed. This exercise can help you get to sleep.

O = Order your mind   to focus on a succinct, positively phrased assignment. I recommend you repeat the four-word phrase "I'm good at ConZentration." Your assignment is to think of that for five minutes. Feel free to design your own personally meaningful sound bite.

C = Chant   your selected phrase silently or out loud. Commit your complete attention to this four-word statement. "I'm good at ConZentration, I'm good at ConZentration." Say it slowly, purposefully, rhythmically. Roll the words around in your mouth and mind. Close your eyes so you're not visually distracted. Intone the phrase as intensely as possible so that it's all you're thinking about.

U = Use thought stoppage.   The instant your mind considers something other than your given task, think "NO!" and return your attention to your chosen project. Don't criticize yourself for becoming distracted and don't tell yourself not to think about this distraction. Ironically, telling yourself not to notice something causes you to think about the very think you don't want to think about! Simply say no and bring your mind back by saying your assigned phrase wholeheartedly and whole-mindedly.

Feel free to create your own thought-stoppage key word. A techie friend of mine prefers to say "delete" or "cancel," which is her cue to erase the intrusive thought and fill her mind with her original assignment. Another friend who has studied Zen thinks saying no is too harsh and employs nonjudging awareness. If her mind strays, she gently observes the thought that's pulling her off track and releases it; then she focuses on her selected phrases more reverently.

S = Stick with it. Remember, giving up or getting frustrated accomplishes nothing. The key to success is consistency. If you continue to bring your mind back every time it gets off track, it learns it can't get away with disobedience. Your persistence will pay off because your mind will learn to stay focused on what you tell it to do, even if it has tempting alternatives.

What's the Point of the Five-Minute F.O.C.U.S. Exercise?

I am extraordinarily patient provided I get my own way in the end.
—Margaret Thatcher

Are you wondering what the purpose of all this is? The point is to patiently teach our mind to be one-pointed. The purpose is to practice bending our mind to *our* will instead of allowing it to wander *at will* . . . so we get our way in the end.

Don't expect immediate, perfect results. As the popular T-shirt says, "If at first you don't succeed, welcome to the club." You wouldn't expect to put on a pair of Rollerblades for the first time and zip effortlessly down the street. Nor can we expect, in these initial efforts, to ConZentrate perfectly the first time and every time.

The good news is, as with any skill, the more you practice, the better you get. If you practice in-line skating every day, you become a better skater. If you F.O.C.U.S. every evening, you become a better ConZentrator. Practice this exercise for the next two weeks, and your mind will say "Aye-aye!" when you give it an order.

Beneficial Brainwashing

Pride is the direct appreciation of oneself.
—Arthur Schopenhauer

ConZentration is the direct result of believing in oneself. The Five-Minute F.O.C.U.S. exercise benefits you in another way. The phrase "I'm good at ConZentration" is an *affirmation*—a statement in which we claim to possess and/or exhibit a *positive* quality. Some skeptics scoff at affirmations and write them off as pop psychology, but respected human behavior psychologist William James stated, "We act in accordance with our beliefs." If you see yourself as a klutz, every time you trip, you'll see it as proof you've got two left feet. A person who doesn't believe he's clumsy will simply think, "I stumbled," and will look for the crack in the sidewalk instead of automatically assuming he stumbled because he was uncoordinated.

Many people's self-talk (what they say to themselves all day, every day) is predominantly negative. "That was dumb." "I messed up again." "What a stupid thing to do." The point of affirmations is to reverse that destructive process by imprinting and thereby producing *constructive* beliefs and behaviors.

I believe affirmations are a type of *beneficial brainwashing*. Repeating the phrase "I'm good at ConZentration" does double duty—it gives us an opportunity to practice mind management and helps convince us we possess this advantageous characteristic. Drumming into our skull the belief that we're good at ConZentration accelerates our acquiring of this ability.

A clever student of mine took this idea one step further and substituted his own phrase: "I ConZentrate *easily* whenever I want." Rob said repeating that sentence helped him reformat his original perception that ConZentration was difficult to do. He said, "My vision of concentration used to be scrunching up my face, furrowing my brow, and trying real hard to focus." Saying "I ConZentrate *easily* whenever I want" changed that perception, allowing him to set up a state of relaxed ConZentration instead of giving himself a tension headache trying to force himself to focus. Try it and discover for yourself the truth of his innovative idea. Consciously repeating "I ConZentrate *easily* whenever I want" will predispose you to do just that.

If you're doubting the value of the Five-Minute F.O.C.U.S., all I ask is you try it when you go to bed tonight. What have you got to lose except a few minutes (and a pessimistic conclusion that this silly exercise won't work)? You're going to be lying there anyway; you might as well put your T.I.M.E. to good use. Invest five minutes a night and you can turn what one man called a spoiled-brat brain into a well-mannered mind. And yes, you can do this exercise silently so you can get your practice in even if you've got a partner who's sleeping.

Want to F.O.C.U.S. to an Advanced Degree?

Man's great misfortune is that he has no organ, no kind of eye-lid or brake, to mask or block a thought, or all thought, when he wants to.
—Paul Valéry

A martial artist asked, "Sam, I already meditate twenty minutes a day, so this will be pretty easy for me. Is there a graduate level of this exercise?"

I told him, "Yes, you can up the F.O.C.U.S. ante by introducing distractions. Do the same exercise, but open your eyes and look around while saying your four-word phrase. Repeat your affirmation with the radio playing. If you start humming along, simply say no and return to your original phrase. Say 'I'm good at ConZentration' more intensely and with exaggerated inflection. Say it loud, say it soft. Do everything you can to make your assignment so compelling there's no room in your thoughts for anything else. The goal is to keep your mind internally focused when your eyes and ears are outwardly focused. Continue practicing this until you can ConZentrate for five minutes despite a distracting environment."

He came back with another question. "What then? Are we just supposed to keep doing this exercise, or do we stop once we feel we've mastered the ability to make our mind mind?"

At about this point, I was thinking I should take this guy on the road with me because he was asking such great questions. I complimented him and then suggested, "Once you feel you can F.O.C.U.S. on command, start using this exercise as a skull session. Replace 'I'm good at ConZentration' with an affirmation that anchors a desired emotion for an upcoming situation. You might want to repeat the phrase 'I wake up refreshed and ready to go' if you have to get up early the next morning. Or use the five minutes to mentally prepare for an upcoming event. Perhaps you could plan a birthday party or rehearse remarks for a presentation you'll be giving the next day."

Author Dan Wakefield tells of participating in a tai chi class that was disrupted by a noisy group next door. He reports that at first he and his fellow students were annoyed with the disturbance until their teacher patiently explained these interruptions were typical of the unwanted distractions that dilute our concentration every day, and that the best response was simply to return to the form. Wakefield took this advice to heart: "There is no use lamenting whatever it is that yanks me physically or mentally or emotionally or spiritually out of a project. The words 'return to the form' are a way of dealing with upsets, the million large and small crises that tug and tear at us through the course of a day, a year, a career, a lifetime."

Wakefield is right: our goal is to devote five minutes of *undivided* thought time to a specific assignment. If your mind wanders ("I can't believe what Sue said to me today at the gym. The nerve!"), return to form. Say no to the irrelevant (for now) intrusion and refocus your mind on the original assignment. Contrary to what Paul Valéry said, we *do* have a tool for blocking out bothersome thoughts—this exercise.

Action Plan 3. ConZentrate on Command

Man's task is simple. He should cease letting his existence be a thoughtless accident.

—Friedrich Nietzsche

We can lead a more thoughtful existence by practicing this mind management exercise every evening before we go to sleep. This F.O.C.U.S. exercise is the first step towards learning how to consciously (instead of compulsively) choose what we pay attention to. Tonight, when you go to bed, use your head. Give your mind an assignment, and if it becomes distracted, return to form . . . again and again. Five minutes a night can help us acquire the skill to make our mind do what *we* want, instead of what *it* wants. Talk about a good use of our T.I.M.E.!

Confusion

Our mind wanders at will
"I don't want to listen to this teacher. I'm going to stare out the window and daydream."

Find fault
"This is a silly exercise. It will never work."

Order your mind to tackle the impossible dream
"I'm never going to let my mind wander again."

Criticize yourself because you can't ConZentrate
"I'm no good at this. I'll never learn how to stay focused."

Use willpower to not think about what you don't want to think about
"I'm not going to let those planes bother me. I will not think about those planes taking off."

Stop when frustrated
"I give up. This is so ridiculous. I can't feel any difference."

ConZentration

Our mind obeys our will
"I'm going to take notes on what the teacher is saying so I learn this."

Find privacy
"I'll sit in my favorite chair and do this right before going to bed."

Order your mind to do a specific positively phrased assignment
"I'm going to repeat 'I'm good at ConZentration' and think of that only for the next five minutes."

Chant your affirmation so you can ConZentrate
"I ConZentrate easily whenever I want."

Use thought stoppage and think about what you do want
"Those planes sure are making a lot of noise . . . I am good at ConZentration. I am good . . . "

Stick with it
"If I keep doing this every night, I know I'll experience improvement."

WAY 4

◎

Focus Pocus

REPORTER: What was it like having dinner at the White House?

YOGI BERRA: It was hard having a conversation because there were so many people talking.

Wouldn't it be great if there was a magic wand you could wave that could help you zoom in and ConZentrate despite distractions? There is, and it's called Focus Pocus.

One of the fundamental principles of ConZentration is **our attention is where our eyes are**. Our eyes and mind focus on whatever is in the center of our visual field. Anything on the periphery is vague unless we turn and gaze directly at it, thereby making it the object of our attention. If our eyes are fixed on one object, our mind will be focused on that object. If our eyes are shifting, our attention will probably be scattered. If our eyes are soft-focused, we're either lost in thought or not thinking about much of anything.

Picture your mind as a camera and your eyes as the aperture. Most of the time, our mind is employing a wide-angle lens so we can take everything in. We're constantly scanning our environment to note what's relevant, interesting, or threatening.

It's normal to think about many things when we're using that wide-angle lens. We can drive on the freeway while considering the chores we've got to do that night. We can watch our son's soccer game while chatting with a fellow parent. We can fold freshly laundered clothes while watching TV. We can operate fairly competently while attending to several things at once *if* (and this is a big if) none of these jobs demands our total attention.

There are times, though, when an activity or individual requires *complete* ConZentration. A brain surgeon must give a delicate operation 100 percent of his or her attention. A gymnast needs to be fully present when competing on the uneven bars. A student wants to be totally focused when taking his SATs. In situations as intense as these, we want to narrow our focus so our eyes operate like a telephoto lens. This can happen naturally (i.e., we zoom in on the face of someone we think we recognize from years ago), but most of the time we need to make a deliberate effort to achieve a one-track mind.

One-Track Mind

We succeed only as we identify in life . . . a single overriding
objective and make all other considerations bend
to that objective.
—Dwight D. Eisenhower

How do we set up a one-track mind? By singling out the object of our attention and making all other considerations disappear from view. The way to compress our attention is to give ourselves a hand.

We can use our hands as blinkers to train our mind's eye to tighten its focus. This physical gesture becomes a way to direct our mental traffic, just like a traffic cop directs vehicular traffic. Try this right where you're sitting. First, scan the room and look at five different items in your vicinity. Then select something close by that is visually appealing—perhaps a bouquet of flowers or a picture of someone you love. Place your hands on the side of your face and slowly bring them forward until they're cupped around your eyes and you see nothing but the flowers or photo.

This motion frames the object of your attention and blocks out your peripheral vision. It helps you to literally and figuratively lose sight of your surroundings so you can become totally absorbed in this one thing. Study your chosen article closely for one minute. Keep your mind in telephoto focus by silently asking yourself questions about the object: "Where was the picture taken?" "How many petals are on that rose?" Now take your hands away and let your eyes (and mind) roam the room again. Note different aspects of the furniture around you. You are now back in wide-angle focus.

Repeat the process of selecting a single item and zooming in on it with your eyes and mind. Experience how easy it is to switch to single-minded focus when you use your hands to physically eliminate your surroundings. From now on, if you want to ConZentrate on one thing in particular, say to yourself, "Focus Pocus." That will be your cue to use your hands as blinkers to give you tunnel vision so you can give total attention to the task at hand.

An insurance claims adjuster reported this method worked wonders for him. "I work in a large open office. I was having a hard time ConZentrating because of all the distractions. The day after your workshop, I tried this technique. When the commotion started to get to me, I cupped my hands around my eyes and gave myself tunnel vision. That simple step helped me stay focused on the paperwork in front of me instead of the people around me."

A man in the same session objected, "I'd feel silly doing this. My coworkers would think I had a headache or suspect I was taking a nap." Good point. Sometimes it's not appropriate or possible to use our hands as blinkers. I told him he could get much the same effect by *imagining* himself doing this. "You don't have to actually cup your hands around your eyes. You can give yourself a one-track mind by mentally holding your hands alongside your face and silently saying, 'Telephoto focus. *This* project, *this* project.'"

Want to Change Your Frame of Mind?

Every year of my life I grow more convinced that it is wisest
and best to fix our attention on the beautiful and the good and
dwell as little as possible on the evil and false.
—Cecil

There are times when, instead of shutting out our surroundings so we can set up single-minded focus, we want or need to do just the opposite. If our mind has become fixated on something that is not good for us, we want to reverse the Focus Pocus process. If you can't stop thinking about an unwanted subject, cup your hands around your eyes and slowly spread them out until they're extended to the side. This physical gesture opens your point of view and moves your mind *off* that obsessive irritant. Derail that negative train of thought by forcing yourself to notice what's around you. Say "Wide-Angle Focus," to yourself, and describe the characteristics of at least five different objects in your area. ConZentrating on items or individuals in your environment is a way to put thinks in perspective and give yourself a more balanced outlook.

I can vouch for this technique because it came in handy while finishing this book. I wrapped up this project over the '98 Christmas holidays while my sons were on the Mainland. Every waking moment was spent brainstorming, editing, and fine-tuning the chapters. I was blissfully caught up in the creative process. I was sleeping, breathing, dreaming about ConZentration. This state of writing reverie is welcome when working on deadline, but I had to pull myself out of it occasionally to re-enter the real world and take care of chores. How did I tear myself away? By tearing my eyes away from the computer monitor. Looking around the neglected house was all it took to remind me that things other than this manuscript needed my attention.

Remember, as long as our eyes stay put, our mind will, too. As soon as our eyes stray, our mind will follow. From now on, give yourself your desired frame of mind by giving yourself the corresponding field of vision. Next time you want to narrow your focus or change your point of view, use your "handy" tools to magically converge or diverge your attention.

Action Plan 4. Focus Pocus

The absence of alternatives clears the mind marvelously.

—Henry Kissinger

The ability to ignore alternatives clears the mind marvelously. Practice putting yourself in the proper frame of mind today by using your hands to switch your style of ConZentration to suit the situation. If you need to focus on a single task, shut out visual alternatives with your hand blinkers and think "Telephoto." If you're stuck in a mental rut, purposely distract yourself by studying multiple items in the area around you. From now on, use your hands to *ignore* distractions (Focus Pocus) or to *invite* distractions (Wide Angle).

Confusion

Failure to focus
"It's a madhouse in here. I give up. There's no way I'll be able to keep my mind on this."

Give yourself a fit
"It's the first snow of the season. Oh, I want to go out and make snow angels."

Taking it all in
"Lynn isn't at her desk. I wonder where she is. And Margaret's gone, too. I bet they went to the deli together."

Obsessive, unhealthy train of thought
"That makes me so mad. This is the third time this week they've taken a long lunch. I'm the one who's . . . "

Wrong frame of mind
"I just can't stop thinking about how unfair this is."

ConZentration

Focus Pocus
"I'm going to shut out those distractions by switching to telephoto lens."

Give yourself a hand
"I'm going to cup my hands around my eyes so . . . "

Tunnel vision
"I'm going to frame my focus so I can stay focused on getting these finished by noon."

Open eyes to wide-angle lens
"Okay, let's put things in perspective here. Today's Friday and I get to . . . "

Right frame of mind
"I'm going to get my mind off this by looking around and . . . "

WAY 5

◉

I WA-WA-WA-Wander. Why?

I can't say I was ever lost, but I was bewildered once
for three days.

—Daniel Boone

What if we've been practicing our ConZentrate on Command
and Focus Pocus techniques, and our mind still occasionally
becomes bewildered?

Laurence J. Peter said, "Real, constructive mental power lies
in . . . your hour-by-hour mental conduct. Develop a train of
thought on which to ride. The nobility of your life depends upon
the direction in which that train of thought is going."

The question is, How do we develop a desirable train of thought
and keep our mind on that track? Follow the example of elephant
handlers in India. The owners often need to walk their elephants
through the narrow streets of town to get to the temple where the
elephants are used for religious ceremonies. Unfortunately, the
streets are often packed with stalls displaying fruits, vegetables, and
shiny trinkets. The elephants can't help but investigate the oh-so-
enticing temptations with their trunks.

The trainers know if they want to get to the temple on time,
they can't let the elephants stop every other step to sample the
wares (not to mention the objections of the stall vendors!). So
these handlers have devised a brilliantly simple solution to help

the elephants stay focused. They give each elephant a short bamboo stick to carry in his or her trunk. The elephants' trunks are now full. They walk right by the stalls and aren't even tempted to check them out because their trunks (and minds) are occupied.

Hold That Thought!

What a man thinks of himself, that is what determines . . .
his fate.
—Henry David Thoreau

Can you relate to the elephant handlers' dilemma? Does it seem no matter how hard you try to keep your mind on the straight and narrow, it wanders all over the place?

From now on, you can stay on track by giving your mind a mental stick to hold so it's not tempted to stray. Help yourself stay focused with the following "**Hold That Thought!**" steps.

Step 1. Predetermine your mental destination. You've probably heard the saying, "If we don't know where we're going, we'll end up somewhere else." If our mind doesn't know where it's headed, it will meander all over the place. It can't stay on track if it hasn't been told what track to take. Identify your destination ("I need to inventory this new merchandise that arrived yesterday") so your mind won't get waylaid.

Step 2. Assign a feasible timeline for the trip. If the elephant handlers don't have to be any particular place at any particular time, it doesn't matter if the elephants get sidetracked. It's okay to turn this into a leisurely stroll. Likewise with our mind. If we don't have a deadline to meet, it doesn't matter if our mind takes its own sweet time getting there.

Usually we don't have that luxury. Most of us need to work purposefully, and the only way to do that is to give ourselves time parameters. You may have heard Parkinson's Law: "A job expands to fill the time allowed for it." If we simply start putting the new merchandise into inventory, that task could take forever because it's endless. If we attach a *measurable* timeline—e.g., "I need to inventory this new merchandise by nine A.M. so I can put it out on the shelves before the store opens"—our mind won't wander because it knows it doesn't have time to waste.

Step 3. Occupy your mind with a mental stick so it's oblivious to detours and distractions. Combining phrases such as "finish," "stay focused," and "complete" with your goal and timeline compels the mind to continue ConZentrating despite tempting alternatives. Examples would be: "I will let the answering machine pick up calls so I can stay *focused* on checking in and pricing these new items." "I will *continue* grading these student essays so I can be in bed by 10:30 P.M."

Step 4. Preface your command with your name. Our mind perks up and pays attention anytime we hear our name, even when we say it to ourselves. "Ted, stay focused on proofing this newsletter copy so you can hand it in by noon." "Andrew, ConZentrate on finishing these vocabulary words by six P.M. so you can watch your favorite sitcom." "Alice, take the next thirty minutes to type up these invoices and then you can break for lunch."

ConZentration Crossroads

When you come to a fork in the road, take it.
—Yogi Berra

From now on, understand that whenever something or someone tries to pull you off track, you are at a mental fork in the road. I call these moments ConZentration Crossroads. **A ConZentration Crossroads is the intersection of intense focus and interrupted focus.** It's the moment in which we're working *on task*, and someone or something asks for or attracts our attention. At that instant, we make either a *conscious* choice or a *compulsive* choice of what to do with our attention. Historically, many of us make compulsive choices. Ideas or images come to mind and we mentally pursue them regardless of whether they're the best use of our T.I.M.E. Something more interesting catches our eye or ear, and we abandon our original project and purpose without a second thought.

From now on, our goal is to think twice when we're at a ConZentration Crossroads. Instead of mindlessly pursuing whatever happens to cross our mental path, we're going to pause and think things through so we can make mindful choices about who and what we give our attention to. As Eddie Rickenbacker said, "I can give you a six-word formula for success: 'Think things through, then follow through.'"

The question we're going to ask when we find ourselves at mental forks in the road is **"Should I stay or should I stray?"** "Should I stick with my current project/purpose or switch my focus to this other individual or event?" "Which is the best use of my T.I.M.E.?"

Imagine you're at your computer imputing data and a coworker asks you to join her for a cup of coffee. Take a second to ask yourself, "Should I stay or stray?" It's an attractive offer, but is getting a cup of coffee the best use of your time right at that moment? Remind yourself of your predetermined destination and deadline. Will taking a break keep you from reaching your goal on time? On the other hand, you may have been working nonstop since you arrived this morning and a fifteen-minute java jolt is just what you need. Asking yourself, "Should I stay or stray?" talks you through the decision-making process so you can make a proactive ("Can I have a rain check? I've got to finish inputting these sales figures.") rather than a reactive choice ("Sure, I'd love an espresso right now.").

Why Am I Thinking This?

The happiness of your life depends upon the quality of your thoughts . . . Take care that you entertain no notions unsuitable to virtue and reasonable nature.
—**Marcus Aurelius**

This "stay or stray" idea can also be used to determine whether we should *purposely* get off a counterproductive train of thought. If we catch ourselves dwelling on harmful ideas or images, we can ask ourselves, "Should I continue to think about this or focus on something else?" If we are entertaining nonproductive thoughts, it's in our best interests to get off that track.

A friend visiting from the Mainland quickly picked up on this idea. She and I were walking along Wailea's user-friendly beach path discussing the recent divorce of a mutual friend. She started sharing the acrimonious custody battle she and her ex-husband had waged years ago. Within minutes, she was red in the face and gesturing wildly as she recounted how she felt her ex had gypped her kids out of their college fund. She got more and more enraged as she relived the unpleasant details of that relationship.

Suddenly she stopped in her tracks, looked at me in shock, swept her arm toward the stunning ocean vista next to us, and asked disbelievingly, "Why am I thinking about this? Look where I am."

She had the presence of mind (understand the importance of that phrase!) to realize she had gotten mentally tangled up in a toxic topic and it was in her own best interest to dump it. Here she was, on vacation in a world-class resort, making herself miserable by dwelling on something that was over and done with. A quick study, she chose to redirect her thoughts to something more pleasant instead of dredging up depressing issues that had occurred years ago. Her created-on-the-spot second thought, "Why am I thinking about this? Look where I am," got her out of her head and back into the present moment. Those painful memories that had consumed her seconds ago no longer had the power to rule and ruin her all-too-short time in Maui.

◉

Action Plan 5. Hold That Thought!

You are your choices.

—Jean-Paul Sartre

Today's assignment is to help yourself stay focused by using the "Hold That Thought" process. Before you begin tasks, (1) give yourself a mental destination, (2) attach a timeline to it, (3) occupy your mind with a mental stick so you're not tempted by distractions, and (4) preface orders to yourself with your name so your mind pays attention.

If you do find yourself at a ConZentration Crossroads, resolve to make thoughtful, not thoughtless, choices. Instead of giving your attention to anything and everything that comes to mind, ask yourself, "What is the best use of my T.I.M.E.?"

If you find yourself focusing on "somethink" other than your chosen task, ask yourself, "Should I stay or stray?" If your mind has latched onto a distressing idea or depressing image, ask yourself, "Why am I thinking this?" Fill your mind with your purpose and give it a mental stick to grip so it doesn't have the room or the inclination to roam.

Confusion	ConZentration
Mental muddle "I wonder what I'll say if they ask about . . . Oops, can't forget to stop by the dry cleaners on the way home. There's Ed. I've got to tell him what happened, but first I better fax this . . . Oh my gosh, it's time for the meeting."	*Mental stick* "I wonder what I'll say . . . Oops, can't forget to stop by . . . Ann, focus completely on memorizing these points in the next 15 minutes."
At the mercy of our thoughts "What if I make a fool of myself?"	*Manage our thoughts* "I am going to do my best to get this proposal approved."
Perpetually preoccupied "How does my hair look? Is my mascara smeared? Did I put on enough lipstick?"	*Fully occupied* "I'm here to inform, not to impress. I'm here to persuade them to fund this program."
Lose your train of thought, stray "Oh, no, there's Bill. He doesn't support this idea. He's going to bring up all the reasons this won't work."	*Hold that thought, stay* "Why am I thinking that? Worrying about Bill won't help. Stay focused on convincing everyone that this is worthwhile."

Confusion	ConZentration
Lose perspective	*Regain perspective*
"I'll die if he asks me something I don't know. It would be humiliating to appear unprepared."	"Look around. I'm glad to have an opportunity to speak to these people about something so important."

WAY 6

◉

Get the Nots out of Your Thinking

When I saw the play *Annie* [at a date's insistence] I had to
hit myself on the head afterward with a small hammer to get
that stupid "Tomorrow" song out of my head.

—Ian Shoales

S urely there must be a better way to banish bothersome thoughts
than hitting yourself on the head with a hammer! Fortunately,
there is. We can eliminate unwelcome thoughts by **replacing,
reframing**, and **removing** them.

First, though, we must grasp the notion that whenever we tell
ourselves *not* to think about something, we focus our attention on
the very think we don't want to think about! If we are snowboard-
ing down an icy slope and say to ourselves, "I hope I don't fall,"
we've just introduced the idea of falling into our consciousness.

The mind can't *not* consider an idea it's just been told not to consider. This may sound convoluted, but it makes sense. Our brain
acts like a computer. It is quite literal and can't interpret what we
really mean. Furthermore, it reacts most readily to word pictures.
Say to yourself, "I'm going to the mall." Your mind probably flashed
an image of a nearby shopping center. Now say, "I will *not* go to the
mall." Chances are, your mind still focused on the word "mall." It
overlooked the ghost word "not" because it can't conjure up the
opposite of a concept.

If you tell yourself, "I'm not going to get mad," the mind is incapable of extrapolating from the word "mad" to what you *do* want to do. Like your computer, it just records and prints out what was keyed in. The word "mad" was keyed in, so that's what it pictures. When that snowboarder thought, "Don't fall," what he wanted was to stay on his feet, but that's not what he told his mind, so he's now probably sliding down the slope on his fanny.

If It's Not One Think, It's Another

My mother is so passive-aggressive. She says things to me like "You just can't seem to do anything right, and that's what I love about you."
—comedian Laura Silverman

Talk about mixed messages! That's what we do to our brain when we tell it to stop focusing on something. Funny lady Paula Poundstone gives a great example of this. "I don't think the New York subway system is scary, but it is a little odd. They have big 'No Spitting' signs everywhere. I never even thought of spitting until they brought it up; then it was all I felt like doing."

Remember your science teacher telling you that "Nature abhors a vacuum"? (Come to think of it, I'm not too fond of them either.) When the mind is told not to stop doing something, it may comply momentarily, but it is now sitting there empty. Unless we immediately fill that vacuum with something more constructive, the mind will fill the void itself by returning to the previous, undesirable thoughts, images, or behavior.

That's why telling ourselves not to overeat or to stop smoking rarely produces the desired change. We are sabotaging our success by riveting our mind on the very activity we want to quit. What to do? From now on, we're going to replace, reframe, and remove counterproductive images and ideas.

Replace Unwanted Thoughts

I keep the telephone of my mind open to peace, harmony, health, love, and abundance. Then whenever doubts, anxiety, or fear try to call me, they keep getting a busy signal—and soon they'll forget my number.
—**Edith Armstrong**

From now on, follow Ms. Armstrong's advice and block out destructive thoughts by filling your mind so full of desired ones, there's no room left at the mental inn. When you talk to yourself, use specific word pictures of *wished-for* states and outcomes. Remember, your mind can't interpret what you really mean and will do what it's told, so be *precise* and fill it with what you hope *will* happen instead of what you hope *won't* happen.

To help us remember this all-important concept, I've created a mental stick that's a variation of the knock-knock joke. (You know, "Knock, knock. Who's there? Boo. Boo who? Don't cry.") I call this mental stick "Not, not."

Here's how it works. The second you think or say something with the word "not" in it (and yes, that includes contractions such as "I won't worry," "I don't want to interrupt her," "I can't be late"), stop and say **"Not, not."** That's your cue to ask yourself "What *do* I want?" Perhaps what you want is to trust that everything will turn out okay. What you want is to let this person finish speaking. What you want is to be early. Rephrase your orders to yourself by replacing won'ts with wants, can'ts with cans, and don'ts with dos.

Baseball player Ken Boswell told manager Yogi Berra, "I'm in a rut. I can't break myself of the habit of swinging up at the ball." Berra said simply, "Then swing down." Yogi must have been Yoda in a different life. He's right. The way to break bad habits is to replace them with their verbal polar opposite. Golfers know they better replace "Stop trying to blast the ball" with "Swing slow and smooth." Parents need to replace "don't" orders—"Don't run around the pool"—with "do" orders—"Jason, please walk around the pool."

There's a Russian proverb that goes: "Once a word is spoken, it flies. You can't catch it." I disagree. I think we *can* catch ourselves in the act of thinking and saying counterproductive words, ideas, and concepts. And when we do, we can choose to replace those negative thoughts with nurturing ones. This **"Catch and Correct Concept"** is the key to producing desired rather than dreaded results.

Reframe Unwanted Thoughts

Drag your thoughts away from your troubles—by the ears, by the heels, or any other way you can manage. It's the healthiest thing a body can do.
—Mark Twain

Another way to drag our thoughts away from troubles is to mentally paint those troubles in a more positive light. The more negative emotion we attach to an event, the more power it has to destroy our peace of mind. Choosing to see the incident, individual, or emotion from a different point of view can often put that event in perspective and neutralize its power to dominate our thoughts.

A perfect example of this happened recently at our local library. After selecting our books, my sons and I went to check them out, only to be told we owed $32 in overdue fines. Suffice it to say, I was not a happy camper. I was sputtering about how this could have happened when Tom piped up with a pearl of wisdom. He said, "Mom, that's nothing. We spend more than that in one visit to Borders." His reframe was right on. I've visited the library dozens of times over the years and borrowed hundreds of its books for free. When looked at this way, $32 was cheap.

Instead of getting locked into a negative interpretation of events, we should derive a lesson from them. As soon as we extract some insight or value from what's taken place, the event will lose its power to make us miserable. We can do this by asking ourselves, **"What's a different way to think about this?"** My sons and I had yet another opportunity to practice what we preach. We had taken a pickup full of stuff to Maui's famous Saturday swap meet with the hope of turning our cast-offs into some cash. Andrew had outgrown his almost new mountain bike, so that was added to our pile of ready-to-be-sold possessions. Unfortunately, while Andrew was away checking other booths, his $250 bike got sold for $25. Suffice it to say, he was bummed and getting more bummed when Tom contributed another pearl of wisdom: "Look at it this way. Some lucky kid just got the deal of the century. He's getting a Christmas present his parents probably never would have been able to afford otherwise." Out of the mouths of teens. Tom's insight turned the situation around. Instead of dwelling on what he lost, Andrew was able to let it go because he focused on what some fortunate kid gained.

Another way to reframe an unhealthy focus is to ask ourselves, **"Can I change what's happened?"** Often we can't undo the mess in which we find ourselves. Andrew couldn't track down the man who bought his bike and demand more money. Getting angry at the librarian wouldn't erase the fine we owed and would only cause senseless mental wear and tear.

The reframing phrase **"Can I do anything about this?"** reminds us of the futility of mentally ranting and raving about something that can't un-happen. Since we can't alter the event, we better alter our thinking about the event.

I once witnessed a memorable demonstration of reframing. The owner of a family-oriented restaurant chain asked me to present a motivational talk at the company's annual Christmas party. The ballroom was standing room only. A few staff members had brought their children and were sitting next to the aisles so their toddlers could crawl around. A baby started crying during the award ceremony, and a couple of the kids were playing hide-and-seek near the front of the stage. The commotion made it difficult to ConZentrate on the program, and I halfway expected the owner to look disapprovingly at the "disturbance" and ask for the children to be taken outside.

Instead, the business partner stopped for a moment, smiled benevolently at the energetic youngsters, and said, "It's good to see life here." He then continued announcing the awards (a little more loudly so everyone could hear).

What an inspiring reframe. Instead of seeing the boisterous children as an annoyance, he saw them as welcome members of their employee family. Carl Sandburg once said, "A baby is God's opinion the world should go on." This wise business owner was of the opinion the meeting could go on . . . and the kids could stay.

A skeptic once spoke up and said, "Reframes might work okay for crying babies and library fines, but I've been downsized three times in the last five years and I don't think this system works for serious problems. It's one thing to reframe my thoughts if I'm charged a late fee for overdue books, it's another if I'm out of work and don't know how I'm going to pay bills and put food on the table."

I posed his comment to the class and asked what they thought. A man named Steve said, "I think reframing is even more important when we're facing hard times. My company reorganized last year and my position was eliminated. I had worked for that company for most of my adult life and was a senior manager. I couldn't believe twenty years of seniority could disappear just like that. I was so depressed I sat around the house and moped for a month. I once read that depression is suppressed rage, and I agree. I finally realized sitting around in my pajamas wasn't going to find me a new job."

Steve continued, "I made an appointment with an outplacement specialist. My company had offered to pay for this before, but I had been too angry to go. This rather blunt career counselor flat out told me my situation wasn't going to turn around until I changed my thinking. Her exact words were 'No one is going to hire a bitter ex-employee with a bad attitude.' She refused to let me complain, because she knew that would keep me stuck in resentment. Instead, she taught me to use the phrases 'Don't go there' and 'Turn it around.' If I said something negative like 'I can't believe that company just tossed me out like I was some bit of trash . . . ' she'd interrupt and say, 'Don't go there.' If I said something pessimistic like 'I'll never find a job . . . ' she'd say, 'Turn it around.' It may sound simplistic, but those phrases motivated me to get off my bottom and do something about being jobless instead of dwelling on how unfair it was."

Do you have a situation in your life that is unfair, unpleasant, or unwanted? Could you reframe it by asking, "What's a different way to think about this?" or "Can I do anything about this?" or by telling yourself to "Turn it around"? Those phrases can help you extract value from the situation so you can mentally move on.

Remove Unwanted Thoughts

Frank Lloyd Wright received a phone call from a man who was living in a house the great architect had designed. The caller complained, "Right now, I am sitting at my dining room table. There's a leak over my head and it's dripping on me." Wright's one-word response was "Move."

Frank Lloyd Wright was a wise man. If we're not able to ConZentrate, perhaps we can remove the *source* of the irritation or remove *ourselves* from the source of irritation. Instead of replacing or reframing our thinking about unhealthy situations, we'd sometimes be better off eliminating them entirely.

"After I had lived with my boyfriend for two years," a woman confided, "he decided he wanted to see other people. He moved out and left me with all the memories. Every time I looked around our apartment I would be reminded of something we did together. There were the videos we had watched together, there was the perfect couch we had found for half price, there was the dining room table where we shared so many meals. I finally realized I'd never be able to get Brad out of my mind as long as I stayed in that apartment. So I gave myself a geographical fresh start. I sold almost all my furniture through free ads in the *Pennysaver*, went out and bought a few basic pieces, and found a different apartment in another part of town. That was six months ago, and I can honestly say I'm over him now, because I (literally and figuratively) moved on with my life."

Instead of trying to assert superhuman willpower and *not* think about this man who broke her heart, this smart woman removed all reminders of him and filled her life with fresh surroundings. Sometimes "out of sight, out of mind" is a good think.

"Life does not consist mainly, or even largely, of facts and happenings," Mark Twain believed. "It consists mainly of the storm of thoughts that are forever blowing through one's mind." Today, evaluate whether the storm of thoughts blowing through your mind and occupying your valuable T.I.M.E. are good for you. If they are, great. If they are not, reframe, replace, or remove them with ones that are.

◉

Action Plan 6. Get the Nots out of Your Thinking

The good mind chooses what is positive, what is advancing, what embraces the affirmative.

—Ralph Waldo Emerson

Today's assignment is to advance your ConZentration cause by choosing to embrace positive, affirmative thoughts. As Michel de Montaigne said, "Nothing fixes a thing so intensely in the memory as the wish to forget it." Start **replacing** and **removing** unwanted thoughts instead of trying to forget them. **Catch** yourself in the middle of saying what you *don't* want and **correct** it by clearly stating what you *do* want. **Reframe** unfortunate circumstances by asking yourself, "What's a different way to think about this?"

Maurice Chevalier's line "Old age is not so bad when you consider the alternative" is a classic case of reframing. His quote shows how we can change gripes to gratitude in a flash if we opt to see thinks from a different point of view.

Confusion	**ConZentration**
Nots in your thinking "I'm not going to let him psych me out."	*"Not, not" thinking* "I'm going to play my own game."
Reinforce unwanted ideas "I can't think about losing. It doesn't matter that he beat me last year."	*Reframe unwanted ideas* "I'm in the best shape of my life. I'm peaking perfectly for this match."
Recall unhealthy images "His spin serve is unreturnable. I won't be able to get it back over the net."	*Replace unhealthy images* "I'll prepare early and stay on my toes so I'll be ready for his serve."
Reintroduce negative thoughts "I can't double-fault or make any dumb mistakes."	*Remove negative thoughts* "I'm going to play high-percentage shots and get my first serves in."

Confusion	ConZentration
Recycle harmful beliefs	*Re-mind with helpful beliefs*
"This is going to be embarrassing. I don't want to let my team down."	"I'm going to give one hundred percent and do my best to help the team win."

PART 3

Focus When You Don't Feel Like It

It's amazing how long it takes to complete something you're not working on.

—R. D. Clyde

WAY 7

◉

Want to Change Your Mind?

LUCY: Do you think anybody ever really changes?

LINUS: I've changed a lot in the last year.

LUCY: I mean for the better.

—Charles M. Schulz

Have you ever told your brain to ConZentrate and it paid you no mind? Remember, one definition of ConZentration is "interest in action." What this means is no interest, no action. Part 2 explained how we can train our brain to pay attention despite distractions. This section explains how we can train our brain to focus when it doesn't feel like it.

A fundamental concept of motivation is that in order to act, we must have a firm reason why. Do you know there are only two reasons why we do anything? Think about it. We do things because we *have* to and we do things because we *want* to. If we do things because we have to, we'll do them either begrudgingly or not at all if we can get away with it. When we tell our mind it *has* to ConZentrate, it rebels. It may eventually comply, but with some reluctance, resentment, or resistance. That's why when it's time to focus we need to move ourselves to a want-to frame of mind. How can we do this? By reminding ourselves of all the benefits we reap when we pay attention.

The Payoffs of Paying Attention

No steam or gas ever drives anything until it is confined. No Niagara is ever turned into light and power until it is tunneled. No life ever grows great until it is focused, dedicated, disciplined.
—Harry Emerson Fosdick

Next time you have to focus and would rather not, review the list below. Reminding yourself of all the tangible advantages of ConZentrating can persuade you to pay attention even when your mind believes it has better thinks to do.

Payoff 1. Tasks take less time. Have you seen the office poster that asks, "If you don't have time to do it right the first time, when will you have time to do it over again?" ConZentration helps us do thinks right the first time. This is particularly important for tedious chores. If you're faced with an unpleasant task (for example, putting up the storm shutters), wouldn't you rather have it over in a couple of hours instead of having it eat up your entire Saturday? Paying attention not only decreases the amount of time you spend on the task initially, it saves the time it would take to correct the mistakes and omissions that are a by-product of inattention.

Payoff 2. Increased productivity. We simply get more done when we are 100 percent focused. We get more letters written, phone calls answered, projects completed, and obligations crossed off our to-do list. There is a direct link between the quality of our ConZentration and the quantity of our output.

Payoff 3. Improved confidence. Ask any actor, musician, or world-class athlete, and they'll tell you ConZentration and confidence are as interdependent as the chicken and the egg. Mark Twain said, "A man cannot be confident without his own approval." The ability to ConZentrate on self-approving, performance-enhancing thoughts instead of debilitating doubts is the key to turning panic into poise and anxiety into assurance.

Payoff 4. Enhanced peace of mind. "Each person has to find his peace from within," said Mahatma Gandhi. "And peace, to be real, must be unaffected by outside circumstances." ConZentration means *we* regulate our thoughts instead of giving stress-inducing events and/or individuals the power to rule (and ruin) our mood. ConZentration helps us maintain a tranquil state of mind despite trials and tribulations because we've developed our own inner-calm system.

Payoff 5. More goals completed. "Patience is the ability to care slowly," said John Clarke. Whether our goal is to finish our taxes or to finish writing our thesis, ConZentration helps us continue to care over the long haul instead of quitting when the going gets tough.

Payoff 6. Improved quality of life. José Ortega y Gasset said, "Tell me to what you pay attention, and I will tell you who you are." Such a simple statement, and yet so profound. The world's greatest thinkers have all come to the same conclusion. The quality of our life is a direct reflection of the quality of our thoughts. As John Milton pointed out, "The mind is its own place, and in itself can make a heaven of hell, a hell of heaven."

Karma means roughly that we reap what we sow. **ConZentration Karma** states that **"What we think about, we become."**

A community college professor named Lani Uyeno approached me after a public seminar and said, "I always knew in a vague way that ConZentration was important, but never really understood just how much it impacts everything we do. I signed up for this seminar because I wanted to learn how to help my students study better. I never realized that ConZentration affects everything from confidence to quality of life. From now on, I'm going to begin every semester with a mini-course in ConZentration techniques. Teaching them this one skill will help them in and out of school for the rest of their lives."

Writer Nancy Thayer said, "It's never too late—in fiction or in life—to revise." It's never too late to change your mind for the better. Just remember the many benefits that will accrue to you and your mind will be motivated to mind.

Action Plan 7. Want to Change Your Mind?

**She changed her mind, but it didn't work any better
than the old one.**

—Henny Youngman

A favorite coach used to tell me the single ability we all have is the ability to change. From now on, if you need to ConZentrate and your mind is saying "No way," review these benefits. They'll provide incentive so you choose to pay attention. Instead of telling yourself, "I really *should* ConZentrate on drawing up those blueprints" or "I *have* to finish these lab reports," say "I *choose* to ConZentrate because . . ." and fill in the many benefits that will be yours if you pay attention. Werner Erhard said, "Live as if your life depended on it." ConZentrate as if your life depends upon it. It does.

Confusion	ConZentration
Have to ConZentrate	*Want to ConZentrate*
"I have to study for this test or I'll fail."	"I want to study for this test so I get a good grade."
Resist paying attention	*Choose to pay attention*
"He's such a boring teacher. I hate his class. I'm not listening to him drone on and on."	"I'm going to take notes so I can learn this material and score well on the oral exam."
Reluctant to focus	*Ready to focus*
"Algebra is such a waste of time anyway. No one uses it in real life."	"I want to pass this course because it's needed for my major."
Resent needing to ConZentrate	*Willing to ConZentrate*
"I'm supposed to go to the library and research that material, but it's Saturday. I'm not going on my weekend."	"I'm going to the library first thing in the morning so I can ConZentrate on looking up material without a lot of distractions."

WAY 8

◉

Vigor Mortis? Try a Little A.R.D.O.R.

No one knows what he can do till he tries.

—Publius Syrus

Remember the laws of inertia and momentum you studied in high school science class? The law of inertia states that a stationary body tends to stay stationary, and the law of momentum states that a body in motion tends to stay in motion.

Inertia can be illustrated by a stalled car. The car will continue to sit there until someone exerts some effort to get it going. Once it's rolling, it can continue on its own without much assistance.

The same principle applies to our brain. A mind in inertia is likely to stay there unless we exert some effort to get it rolling. Once we put our mind in gear, though, it achieves mental momentum, that wonderful state in which it seems to coast along of its own accord. This highly desirable frame of mind doesn't turn on instantly like a faucet. Just like a finely tuned sports car, our mental engine needs to warm up before it operates optimally.

How does this apply to ConZentration? Many times when we don't feel like focusing, it's not that the task we're attempting is so awful; it's just that our mind is in a state of inertia. If we can just get started and persevere through those uncomfortable first few minutes, our mind will soon be rolling along without a lot of exertion on our part.

Sigmund Freud once said, "When inspiration doesn't come to me, I go halfway to meet it." Smart man. He didn't sit and wait for divine intervention. He knew good things come to those who . . . initiate.

This chapter suggests a variety of ways we can meet inspiration halfway. As the title says, if we find ourselves suffering from vigor mortis, the solution may be to try a little **A.R.D.O.R.**

A.R.D.O.R. = Act Now, Feel Later

You can't learn anything from experiences you're not having.
—Louis L'Amour

From now on, instead of allowing inertia to immobilize us, we're going to get our mind out of Park and into Drive with the "Act Now, Feel Later" Approach. In essence, when we use this approach, we state to ourselves: "I will start this task and work on it for five minutes. If at the end of five minutes, I don't feel like continuing, I can quit." Of course, what happens is, after working on the task for several minutes, we discover it's not nearly as onerous as we've made it out to be. As novelist Madeleine L'Engle said, "Inspiration usually comes during work, rather than before it." Now that we're out of the sedentary state, we're glad to finally be getting this chore *out* of the way (instead of it being *in* our way) and we are intrinsically motivated to continue. We may even find we enjoy the task.

Respected psychologist and philosopher William James believed one of his most important findings was: "Action produces feeling more often than feeling produces action." If we wait until we *want* to do something, we will probably never do it. The key is **"No debate."** Don't ask yourself whether you'd like to begin, just begin. If you pay attention to any protests from that lazy person in your head—"But it's cold" or "I stayed up late last night"— you'll end up arguing with yourself. Since emotions are more compelling than logic, we will almost always go with what feels good at that moment instead of doing what's good for us.

That's why it's so important not to engage in dialogue with yourself. It doesn't matter how you feel, just start. Work on the task for five minutes without acknowledging any whining from the mind, and you'll find that taking action produces motivation rather than the other way around.

A woman used this idea to finally act on her intentions to get physically fit. "Our community recently installed an Olympic-sized pool two minutes from my house, which meant I didn't have an excuse anymore for not getting back into swimming. I had been a decent backstroker in college and enjoyed being part of a team. The problem was, I'm overweight and I wasn't too thrilled about the prospect of parading around in public in a swimsuit. It was one of those catch-22 deals. I was out of shape because I wasn't exercising, and I wasn't exercising because I was out of shape.

"I finally faced the fact that the only way I would ever reverse this vicious cycle was to show up for workouts, regardless of how I looked. The key was not giving myself a chance to talk myself out of it. I banned my brain from thinking. I didn't let my mind conjure up images of pudgy thighs and dimply arms. I just put my swimsuit on, drove to the pool, dove in, and started doing laps. That was three months ago, and it's the best thing I've done for myself in years. I've made new friends, can swim a mile without stopping, and perhaps best of all, feel good about gutsing through my self-created dread. This sure beats sitting home and worrying what people think of how I look in a bathing suit."

Comedian Marsha Doble said, "I have to exercise in the morning before my brain figures out what I'm doing." She's right. It's better *not* to engage our brain when we want to exercise our body. If we do, it will tell us all the reasons it would rather stay home. Keep that mind turned off. No dialogue, none.

What is something you want to do, but for some reason haven't? Could you put your head on hold and get yourself in motion? Could you act yourself out of inertia so you don't look back with regret at opportunities not taken, people not met, activities not experienced? You won't regret taking action, you'll only regret taking yourself out of the action.

A.R.d.O.R. = Realistic Goal Lines

*It must be born in mind that the tragedy of life doesn't lie in
not reaching your goal. The tragedy lies in having no
goal to reach.*
—Helmut Schmidt

Imagine the game of football without five yard markers and a goal
line. Players would have nothing to measure progress, nothing to
indicate when they scored, nothing to celebrate. Without a goal
line, their efforts would become pointless.

Just as a football field has a goal line at both ends of the field, we
need a goal line at both ends of our project. Our undertaking needs
a beginning and an ending time. Without a specific starting time,
we have no commitment to begin, only a vague understanding that
a certain task needs to be attended to—sometime. If you say, "I
really need to work through my in-basket," your mind won't get to
work. Why should it? You observed that your in-basket needs attention, but you didn't order your mind to attend to it now or at a later
scheduled time.

We also need to agree to, in advance, a finish time. It's one thing
to start ConZentrating on a task, it's another to *continue* ConZentrating until it's completed. Unless we commit to having that task
done by a particular time, we will work lackadaisically. Why push
ourselves? There's no pressing deadline.

Remember Parkinson's Law, which states that work expands to
fill the time available for its completion. If you tell your children to
take care of their chores and don't let them know by when, there
will be no purposefulness to their efforts. They'll probably lazily
pick up their room, shoot some hoops while taking the trash out,
and even engage in a water fight while washing the car. Those
chores could take hours to finish. That's fine if you don't have other
plans for the day, but if you need to get out of the house by a certain time, assign goal lines to those chores. Telling your kids they
can go to the video arcade if the house is clean by noon will transform them into whirling dervishes. Their indulgence will be transformed into industriousness.

Completion times are crucial to ConZentration. With no end in sight and with all the time in the world, our mind has no incentive to apply itself. Intentions will remain just that unless we assign a start and a finish time to every task. Time parameters create a faster, focused pace. Our mind will know we mean business and it will get down to business.

It's also important to establish interim goals, the equivalent of first downs in football. Imagine how ridiculous it would be to expect football teams to go the entire length of the field in one play. That's an impossible, or at least improbable, expectation. Teams would fail every time and would probably give up out of frustration and a sense of hopelessness.

Yet that's exactly what many of us do to ourselves when we tackle complex projects. We think of the task in its entirety and end up quitting (or not even starting) because we know we'll never be able to finish the whole thing.

From now on, assign interim goals to each long-term task. Break complicated tasks into increments that are significantly challenging, yet achievable—the equivalent of ten yards in four plays. Football teams who successfully complete ten yards are rewarded with a first down, which inspires them to continue making progress toward their goal. The same psychology works for us. Successfully completing one portion of our project makes us feel proud ("I can do this"), gives us something to celebrate, and provides an incentive to keep working toward our goal.

Pope John Paul II said, "The future starts today, not tomorrow." What's something in your life you want or need to do, but haven't started? Could it be you haven't specified a "time in" and a "time out"? Is there something you initiated and then abandoned because you were intimidated or overwhelmed? Was it because you didn't give yourself "first downs"? You may have heard the aphorism "An obstacle is something you see when you take your eyes off the goal." Obstacles will be *all* we see unless we assign our project realistic start and finish times and achievable interim objectives.

A.R.D.O.R. = Deal You Can't Refuse

We have got but one life here. It says . . . to try and accomplish things in this life and not merely to have a soft
and pleasant time.
—Theodore Roosevelt

Another way to motivate our mind is to make it a deal it can't
refuse. For obvious reasons, I call this the Godfather Approach.

The brain takes bribes. It will focus on and accomplish something it doesn't want to do if we promise it a soft and pleasant time
later. A seminar participant called this approach "Let's make a
deal." Rewards work. We can develop a mutually beneficial relationship with our mind by establishing a quid pro quo in which we
give it what it wants and it gives us what we want.

One entrepreneur I know uses this system to file his general
excise tax report each month. Finances are not his strength, and he
used to dread dealing with all the forms and having to write that
BIG check every thirty days. He now blocks in the first Friday of
every month and dedicates his morning to updating and resolving
his records for the previous month. When lunchtime rolls around,
he rewards himself with his once-a-month golf date with his buddies. Those mornings still aren't pleasant for him, but he no longer
postpones his tax reports because that onerous obligation is offset by
his trip to the golf course that afternoon.

What if you've racked your brain and can't come up with any
trade that will make ConZentrating on this task worth the effort?
Could you increase the consequences for *not* acting? What task
don't you want to do? What will happen if you don't do it? The
answer to this question will cause you either to spring into action or
to realize you can postpone this task with no dire consequences.
Identifying the negative ramifications of inaction can help change
"I don't want to, so I'm not going to" resistance into "I don't want
to, but I will because . . . " resolve.

If you've been ConZentrating intensely for a while and your
mind is chafing under the control, make a gentleman's agreement
with it. Say, "I will finish reading this assignment, and then I get to
sit in my favorite chair and kick back for the rest of the evening."

Tell the mind the task it needs to attend to now and the treat it will get later for cooperating. It's a way of saying, "If you'll keep your end of the bargain, I'll keep mind." Our brain will more readily ConZentrate on what we want, when we want . . . because it knows its time is coming.

Marvin was a self-confessed right-brained person in a left-brained world who was falling further and further behind his peers because of his computer illiteracy. His favorite line about anything electronic was "It's geek to me." He was reluctant to sign himself up for some training because he didn't relish the thought of some "twenty-year-old techie hotshot" treating him "like an idiot" (his words). He finally persuaded himself to bite the bullet by using a combination of bribes and threats. His reward was that he got to leave work an hour early every Tuesday and Thursday for the six weeks of the program, and his threat was realizing he could be demoted for his lack of computer skills unless he took these courses.

Lord Byron once said, "The Head is the dome of thought, the palace of the soul." We've all heard that Dome wasn't built in a day, and neither is the ability to ConZentrate. After years of doing *what* it wants *when* it wants, it may not like the idea of obeying orders. That's why it's important to give our head its head every once in a while. If we swap quid pro quo time with our brain, it will mind more willingly.

A.R.D.O.R. = Objectives Versus Objections

I was underwhelmed.
—George S. Kaufman's review of a play

It's ironic; the mind refuses to work when it's overwhelmed *and* when it's underwhelmed. When it's overwhelmed, our brain throws up its mental arms, says, "I see no way I can do that," and refuses to budge. When it's underwhelmed, it says, "I see no reason to do that," and refuses to budge.

You've heard the phrase "mind over matter"? We're going to modify that: If it doesn't matter, our mind won't move. To apply itself, the mind must feel the outcome will be worth the effort. What I've observed in years of studying this topic is that when we're not ConZentrating, it doesn't necessarily mean the advantages don't outweigh the obstacles; it's just that we're focusing exclusively on the obstacles.

For example, do you owe someone a letter? (Is this a rhetorical question or what?) Almost all of us owe at least one person a letter. Chances are you've been focusing on your why-nots (for example, you don't have time, the letter's been postponed so many times you're going to have to write a ten-page epistle, etc.). As long as you stay locked on those objec*tions*, that letter won't get written.

Instead, switch your focus to your objec*tives*. *Why* would you like to stay in touch with this person? Is keeping this friendship "in repair," as Samuel Johnson put it, worth fifteen minutes of your time?

Now for the kicker. Instead of dwelling on your emotions (you're not looking forward to writing a letter), dwell on your friend's emotions (how much she'd enjoy receiving your letter). This is a time when projecting into the future (imagining her reaction) is preferable to being in the moment (anchoring your resistance). Picture how pleased she'll be to know you care enough to reconnect. Keep that motivating image in mind, ConZentrate on how *she'll* feel (instead of how you feel) and then sit down and write that letter. You'll be glad you did (and your friend will be, too).

An empty-nester, Wanda didn't know what to do with herself now that all her kids were out of the house. When I asked what she wanted to do, Wanda said she wanted to go back to school and get her degree. When I asked why she hadn't followed up on her wish to return to college, she started listing all the difficulties. She dreaded the time it was going to take to track down her long-lost transcripts. She wasn't sure what major to select. She was afraid of being the oldest person on campus.

I then asked Wanda to list all the reasons why going back to college would be worth her while. I suggested she imagine how rewarding it would be to stretch her mind and study subjects she found fascinating. I recommended she see this as a welcome opportunity to reinvent herself. I proposed she picture herself striding across the stage, proudly receiving her diploma, and then tossing her mortarboard up in the air to celebrate. Wanda switched her focus to the advantages of returning to college, and last I heard, she was attending classes and enjoying every minute. Why's woman!

Imagine that you give yourself piano lessons for a birthday present. You regret not learning as a youngster and decide better late than never. The problem is, it's lesson night and you're exhausted from a long day at work. The last thing you want to do is get back in the car and drive across town to your teacher's house for your weekly lesson. You're sorely tempted to call and cancel.

Instead of dwelling on your vigor mortis, fast-forward in your mind to already being at your instructor's home. Imagine listening as she demonstrates a new song and eagerly trying it yourself. Think about the years of fun you've got ahead of you. Enlarge those "why I want to play the piano" images and bring them to the forefront of your mind so they are all you're thinking about. Instead of using apathy as a *reason* for not acting, understand that it is the *result* of not acting. Picture that birthday party you've promised yourself with your friends gathered around singing Broadway show tunes . . . and then get in the car and get yourself to that lesson!

Do you have a commitment you're supposed to keep (e.g., weekly choir practice, volunteering at the hospital, attending AA meetings); but when it's time to be on your way, you often find your get-up-and-go has got up and left? Could you fast-forward in your mind to how you'll feel *after* you've successfully completed this obligation? Runners invariably say, "I'm always glad I've run, even when I started out feeling awful." Make keeping this commitment a fait accompli by adopting a mindset where not going isn't an option. Relegate resistance to a think of the past by focusing only on why this will be worth your while.

A.R.D.O.R. = Remember Mortality

Just when you think tomorrow will never come, it's yesterday.
—Anonymous

If you think about it, we have an underlying assumption every time we postpone ConZentrating on something. The unspoken presumption is: We can do this later if we choose. We take for granted the opportunity will wait for us and still be there when we want to take advantage of it. We count on having the health, time, money, or capability to start when we're good and ready. That may not be the case.

Yogi Berra said, "It gets late early out there." As usual, Berra's seemingly off-the-cuff remark has enduring insight. Keeping our mortality in mind is one way to turn around a laissez-faire attitude. We won't be so casual about taking our T.I.M.E. for granted if we stop to realize how fragile life is, and that there are no guarantees.

Years ago, I spoke at a convention in Waikiki about how to ConZentrate on intentions so they become actions. I suggested the group take advantage of their trip to the islands by getting up early the next morning to watch a Hawaiian sunrise. This was the first and only time some of them would be visiting the fiftieth state, and I suggested it would be worth their while to set their alarms for six A.M. so they could have the "chicken skin" (Hawaiian slang for goose bumps) experience of seeing the sun peek over Diamond Head and illuminate the sky in shades of pink, yellow, and orange. I mentioned they could make the morning even more memorable by watching the sun come up while bobbing in the gentle waves offshore.

Human nature being what it is, I warned them that when their alarm rudely woke them the following morning, they'd be sorely tempted to turn the darn thing off, curse me for proposing this idea, and roll over and go back to sleep. At that instant of temptation, they were to ask themselves, "What will matter a year from now?" Would it matter that they got an extra hour of sleep? Or will it matter that they saw the golden sun coloring the sky as it peeked over that world-renowned landmark? Would they remember the extra winks, or would they remember the fragrant tropical air, the gentle trade winds ruffling the palm fronds, and the freshly plucked plumeria flower behind their ear?

Several couples tracked me down the following day to tell me those seven words, "What will matter a year from now?" were just the incentive they needed to get up and outside. They all agreed that the memory of a lifetime sure beat staying in bed.

Author Rita Mae Brown said, "A deadline is negative inspiration. Still, it's better than no inspiration at all." The next time you're tempted to forgo an experience, for whatever reason, ask yourself, "**What will matter a year from now?** Will I be glad I gave in to the temptation to do nothing, or will I be glad I made the most of my T.I.M.E. while I could?" Remember La Rochefoucauld's wise insight: "Our minds are lazier than our bodies." Our bodies are usually ready and willing, but they are often betrayed by a mind that would rather stay in bed. Remembering your mortality—your deadline—can inspire you to act on opportunities now, not someday.

◉

Action Plan 8. Vigor Mortis? Try a Little A.R.D.O.R.

Iron rusts from disuse, stagnant water loses its purity and in cold weather becomes frozen; even so does inaction sap the vigors of the mind.

—Leonardo da Vinci

What is something you've been meaning to ConZentrate on, but you've been mired in mental rigor mortis? What will it take for you to invigorate your mind? Could you kick-start your mental engine with the "Act Now, Feel Later" plan? Could you divide your wished-for results into "first downs" so your mind feels more motivated? Could you ConZentrate on your objec*tives* rather than your objec*tions*?

"We accept the verdict of the past," observed Judge Learned Hand, "until the need for change cries out loudly enough to force upon us a choice between the comfort of further inertia and the irksomeness of action." We can know how to ConZentrate, but that knowledge is incomplete unless we know how to ConZentrate when we don't want to.

I've provided two pages of don'ts and dos to help us overcome the comforts of inertia. Photocopy them and place them where you'll see them frequently throughout the day. If your mind's about to balk, focus your eyes and attention on all the reasons it will be worth your while to ConZentrate. As George Eliot said, "It is never too late to become what you might have been." It is only too late if we don't start.

Focus and Maintain Attention—When You Don't Feel Like It

Confusion	ConZentration
Mind is underwhelmed, overwhelmed "I really want to have a garage sale, but there's so much stuff, it's more trouble than it's worth."	*Mind knows it's worthwhile* "I want to get rid of this junk and make some cash, so I'm going to have a garage sale."
Focused on objections "It's going to take me hours just to organize all this junk."	*Focused on objectives* "I'll place an ad in the paper so we get lots of people."
Why not "I bet no one comes. It would really be a bummer to go to all that effort and have two people show up."	*Why* "It's going to feel so good to have a clean garage so I don't feel guilty when I go in there."
Difficulties "I have to make and put up signs so people can find our house. And I've got to wash down the driveway, yuck."	*Benefits* "I'm hoping to get to know some of my neighbors. I've been so busy, I haven't met many people."
No goal line "I really ought to get back in shape for my high school reunion."	*Bookend goal lines* "I'm going to start dieting today and lose twenty pounds by June 28."
Impossible-to-achieve objectives "I'm not going to have any desserts for the rest of my life."	*Achievable, interim objectives* "I'm going to join Weight Watchers and plan on losing two pounds a week."
No end in sight "Man, this is hard. I'm hungry all the time. I don't know how much longer I can keep this up."	*Start with end in mind* "I'm going to feel proud walking in that door on June 28. I'll wear that suit that's been too small."

Confusion

ConZentration

Do it all or not at all
"I'll never be able to keep this up.
I guess I just love food too much.
Maybe I won't go to the reunion."

Divide it up
"Okay, I've lost ten pounds and I'm
halfway there. Good for me.
Five more weeks, I can do it."

Roll over and go back to sleep
"I didn't get to bed until late last night.
I'm going to get a few more z's."

Roll out and get up
"What will matter a year from now?
I won't remember the extra hour of
sleep. I'll take a shower to wake up."

Indulge and feel remorse
"I'm so mad at myself for going back to
sleep. Why didn't I get up like I promised
I would?"

Initiate and produce results
"I'm so glad I got up early this morning.
I've been promising myself for weeks
that I'd do this."

Assume we can do things later
"They hold those services every year.
It's no big deal that I didn't go today. I'll
have another chance."

Act and do things now
"I'm going to approach the choir director
to see if she has room for another
soprano. I'd love to get back into
singing."

The brain is blocked
"I don't want to run these errands.
Traffic is going to be jammed up."

The brain is bribed
"I will run these errands and then stop
by that new deli."

The mind says "no way"
"I'm tired. These errands are going to
have to wait."

The mind says "okay"
"I'll sleep in and then grab a coffee and
hit the road."

Law of inertia
"I hate doing my taxes. They take so
long and I can never understand the
directions."

Law of momentum
"I'm going to gather all the necessary
paperwork and start my taxes at nine
A.M."

Mind in park
"It's April 13 but I still don't feel like
doing my taxes."

Mind in drive
"Okay, I've collected all my W-2s.
I'll start on Schedule C first."

Confusion	ConZentration
Wait 'til we feel like it	*Initiate even though we don't feel like it*
"I really don't feel like staying inside on a beautiful day like this. I'll tackle those taxes tonight."	"I'm going to work until noon and then I'll take Fetchit to the park for some Frisbee."
Just say no	*Just say go*
"I know I promised myself I'd do the taxes tonight . . . but I didn't know my favorite movie was going to be on TV."	"I don't care if I don't feel like it. I'm going to sit down and finish those taxes like I said I would."

WAY 9

◉

Put Procrastination Behind You

Procrastination Club motto:
We're behind you all the way.

Have you ever driven by a service station, told yourself you needed to buy gas, and then sped by, vowing to get it the next day? Have you ever noticed a couple of out-of-date yogurts at the back of the shelf in your refrigerator and thought, "I should throw those away" . . . and then closed the door and gone about your business?

That's procrastination, defined as the automatic postponement of an unpleasant task for no good reason. The key word here is "automatic." When faced with something we need (but don't want) to do, we simply say, "I'll do it later," without considering the downside of our delay.

Newscaster Ted Koppel 'fessed up to being a procrastinator and commented, "What can I say? My parents and teachers used to be exasperated by the fact I would wait until the last minute, and now people are fascinated by it. I need the pressure." For some people, procrastinating until they can't put off a project anymore provides the urgency they need to produce. The question is, does brinksmanship contribute to or compromise your ability to ConZentrate?

Adopt a Face the Music Philosophy

Life, as it is called, is for most of us one long postponement.
—Henry Miller

What's a project you've been postponing? From now on, if you're about to put something off, ask yourself these three questions:

1. Do I *have* to do this?
2. Do I *want* to have this finished?
3. Will this be any *easier* later?

If we need and want to get this finished and it won't be any easier later, **do it now.** These three questions comprise what I call the Face the Music Philosophy. They help us tackle unwelcome tasks when we're supposed to, instead of automatically relegating them to some fuzzy future date. Talking ourselves through these questions helps us reverse the knee-jerk habit of procrastinating because they bring us face-to-face with the consequences of our delay.

Look what happens when you apply the Face the Music Philosophy instead of promising to fuel up the next day. Asking "Do I *have* to buy gas? Do I *want* to fill my tank now so I don't run out on the freeway? Will it be any *easier* to buy gas later?" forces you to realize you're right in front of a gas station and it's to your advantage to pull in now. Instead of giving yourself an excuse to take a rain check, you've given yourself incentive to take action.

There's another technique you can add to this Face the Music Philosophy to make it even more effective. After asking yourself the three questions, *verbally minimize the time required* to complete the task. Say, "It'll take only five minutes to get gas." "It'll take only five seconds to toss these yogurts in the trash." Noticing how little time a task actually takes can spur you into action because it seems almost silly not to do something that will take only a few moments.

Margaret Thatcher said, "Look at a day when you are supremely satisfied at the end. It's not a day when you lounge around doing nothing. It's when you've had everything to do, and you've done it."

A mother of five says she remembers Thatcher's quote when

she's tempted to procrastinate. She's reversed her habit of automatically putting things off by talking herself through the Face the Music Philosophy every time she looks at the dirty dinner dishes in the sink and thinks, "I'll do them tomorrow." She said, "Asking those three questions makes me realize the dish fairy isn't going to magically appear in the middle of the night and wash them for me. And they're not going to be easier to do in the morning. In fact, they'll probably take twice as much time because everything will be crusted on. Those questions bring me face-to-face with the fact that it's better to take ten minutes to take care of them now so I'll have a nice clean kitchen waiting for me in the morning."

"I Used to . . . and Now . . . "

My parents told me I'd never amount to anything because I procrastinated too much. I told them, "Just you wait."
—comedian Judy Tenuta

Being given a derogatory label early in life is no laughing matter. Were you branded with a similarly harmful stereotype? You may have concluded you couldn't ConZentrate because parents or teachers said you were absent-minded and never did anything on time.

It's time to ask if the labels attached to you earlier in life (whether by you or someone else) are still true, or in fact if they were *ever* true. If these negative beliefs are blocking your potential, it's time to update your image instead of allowing yourself to be limited by this harmful status quo.

If only we all had been lucky enough to have mothers like the artist Picasso. He once said, "My mother said to me, 'If you become a soldier you'll be a general; if you become a monk, you'll end up as the Pope.' Instead I became a painter and wound up as Picasso." His mother's confidence in him was contagious. Unfortunately, contempt is also contagious. The question, of course, is how we can turn around a negative perception of our capabilities.

Instead of accepting a negative label and allowing it to undermine our ability to ConZentrate, say, "I used to . . . and now . . . "

"*I used to* think of myself as a procrastinator, *and now* I use the Face the Music Philosophy to motivate myself to do things when they're supposed to be done." Say, "*I used to* give up when the going got tough, *and now* I get going when the going gets tough." Say, "*In the past* I would put off unpleasant tasks; *now* I verbally minimize them to inspire myself to take action now."

An office manager told me, "My parents used to tell me I was a space case living in a world of my own. Instead of being motivated to prove them wrong, like Judy Tenuta, I accepted what they said as gospel and behaved accordingly. I saw myself as a daydreamer who didn't have anything to offer. I took a low-paying receptionist job out of high school because I didn't feel smart enough to apply for anything else. Luckily, I had a boss who saw my potential and mentored me. He sent me to business seminars, signed me up for Dale Carnegie classes, and gave me more and more responsibility. After six years, I ended up running his office for him. If it hadn't been for his belief in me, I might still have been living down to my parents' expectations."

Give Yourself a Faith Lift

Skepticism is not intellectual only; it is moral; a chronic
atrophy and disease of the whole soul.
—Thomas Carlyle

Have you accepted someone else's negative categorization of you and allowed their label to limit your potential? Doubting ourselves is the worst sort of self-sabotage. Skepticism atrophies the mind also because it keeps us from trying. From now on, if you find yourself slipping back into your old pattern of procrastinating, give yourself a faith lift. Say, "I believe in myself, and I ConZentrate when I need to."

St. Francis of Sales said, "Have patience with all things, but chiefly have patience with yourself. Do not lose courage in considering your own imperfections, but instantly set about remedying them; every day begin the task anew." Today, vow to give yourself a silent pat on the back each time you begin a task. Compliment yourself for patiently sticking with a project when it becomes mentally challenging. Congratulate yourself for tackling a technical book instead of promising yourself you'll read it later.

"An optimist expects his dreams to come true," noted Laurence J. Peter, "a pessimist expects his nightmares to." Are you an optimist or pessimist about your own potential? Remember, we don't get what we deserve, we get what we expect. From now on, instead of expecting to procrastinate (which will produce your worst nightmare), expect to ConZentrate (which will help produce your fondest dream).

Re-examine Your Rainy-Day Philosophy

You don't save a pitcher for tomorrow. Tomorrow it may rain.
—Baseball manager Leo Durocher

Are you saving something for a rainy day? Sometimes when we procrastinate, it's not because we're lazy or suffering from low frustration tolerance; we're *purposely* delaying an activity for what we think is a rational reason.

The problem, as Durocher pointed out, is there's a risk of losing out altogether if we don't act when we have the chance. It's presumptuous to assume an automatic tomorrow. Are you putting something off right now because you're waiting for a better set of circumstances? Maybe you're planning to spend more time with your grandchildren when you retire. Perhaps you intend to fulfill your lifelong dream of flying a biplane when you come into some money.

In every seminar I ask participants for their favorite quotes. Often people will pull from their wallet a wrinkled article they tore out of a newspaper or magazine long ago. Sometimes they'll share an aphorism from a favorite relative. The "Points to Ponder" section from the *Reader's Digest* has been the source of many of these meaningful passages. Many people don't remember where they picked up the saying, but the message has stuck with them through the years. The following quote was from one of those anonymous benefactors, and it has remained with me for many years: "Every man dies, but not every man has lived."

If you were to die tomorrow, would you be able to go with the satisfaction that you acted on the opportunities that came your way? Or would you be filled with remorse, knowing you had forfeited many chances to fully experience this gift of life? Anne Morrow Lindbergh said, "Perhaps we never appreciate the here and now . . . until it is challenged." Resolve today that you will not wait until your here and now is challenged to appreciate it.

Years ago I had the privilege of being asked to speak on the Royal Viking Sun cruise ship on a leg of their round-the-world tour. My son and I were aboard only one week (and what an incredible week it was!), but many of the passengers signed up for the entire eighty-day journey that included many major ports in a dozen different countries.

The most enjoyable part of this adventure was hearing the vacationers' fascinating stories about the people they'd met and the sights they'd seen. The saddest part was that many of the passengers were widows in their sixties and seventies who were making this voyage sans their spouses. They had postponed their travel plans until retirement. After finally getting to the stage in their lives when they had the time and the money to travel, they no longer had the loved one they'd planned to travel with. To a person, they all said they wished they had acted on their dream earlier.

Your often-postponed event may not be as grandiose as a cruise around the world, but is it worth risking the regret you'll feel for not doing it? This is not meant to be gloomy, it's meant to help you be grateful for your T.I.M.E. and to demonstrate that gratitude by not taking them for granted. William James said, "In the dim background of our mind we know what we ought to be doing, but somehow we cannot start. Every moment we expect the spell to break, but it continues pulse after pulse and we float with it." Vow to stop floating on the sea of postponement. Break the spell and take an action today on something that will make your life more meaningful and rewarding.

Action Plan 9. Put Procrastination Behind You

Genius is the ability to put into effect what is in your mind.

—F. Scott Fitzgerald

From now on, if you're about to automatically put off something off, ask yourself, "Do I *have* to do this?" "Do I *want* to have this completed?" "Will it be any *easier* later?" Verbally minimize tasks so they don't seem so daunting: "I'd rather take an hour and handle it now instead of having it hang over my head the next few days."

And finally, re-examine your rainy-day philosophy. Could you lose this opportunity if you don't take advantage of it now? J. C. Penney said, "The hardest part of any job is . . . getting started." Kick-start your ConZentration by adopting a "do it now" instead of a "do it later" mentality. Be a genius by taking advantage of your precious mind and using it to ConZentrate on some worthwhile project today. You won't be sorry you started; you'll only be sorry if you don't start while you have the chance.

Confusion	ConZentration
Do it later	*Do it now*
"I know I should winterize the house, but it's such a dreary job. I'll do it next weekend."	"I'm going to winterize the house so we don't get caught unprepared by a bad storm."
Automatically postpone unpleasant tasks	*Apply ourselves to unpleasant tasks*
"I really should insulate the attic. I know we're losing a lot of heat up there. I don't feel like making a trip to the hardware store. I'll go tomorrow."	"It won't be easier to go to the hardware store tomorrow. I'll drive over there today and buy the insulation."
Floating on a sea of procrastination	*Face the Music philosophy*
"This is what I hate about living in the Northeast. Maybe I can get away without putting up the storm shutters this year."	"Do I have to put up those storm shutters? Yes! We will be in big trouble if I don't."
Believe in pessimistic label	*Believe in potential*
"I'm so lazy. I just can't get myself to do the responsible thing."	"I'm going to do the right thing so my family and house are safe this winter."
Expect to put things off	*Expect to patiently stick with it*
"Okay, I've cleaned out the gutters. I'll take a break and do the rest later."	"The gutters are cleaned out. I'm going to keep working now that I'm outside."

Confusion

Save for a rainy day
"Look what I found in the attic. That box of photos Denise and I were trying to find. I should take them downstairs, but I don't feel like making the extra trip. I'll retrieve them later."

ConZentration

Start today, not someday
"There's that box of photos. I'm going to take them downstairs and put them on the kitchen table. We can go through them during dinner."

PART 4

Mind Your Own Business

You must know I am entirely
absorbed in my work.

—Claude Monet

WAY 10

◉

Give Me Some S.P.A.C.E.

My husband said he needed more space.
So I locked him outside.

—Roseanne Barr

Do you find it difficult to get absorbed in your work because your office space is crowded, cramped, and chaotic? Do you long for some peace and quiet in which to ConZentrate?

There is a way to set up your work space so it's conducive to ConZentration—it's called ergonomics. Ergonomics is the science of designing our environment so it enhances our effectiveness. It includes everything from placing our chair and computer at optimal heights so we can work without getting a backache, to providing plenty of light so we can focus without getting eyestrain.

This chapter explains how we can create an office S.P.A.C.E. that is *aesthetic* (appealingly designed so we feel good) and *functional* (efficiently designed so we ConZentrate "good"). These five steps can help you set up surroundings that support your efforts to get work done in a timely manner.

S.P.A.C.E. = Silence!

True silence is the rest of the mind; it is to the spirit what sleep is to the body; nourishment and refreshment.
—William Penn

Is it hard to ConZentrate in your office because there is too much noise, or what Ambrose Bierce called "audible grime, a stench in the ear"?

The problem with noise is that our mind is programmed to pay attention to it. One of our brain's responsibilities is to be aware of sounds in our area to determine whether they pose a threat. Every time we hear something out of the ordinary, our mind checks it out to see if it is hazardous. If it perceives whatever is causing this noise is not dangerous, it decides it can safely ignore it and returns to what it was ConZentrating on previously.

Fortunately, our brain has devised an adaptation to constant noise so it's not always on red alert, checking out the hundreds (thousands?) of sounds bombarding our senses throughout the day. You've probably heard the term "white noise." If the mind hears the same sound repeatedly and it never poses a risk, the mind concludes it is safe not to notice it. Perhaps you have friends who live next to an airport or freeway. When asked, "Doesn't that noise bother you?" they say, "What noise?"

Are you wondering what this has to do with ConZentration? What sounds in your work area are *not* white noise? What noises pull your mind away from your work? How can you remove or reduce them?

A secretary said, "Your workshop gave me the courage to go back and ask my supervisor to relocate our office copy machine to the supply room. It used to be right next to my desk and it drove me crazy. It wasn't just that it was noisy; half the time coworkers were hanging around waiting to make copies. They'd be talking, laughing, having a great time, and didn't seem to notice or care that I was trying to get some work done. Plus, every time the machine jammed or ran out of paper, guess who got asked to help out? Some days it seemed like I was interrupted every other ten minutes. It's such a huge relief to not have to deal with that distraction anymore."

What can you do to create the "sound of silence" in your work area? Could noisy machines be moved down the hall? Could the bells of phones and faxes be muted? Could the "You've Got Mail!" announcement be silenced so it doesn't derail your train of thought? Take steps to give yourself some peace and quiet and you'll reap the rewards of uninterrupted thought flow.

S.P.A.C.E. = Proper Posture

It's a sure sign of summer if the chair gets up when you do.
—Walter Winchell

What else happens when you get up from your chair? Is your neck tight? Do your wrists throb? Is your tailbone sore?

A rule of thumb is that ergonomic injuries are easier to prevent than they are to reverse. If we're not standing or sitting up straight, it is only a matter of time before something starts to ache—and as anyone with a bad back can attest, it's almost impossible to pay attention when we're in pain. Whether we process paperwork at a desk, input data on a computer, or answer a switchboard we can prevent muscular aches and pains (and facilitate ConZentration) by practicing proper posture. From now on, be sure to have your:

1. feet flat on the floor. It's okay to occasionally cross our legs or ankles, but doing it for hours at a time places unnatural stress on joints.
2. knees slightly up. This places our weight on our bottom where it belongs instead of being transferred to our knees.
3. back supported. Those small inflatable cushions can support our spine and encourage us to sit tall.
4. elbows at right angles and wrists straight. If our hands are higher or lower than our elbows, tension will accumulate in our wrists and fingers because they're being used improperly. Wrist rests are okay as long as you don't press against them.
5. computer monitor at eye level. if it's below eye level, we tend to collapse our spine and hunch down, which plays havoc with our neck and back.
6. If you're standing, wear cushioned, orthopedically correct shoes, and keep a stool handy so you can take a load off every once in a while.

There's another helpful rule of thumb when it comes to proper posture. As soon as you feel an ache, do something differently. An ache is our body's way of saying, "This muscle/joint is overworked.

Give it a rest." Try getting up from your desk and stretching, doing some shoulder/neck rolls to relax tight muscles, massaging sore spots, shifting in your seat to redistribute weight, or repositioning your chair.

Carpal tunnel syndrome (CTS) and other repetitive motion disorders account for 48 percent of workplace injuries, as reported by the U.S. Department of Labor. Reporters, assembly-line workers, supermarket checkers, data processing clerks—anyone whose job requires them to perform fast-moving, repeated actions can help prevent repetitive motion disorders by taking breaks, using different equipment, varying work tasks, and purposely changing position and posture every ten minutes.

I can attest to the importance of this. I developed a bothersome soreness in my left arm while writing this manuscript. I couldn't figure out why my arm hurt so much, and was having a tough time ConZentrating because I had to stop every few minutes to massage my elbow. It baffled me until I retracked my movements and pinpointed the one activity that put a constant strain on that particular spot.

A file cabinet was blocking my chair from facing the computer straight on, which meant I'd been typing on the computer keyboard at an awkward angle, often for hours at a time. Once I identified what was wrong, it was easily corrected. I hate to think what would have happened if I hadn't diagnosed the problem and made appropriate adjustments. That writer's cramp could definitely have cramped my ConZentration style.

S.P.A.C.E. = Access

Cleanliness and order are not matters of instinct; they are matters of education, and like most great things—you must cultivate a taste for them.
—Benjamin Disraeli

A goal of ergonomics is to design your work environment so there are as few stops and starts as possible. Picture your office. Can you reach high-use items quickly and conveniently, without having to interrupt your work efforts? If not, you may be needlessly breaking your ConZentration by having to get up from your chair to access files or equipment that could be kept close by.

Figure out how you could rearrange your workspace so often-used items are in your comfort zone. If you use your fax machine frequently, move it next to your desk so you can send and receive faxes without having to get up from your chair. If you file forms throughout the day, relocate your file cabinet so you can reach it from your desk. A good rule of thumb is "If you use it more than three times a day, it needs to be within an arm's reach of your main work area."

A college student said, "I never realized how much something as simple as getting up from my chair to sharpen my pencil or find a dictionary kept me from achieving quality ConZentration. I understand now those little side trips were often a form of creative procrastination. I put together a homework checklist, and now I make sure to gather everything I need *before* I sit down to study so I'm not popping up and down like a doggone toaster."

This rule is the ConZentration version of the carpenter's motto: "Measure twice, cut once." B. F. Skinner said, "I spent a lot of time creating the environment where I work. I believe people should design a world where they will be as happy as possible." Collect everything you need *before* starting a task, and you'll create a work world where you can ConZentrate more efficiently.

S.P.A.C.E. = Clear Away Clutter

It's not the tragedies that kill us. It's the messes.
—Dorothy Parker

While Parker's statement may be a bit of an overstatement, she's right in that messes do kill ConZentration. It's almost impossible to be clearheaded in the midst of chaos.

Please picture your desk. Arrgghh! Ask yourself, "Is my desk a *work* space or a *storage* place?" One of the key steps to ConZentration is to clear away needless distractions by instituting this idea: "If I don't use something at least once a day, it doesn't belong on my desk." Be ruthless. Start at one end of your desk and evaluate every item. Those stacks of letters that don't need to be answered until the end of the week? Off the desk. Those bills that aren't due until the end of the month? File them elsewhere.

Why is this so important? Remember the expression "out of sight, out of mind"? What's the opposite of that? You're right: "in sight, in mind." Stress is feeling overwhelmed and out of control. If we're trying to work at a desk that's covered with U.P.O.s (unidentified piled objects), we stress ourselves every time we look down. We see that in-basket overflowing with overdue paperwork and think despairingly, "When am I ever going to have time to get to that?" Our eyes happen to fall upon a pile of pink message slips, and we think, "I should have answered those hours ago." These observations (a) distract us dozens of times throughout the day, (b) scatter and drain our mental energy, and (c) produce a feeling of hopelessness: "I'll *never* get caught up."

A claims adjuster said, "I work for a company that *requires* every employee's work area to be neat. Management wants us to be able to find files on each other's desks in case that employee is out of the office and we need to answer a question regarding their caseload. Our supervisor told us about a study that found if you walk into a public rest room and it's neat, most people will follow the precedent that's been set and make an effort to keep it clean. Some people even wipe down the sinks to keep it looking nice. If there's even one paper towel lying around, though, people feel no obligation to pick up after themselves and the place quickly becomes more and more messy." The same theory holds true for our office. If we organize our work area before we go home so it's nice and neat when we arrive in the morning, we have an incentive to keep it that way. If we walk in and the place is a disaster area, it will only become worse.

When will you be at your desk next? Plan to arrive early and dedicate thirty minutes to turning your desk into a work space that aids rather than abets your efforts to ConZentrate. Perhaps that in-basket can sit on the credenza next to your desk so it is within reach, but out of sight. Phone message slips can be posted on the bulletin board at your side so you can see them when you want or need to but not every time your eyes look down.

By eliminating irrelevant (for now) matters, you've just made it easier for your eyes and thoughts to stay focused on your top priority. From now on, remember that visual clarity produces mental clarity.

When you're ready to start a task, place it in the center of your desk, move other papers "out of sight, out of mind," and begin. You'll be able to keep your attention where it belongs because you've given yourself a single visual and mental focal point.

Another way to facilitate work flow is to incorporate the principles of feng shui (pronounced *fung shway*). The philosophy of feng shui (which means wind and water in Chinese) has been practiced for over three thousand years in China and is based on three basic beliefs: everything is alive, everything is connected, and everything is changing. The goal is to create space that has a harmonious, positive energy flow. Look at how your work space is laid out. Does it have a feeling of vitality? Is the overall impression one of darkness or light? Can you move easily through the room, or are there obstacles in your path? It's worth checking out a book on feng shui from your library and experimenting with some of its suggestions. You may even want to bring in a feng shui consultant. A friend who did said, "It's hard to put my finger on it, but I just feel more like working in my office now that the furniture placement, mirrors, windows, and traffic patterns have been brought into alignment with these principles."

S.P.A.C.E. = Eyes Have It

There is more to seeing than meets the eyeball.
—N. R. Hanson

Whoever said "Let there be light" knew what he was talking about. Remember this phrase: "Watts up." Ergonomic studies have shown that increasing the wattage of a reading lamp from 60 to 90 watts literally and figuratively sheds more light on the subject so we can focus for longer periods of time without having to strain our eyes.

Furthermore, the National Institute of Health in Bethesda, Maryland, has conducted research that shows some people suffer seasonal depressions caused by the waning of the sun's natural light during winter. While never clinically diagnosed with SAD (seasonal affective disorder), I realize now I had all the classic symptoms while living in Washington, D.C., during the late 1970s. During the gray months of November to March, I felt lethargic. All I wanted to do was crawl under my covers and hibernate like a bear.

Afternoons in the office were almost un-bear-ably long and sleep was on my mind a lot more than ConZentration. That's no longer a problem since I've moved to Maui, land of perpetual sunshine. Mainlanders ask if I miss the seasons. Not a chance.

You may be thinking, "So, if I'm listless during winter months, I'm supposed to move to Hawaii?" Not necessarily. This malaise can be at least partially reversed by introducing more bright white light into your environment. Keep the lights up, move your desk close to a window, or failing that, take a quick walk outside if the sun peeks through the cloud layer. Sunlight can counteract a gray mood and energize a sluggish mind.

A corporate trainer contributed her experience. She said, "Presenters have always known that when we dim the lights to show films we lose half our audience. Low light makes it too tempting for participants to study the inside of their eyelids. Every trainer also knows that in all-day workshops, the group's energy will sag after lunch. We know where the blood is, and it's not in their brain. After I attended your workshop, I started turning the light up as far as it would go during afternoon sessions. I've noticed a big difference in the attention level of the group. Bright white light really does help them stay awake and stay focused."

Would you like to learn an eye-opening way to relieve eyestrain? Close 'em. Hectic offices with their nonstop visual traffic are an assault on our senses. If you're mentally exhausted, give your brain a break by shutting your eyes for two minutes. Cup your palms over them so no light gets through. You'll probably still see dancing white shapes for up to a minute after you close your eyes. This gives good insight into how bombarded your eyes and mind are with nonstop stimuli.

The next step is to say and see black. Thinking "black" gives your eyes and mind a moment of nothingness, so they can rest. While your eyes are shut, you may even want to gently roll them up, down, and around. Think of how good it feels to stand and stretch your neck, shoulders, and back after you've been sitting for a long time. This "rest and roll" exercise is the mental and visual equivalent of stretching your eyes after they've been tightly focused for hours at a time.

Action Plan 10. Give Me Some S.P.A.C.E.

If a cluttered desk is an indication of a cluttered mind, what is indicated by an empty desk?

—coffee mug slogan

An empty desk is an indication of a concentrated mind. It is the mark of a wise individual who has created visual order in order to have mental order.

What can you do to give yourself some S.P.A.C.E.? Can you reduce noise pollution by muffling the sounds of the office machines? Can you align your spine and turn a slouching you into a sitting-up-straight you so you avoid an aching back? Can you move frequently used items closer so you can reach them without sidetracking your train of thought? Can you give yourself a clean slate by moving lesser-used items "out of sight, out of mind"? Give yourself the gift of an ergonomically correct office and you'll be better able to keep the work flow flowing.

Confusion	ConZentration
Noisy	*Silence!*
"I can't get anything done with that paper shredder making that racket."	"I'm going to see if we can move the shredder down the hall."
Lousy posture	*Proper posture*
"I can't stay focused. My back hurts too much."	"I'm going to stand up and stretch for a few minutes."
Inaccessible	*Accessible*
"This is the third time this morning I've had to get up to sharpen my pencil."	"I'm putting the pencil sharpener on my desk."
Cluttered	*Clean*
"Now where is that report for today's meeting? I can't find anything in this mess."	"Here's the report. I'm going to place it in the center of my desk and study it."

Confusion	ConZentration
Eyesight impossible	*Eyesight optimal*
"It's so dark in here. I can't read the small print in this document."	"Let me aim this light at this contract so I can read it."

WAY 11

◎

Office ER

Any idiot can face a crisis—it's this day-to-day living that
wears you out.

—Anton Chekhov

Does it sometimes seem every day is a crisis? Do you throw your
plan out the window five minutes into your workday because
changing priorities and emergencies render it obsolete? Do you
wonder how you're supposed to figure out what to focus on first
when everything is urgent? You're in luck. There is a system that
can help us deal with daily crises; it's called workplace *triage*.

Have you ever watched the TV drama *ER*? If there's been a terrible accident or natural disaster, the ER is swamped with multiple
admissions. They don't have enough personnel to take care of all
the injured individuals at once, so they use a system called triage to
quickly evaluate who can be saved and who can't, and of those who
can be saved, who has the most serious injuries. Their goal is to
maximize the number of survivors, so they use triage to assess the
relative severity of the various patients' wounds in order to make
sound split-second decisions about whom to treat and in what
sequence.

Task Triage

The challenge to think systematically about large, ambiguous questions is inherently daunting. But if we are to manage events, rather than be managed by them, there is no alternative.
—W. S. Rukeyser

Many of us face similar challenges in our jobs. We have multiple admissions and don't have enough resources to handle everything or everyone at once. Just like the ER staff, we need to decide whom or what to attend to first.

Fortunately, most of our dilemmas don't involve life-or-death decisions—although some customers and coworkers act as if they do! Some people are convinced we should drop whatever we're doing and take care of their needs first. That's why it's important to design our own personal triage system so we can manage ambiguous events instead of the other way around. Our goal is to make sound judgment calls about who and what needs our attention most, in what order, instead of mindlessly trying to treat all our multiple demands at once. If someone or something is going to get deferred, we want to make sure he or it is of lesser importance.

Trying to accomplish too many things at the same time ultimately proves ineffective. Plato cautioned, "Each man is capable of doing one thing well. If he attempts several, he will fail to achieve distinction in any." Our challenge is, how do we distinguish, in today's crisis-a-minute workplace, what one thing is the best use of our T.I.M.E. (Thoughts, Interests, Moments, Emotions)?

What Should I ConZentrate on First?

Beware of dissipating your powers; strive constantly to concentrate them.
—Goethe

The key to distinguishing what to ConZentrate on first is to compare competing priorities to our primary purpose instead of to each other. Comparing our many demands to each other and asking,

"Should I do this or that?" will only create further confusion. From now on, when we can't decide what to focus on first because everything's urgent, take these three **Task Triage** steps.

Step 1. Clarify your primary function. What is the overall purpose of your work? What can only *you* do? State this mission in one, succinct statement and post it in your work area. It will help guide your actions and keep you on track when deciding what deserves your attention most. If you are the training director of an organization, perhaps your primary purpose is to give employees the aptitudes and attitudes to deliver first-rate service to everyone you do business with.

Step 2. List tasks competing for your immediate attention. (I'm assuming this is a have-to-decide-now situation, not a normal planning session for the day.) If you can, write them down so you can see them in black and white instead of having them crowd and cloud your brain. Imagine the tasks you need to do today include planning the company Christmas party, teaching an employee workshop on communication, conducting interviews with potential new hires, and printing up and distributing the monthly in-house newsletter.

Step 3. Compare each task to your overriding purpose. Which will help you achieve your chief responsibility *most*? The task that will contribute most to accomplishing your primary function is your high-payoff priority. Comparing these different tasks to your primary purpose helps you see that ConZentrating on delivering a great workshop to current employees on how to better communicate with customers and coworkers is the best use of your T.I.M.E. The other commitments are important, but not as important as this activity that will directly influence employees' ability to deliver top-notch service.

ConZentrate on High-Payoff Priorities

What saves a man is to take a step. Then another step.
—**Antoine de Saint-Exupéry**

The high-payoff priority concept is sometimes easier to grasp when it is illustrated with a real-life example. I had an opportunity to speak at an annual convention for a national campground chain. My topic was how these family-owned-and-operated businesses could get the biggest bang for their ConZentration buck. These mom-and-pop owners handled dozens of chores themselves every day and wanted to make sure they were ConZentrating on the right ones. I suggested they devise their own triage system for determining how best to spend their T.I.M.E. They used the following process to do just that. They:

1. Identified their overriding objective. They decided their mission was to make every customer a repeat customer, which is a great objective for any for-profit, service-oriented business.
2. Listed all the activities required to operate and maintain their business. This included everything from taking out the trash to taking reservations.
3. Solicited feedback from their customers (they're the ones who know!) as to what attracted them to their campground and what kept them coming back. They created a checklist with all their amenities and attributes and asked guests to rank the top five that convinced them to visit and revisit.
4. Tallied the results. Of the fifty items listed (for example, an on-site convenience store, a swimming pool, friendly service, reasonable prices, easy access from the freeway), two features were far and away the most popular. Clean rest rooms/showers was number one, and a quick check-in was number two.
5. Took tangible steps to make sure those two high-payoff items were attended to—no matter what. The entrepreneurs knew they couldn't afford to overlook these primary attractions, so they instituted a policy of checking the bathrooms/showers every two hours. They bought walkie-talkies and agreed to page their partner to come help out if more than two people were waiting to check in. If Pop was pulling weeds and saw several RVs pull in, he would abandon the yard and head for the lobby. If Mom was in the

back taking inventory and someone walked in, instead of calling out, "I'll be with you in just a minute," she would immediately come out front to greet their guests. They knew focusing on these high-payoff priorities would give them the biggest bang for their ConZentration buck.

Are you wondering how you can apply this to your life? "A weakness of all human beings," Henry Ford said, "is trying to do too many things at once. That scatters effort and destroys direction. It makes for haste, and haste makes waste." The next time all hell breaks loose and you have several emergencies competing for your attention, you can make haste and tackle them all at once or you can perform task triage. What's it going to be?

Put the 80/20 Rule to Work for You

He flung himself from the room, flung himself upon his horse,
and rode madly off in all directions.
—Stephen Leacock

There's another system that can help us determine what most deserves our ConZentration instead of going off in all directions. If you've taken time management workshops, you've probably read about the Pareto Principle, or the 80/20 rule, as it's popularly called. Pareto was an economist who discovered that 20 percent of the population possessed 80 percent of the wealth. Since then, people have been fascinated to find that his generalization "20 percent of the whole produces 80 percent of the value" applies to many other situations.

Publishers know 80 percent of their income will come from 20 percent of their authors. Twenty percent of an organization's employees usually cause 80 percent of the personnel problems. Most stores know that 80 percent of their sales come from 20 percent of their items on the shelf (staples such as dairy products, meat, bread, fruit, and vegetables). They use that insight to increase profits by strategically locating the vital few items on the perimeters of the store so shoppers must pass by hundreds of impulse buys.

United Airlines brilliantly capitalized on this concept by originating the Frequent Flyer program. Their research revealed that focusing on business travelers (the vital few who produced a majority of United's revenues) would exponentially increase their income. They set up a strategic program to recruit and reward these high-priority passengers and reaped impressive financial rewards for their resourcefulness.

Next time you're so busy you can't think straight, stop for a second and ask yourself, "What is my 20 percent? How can I set up a system to ConZentrate on the vital few—no matter what?" As the saying goes, the main thing is to keep the main thing the main thing. Focus on the main thing, and at least you'll know you're spending your T.I.M.E. where it will do the most good.

Action Plan 11. Office ER

There can't be a crisis next week. My schedule is already full.

—Henry Kissinger

Many of us feel we can't have a crisis *any* day because our schedule is already full. From now on, when you're so busy your head is spinning, stop. Ask yourself: "Which of these crises can be saved? Which are a lost cause?" Compare your multiple demands to your purpose, not to each other. As Henry David Thoreau said, "It is not enough to be busy, so are the ants. The question is, what are we busy about?" Ask yourself which of these many activities will give you the biggest bang for your ConZentration buck. Devise your own personalized system so you attend to your high-payoff priorities no matter how busy you are.

Confusion	ConZentration
Fling madly in all directions	*Task triage*
"I've got to answer that e-mail. Oh, no, I was supposed to call Shirley an hour ago; and wasn't there a meeting?"	"Of everything I have to do, what is most important right now? What can't wait?"

Confusion	**ConZentration**
Ignorant of primary function "Someone else can take care of that customer. It's my break."	*Identify primary function* "Our top priority is to motivate every customer to come back."
Compare tasks to each other "Should I process these invoices or input those sale figures first? Or maybe I should fax these orders to our main office. I don't know."	*Compare tasks to purpose* "Of all the things that need to be done, which will contribute most directly to serving our customers?"
Attend to any and all activities "I'm so tired I can hardly see straight, but I've got to get all these finished before I can go home."	*Attend to high-payoff activities* "I'm going to place these orders first so our customers receive these items on time."
Handle items as they emerge "Okay, I'll show you how that computer program works," while thinking to yourself, "This will make me late."	*Handle emergencies in order* "I need to go to this meeting in ten minutes. I'll be glad to help when I get back."

WAY 12

◎

Avoid ConZentration Interruptus

If you don't have anything to do, don't do it here.

—sign on office door

Has your work area become the office hangout? Do people gather around uninvited to shoot the breeze and exchange the latest gossip?

Dancer Anna Pavlova said, "To follow without halt, one aim; that's the secret of success." To ConZentrate on one aim without halt seems improbable, if not impossible, in today's open-office cubicle culture. I once read an article that said we are interrupted up to sixty times a day. (You may be thinking, "That'd be a good day!") The goal of this chapter is to suggest ways to prevent and minimize interruptions so we can maintain mental momentum. An attorney jokingly referred to these as Privacy Acts. Great name. Take these three actions to give yourself more privacy so you can ConZentrate with as few disruptions as possible.

Privacy Act 1: Close Your Open-Door Policy

Here, let me drop what I'm doing and work on your problem.
—coffee mug slogan

For most people, an open door is an open invitation to come in and converse. It is the equivalent of putting out a welcome mat for intrusions. It's time to institute the door-ajar policy. A partially closed door is a visual way of saying, "Think before you interrupt." It curtails mindless interruptions because it says, "I'm occupied, so please don't come in unless it's important."

One personnel director was amazed at the difference this one change made. Joan said, "My desk used to face the main hallway. Every time someone walked by, I'd look up to see who it was. They'd look in, our eyes would meet, and it seemed rude not to say hi. The next thing I knew, they'd step into my office and start chatting. Following your workshop, I did two things. I partially closed the door and I turned my desk so it faces the side wall. Now, I don't even notice the foot traffic and I hardly ever get interrupted unless it's on purpose."

Privacy Act 2: Practice ConZentration Courtesy

Opportunity knocks. People barge right in.
—office sign

There is a more direct way to make sure that people don't barge in unannounced and uninvited. It's called ConZentration Courtesy.

Years ago, Challenger astronaut Gordon Lowe visited Maui and spoke about his experiences aboard the shuttle. I asked Gordon, "What was one of the most difficult things about being up in space?" His answer? "Lack of privacy." He went on to explain they were crammed together in a cramped space (sound familiar?) and they kept bumping into each other all the time. They couldn't go out for a cup of coffee or a walk around the block to get away from each other, so they agreed not to mindlessly interrupt each other unless it was important. This simple agreement helped them have pockets of privacy in the midst of their crowded environment.

I've structured and formalized their agreement so it can be applied to everyday work settings. From now on, practice these **ConZentration Courtesy** steps to honor each other's need for uninterrupted work time.

Step 1. Before interrupting coworkers to ask or tell them something, **look at them!**

Step 2. If they're busy, **ask yourself, "Can this wait?** Is what I need to ask or say urgent? Does this have to be handled now?"

Step 3. If it *can't* wait, say, **"I know you're busy, and could I have two minutes of your time, please?"** Acknowledging that they're in the middle of something lets them know you know they have a lot to do. They'll realize you're not mindlessly interrupting; you have a good reason to ask for their valuable attention. Attaching a number (e.g., "Can I ask one quick question, please?") makes your request for their T.I.M.E. finite, and they'll be more willing to give you their ears because they trust you won't insensitively carry on ad infinitum.

Step 4. If it *can* wait, then accumulate your questions and news and interrupt that person once an hour with several things instead of several times an hour with one thing.

Simple, huh? I'll never forget the time I introduced this idea at a management seminar and a man in the front row blushed beet red. I asked what was the matter, and he said he understood, for the first time, how much he'd been undermining his secretary's efficiency. He said, "Up until now, if I *thought* something, I *said* it. If I wondered if the agenda was completed, I'd say, 'Laura, do you have that agenda ready for the meeting?' If I noted that it was the end of the month and payroll needed to be completed, I'd say, 'Laura, make sure to process those checks today.' If I flashed on a chance encounter I'd had the previous day, I'd say, 'Laura, did I tell you I ran into Mike yesterday?'

"My poor secretary probably never had more than ten uninterrupted minutes in an entire day. When I get back to the office, I'm going to call a staff meeting and suggest we all observe ConZentration Courtesy, me included."

That's exactly what he did, and reported back that this simple system produced tangible results. "Staff members say they get so much more done now. We all realized how frequently we broke each other's ConZentration. We'd strike up a conversation and never even stop to think if this was a good time for the other person. We'd barge into a coworker's office to discuss a problem, never realizing how presumptuous we were being to assume our priority was theirs."

So true. Have you seen the tongue-in-cheek poster that says, "A lack of planning on your part doesn't constitute an emergency on my part"? Discuss this idea at your next staff meeting and propose that everyone practice ConZentration Courtesy for a week on a probationary basis. The results will speak for themselves at the end of that time. Workers will appreciate their newfound pockets of privacy and will find they're better able to establish and maintain work flow. They will also appreciate the uncommon courtesy shown by coworkers and will be more likely to reciprocate in kind.

Privacy Act 3: Give Yourself Peace and Quiet

I dote on his very absence.
—Shakespeare

Do you work out of your home? Do yourself a favor and institute a privacy policy with family members. My sons know that trying to get my attention while I'm on the phone during business hours is a no-no. Unless it's urgent, it can wait. If it's an emergency, they either quietly place a hand on my shoulder, which means they need to talk to me immediately, or they put a note in front of me with a couple of key words explaining what's going on. This is a win-win system because I get peace and quiet so I can stay focused on my writing, and they have access to me when they need/want my attention for something important.

A friend operates a desktop publishing business from her home. Elaine designs and produces newsletters for entrepreneurs and associations. We were catching up at a convention and she told me she was having trouble ConZentrating in her home office. Salespeople and friends who knew she was home during the day would call and sometimes even drop by without notice. She didn't want to be unfriendly, but these frequent interruptions were seriously compromising her productivity. When I asked why she just didn't leave her answering machine on, she said she felt obligated to be accessible to clients and didn't want to hurt people's feelings by ignoring their calls.

I talked with Elaine about the third definition of ConZentration (controlling our T.I.M.E.) and reminded her that she had the right and need to diplomatically take charge of her office hours so she could keep her mind on her work. As a result, Elaine instituted phone hours. She wrote a friendly letter to her professional and personal associates announcing the arrangement. She also explained her policy when handing out business cards. She told people they had the best chance of catching her in person between eight and ten A.M. and two and four P.M. During other hours, her voice mail would collect their messages and she would return their call during the next phone period.

I talked with Elaine several weeks after the convention and she said her new system was working wonders. "I get more accomplished in those four hours from ten to two than I used to get done in an entire day. Better yet, not only are people not offended when I explain my system to them, they're impressed! Several people have complimented me and asked how they could set up a similar system."

How are you going to take charge of your workday by preventing or reducing unwanted intrusions? "Privacy is the most comprehensive of rights," believed Louis D. Brandeis, "and the right most valued by civilized men." Understand and honor others' right and need for privacy, and ask that they honor yours. You'll improve your ability to ConZentrate because you don't have to drag your mind away every few minutes to handle nonurgent requests for your T.I.M.E.

Action Plan 12. Avoid ConZentration Interruptus

Great men accomplish significant deeds through an enduring effort in a consistent direction. When you wish to achieve an important aim, direct your thoughts along a steady, uninterrupted course.

—Proverb 57 from the *I Ching*

If we want to accomplish significant deeds and achieve important aims at work, we need to take responsibility for establishing a consistent, enduring effort. That means setting up systems to create an absence of intrusions so we can direct our thoughts on a steady course with as few disruptions as possible.

How are you going to practice what Judith Martin (Miss Manners) calls "preventative hospitality"? Are you going to institute phone hours? Will you practice ConZentration Courtesy with your coworkers and family members? If you respect others' need for peace and quiet, they'll be more likely to return the favor and respect yours.

Confusion

ConZentration Interruptus
"Hey, Tom. Did you see the Forty-Niner game last night? Can you believe they lost to the Chiefs?"

Office hangout
"How am I supposed to get anything done with people stopping to chat every five minutes?"

Mindless interruptions
"That open door is like putting out the doormat for distractions."

Think it; ask/say it
"I wonder if Alice is out sick. Jessie, do you know where Alice is? I haven't seen her around today."

Taking up T.I.M.E. ad infinitum
"Did I tell you about the time I birdied the ninth hole on that course? I used my 3-wood and was on the green in one and then I . . . "

ConZentration

ConZentration Courtesy
"Hmmm. Tom's obviously in the middle of something. I'll talk to him about this later."

Office hideaway
"I'm going to post this tongue-in-cheek sign so people will think before interrupting."

Mindful interruptions
"I'm going to half close my door so people don't barge in whenever they want."

Think it; ask, "Can it wait?"
"Is it important enough to interrupt Jessie to find out where Alice is?"

Finite taking of T.I.M.E.
"Mark, can I ask one quick question, and then I'll get out of your hair? Thanks."

WAY 13

◎

Make Communication T.I.M.E. Sensitive

We need a twelve-step group for compulsive talkers. They could call it On Anon Anon.

—Paula Poundstone

A grocery checker said, "I agree with the concept of ConZentration Courtesy, but I've worked in the same small market for years and most off our customers know me. They love to talk about their kids, colds, and vacations. We pride ourselves on being the friendliest store in town, but I can't stand there all day and listen to Susie or Johnny's newest venture. What can I do when someone is talking my ear off and I've got to move on?"

This woman's challenge is one shared by almost anyone in a service position. How can we be friendly and efficient at the same time? How can we give the personalized attention customers want, need, and deserve while still getting all our work done? The key is to balance our people and procedural needs so we're serving both, not one at the cost of the other. I call this being Suitably Sociable.

Easier said than done, huh? Horace Mann said, "You may as well borrow a person's money as his time." These three Suitably Sociable techniques are tools we can use to courteously keep people from borrowing our T.I.M.E. (Thoughts, Interest, Moments, Emotions) when we've got better things to do.

Technique 1. Tactfully Terminate Overlong Conversations

My wife never has the last word. She never gets to it.
—Henny Youngman

These following four steps can help us get to the last word in conversations. Ideally, people would understand that time is mental currency, and they would take ours only if they believed the resulting conversation would pay off for both of us. Unfortunately, some people prattle on regardless of whether we want or need to hear what they have to say. Starting today, we are no longer going to passively allow people to hold us spielbound (in other words, talk our ear off). We're going to assert "mind over patter" and learn how to politely say adieu.

First, it's important for us to **update our perception of interrupting**. Most of us were taught that it's not acceptable to interrupt under any circumstances. We were told cutting in is impolite and rude, simply not an option. Unfortunately, some people take advantage of this and talk on and on and on while we suffer in silence and pray that they'll eventually come to their senses and put a sock in it. We may even resort to sending subtle signals (for example, glancing at our watch, tapping a foot, looking at the neglected task awaiting our attention). Unfortunately, anyone insensitive enough to blab on ad infinitum (or is it ad nauseam?) will ignore our polite attempts to wrest the conversational ball out of their greedy mental hands. They'll run roughshod right over our signals and continue to hold forth.

In today's busy workplace, we simply don't have the time to passively wait out a customer or coworker who's waxing eloquent (or not so eloquent). We need to serve many people, not just one—which is why I believe **it's okay to interrupt long-winded individuals when the needs being met are out of balance and we're serving our minority instead of our majority**.

I'll explain. Please picture an old-fashioned scale like the one shown on the following page. If someone's been talking to us for ten minutes, their needs are probably being met. How about our needs? How about the needs of the two customers waiting in line to purchase

groceries? How about the needs of the person who called and was put on hold? How about those e-mails that aren't getting answered because we're being held up by this individual?

See, we're serving *one* person instead of many. In this situation, it's not selfish to diplomatically bring this overlong conversation to a close, it's smart! It's appropriate to bring the needs being met back in balance so we can serve several customers instead of just this one.

Once and for all, understand that we're not the one being rude when we end an overlong conversation. The other person is the one who's being rude by monopolizing our time without bothering to consider we may have other things to do than listen to him/her. The question is, how can we wrap up the discussion diplomatically without dissing (American slang for "disrespecting") the other person? With these **Tactful Termination** steps:

Step 1. Say their name. If we just start talking over them, they'll either exclaim, "Hey, I'm not finished yet!" or continue to talk . . . louder! Saying their name will cause a pause, and that's our chance to get our verbal foot in the door.

Step 2. Summarize what they've been saying. If we paraphrase what they've said— "Mr. Summer, I'm sorry we're out of that sale item"; "Tina, I can understand why you're proud of your daughter for placing first in the swim meet"—they'll know we've heard and understood their message.

Step 3. Use an action statement. Say, "I'd like to give you a rain check so you're guaranteed the discount price on that item next time you come in." Or say, "As soon as we're finished talking, I'll make a note to Charlie to order more sandwich bags." This wraps up the discussion and moves it to a resolution.

Step 4. Close with friendly phrases. Warm words offset any perception of abruptness and transform potential resentment into rapport. Saying "I *appreciate* your telling me this," "I'm *glad* you brought this to my attention," or "I *look forward* to hearing more about your Las Vegas trip at the PTA meeting tomorrow" will provide an emotional context to your conversation so they don't think you're coldly cutting them off.

Step 5: Physically break contact with dis-engaging body language. If the person persists in talking, you can be more appropriately assertive by taking a few steps backwards, standing up, or turning to the next person. Be sure to maintain some eye contact while you distance yourself so they don't feel you're turning your back on them.

I had an opportunity to work with a Miss Hawaii and she found this idea invaluable. She said, "I go to many social events where my role is to be a gracious hostess and meet and greet as many people as possible. This was tough for me to do, because some auntie [Hawaiian slang for "respected or related adult woman"] would want to talk and I would feel terrible tearing myself away. This technique helps me exit conversations gracefully and comfortably. It's been a godsend."

Technique 2. Limit the Length of Phone Calls

> The technological advance I wish I could get is an addition for
> my answering machine: a get-to-the-point button.
> —comedian Alicia Brandt

A bookkeeper spoke up. "Tactful Termination sounds like it would work great in person, but I handle most of my clients over the phone. How can we physically break contact when they can't see us?"

Good question. Say, "*Before we hang up*, I wanted to clarify one last thing," or "*Right after this call, I'm going to . . .* " These phrases actually encourage the caller to wrap things up, because they know you can't take action until you get off the phone.

Also, be sure to end the farewell statement with a downward inflection. Descending the vocal register on the last words of the last sentence adds a feeling of finality. Signing off with upward inflection or adding an "Okay?" (for example, "I'll call back as soon as I have an answer to that, okay?") connotes a question and will kick off the conversation all over again—which is probably the last thing you want to do. It puts the ball right back in their court and they'll probably start up again. Having your voice go down on the last word means that this conversation is over.

The bookkeeper spoke up again. "What if there's no action to be taken? What if the person is just 'talking story'?" We can politely exit personal conversations without hurting people's feelings by saying, "*I wish I* had more time to talk with you, *and I need* to . . . [insert an appropriate activity] . . . get ready for my next client meeting." Instead of rejecting them with an *apathetic* "I've got to go" or an abrupt "I can't talk anymore," we use the *empathetic* words "I wish" to soften our departure.

A workshop participant named Patricia said, "I wish I'd known this technique last night. A telemarketer called right in the middle of dinner and kept me on the phone for twenty-five minutes! I kept waiting for him to stop talking, but he never did! It made me so mad because that's the only time of the day I get to sit down with my family. From now on, I'll use Tactful Termination so *I* control the length of my phone calls instead of passively waiting for the other person to run out of things to say. I realize now that no one can keep me on the phone unless I let them!"

Remember what Patricia said. Never again blame someone else for bending your ear. Take responsibility for how much T.I.M.E. you spend in conversation—whether in person or on the phone. If you don't courteously control the length of your conversations, other people will continue to compromise (whether intentionally or not) your efforts to ConZentrate.

After discovering the caller was a telemarketer and being clear she had no intention of buying his product, Patricia had every right to interrupt and say, "Thank you. I'm not interested," and gently hang up the phone. Some unscrupulous telemarketers are taught not to stop talking. They're told the longer they keep prospects on the phone, the more likely those prospects will give in and buy something, sometimes simply because they're worn down and want to get off the phone.

Patricia wouldn't be rude to politely end the conversation, she would simply be taking responsibility for how she was going to spend her evening. Instead of mindlessly serving the telemarketer's needs and letting him impose his priorities on her, she would be taking appropriate action to ConZentrate on her priority of enjoying dinner with her family.

A sales rep devised his own technique to keep phone conversations T.I.M.E. efficient. He said, "That Tactful Termination idea is worth a thousand dollars to me." I kiddingly replied, "You can make the check out to Sam Horn," and then asked why. He said, "I'm responsible for a large region. I spend one week out of every four on the road, and the rest of the time I keep in contact with my clients via phone, fax, and e-mail. I also chair our county's Democratic Party and manage the campaign of the leading council candidate. I used to make courtesy calls to my clients to make sure everything was okay, and the next thing I knew, I'd be in the middle of a political debate. Following your seminar, I put an egg timer on my desk so I had a visual reminder to keep calls to three minutes."

He continued, "You also said in your seminar to never preface a call with 'How are you doing?' unless we've got the time and interest to be on the phone for a while. When a client calls, I say, 'Nice to hear from you. *How can I help you?*' to keep the discussion focused on business. If they ask, 'Have you got time to talk?' I respond with a timeline—'Sure, I've got five minutes'—so they don't ramble. If they start in on the latest political controversy, I interrupt with 'Al, I wish I had time to go into that, and I need to call so-and-so back.' And when I call my customers, I always start with 'I know you're busy, so I'll keep this short.' These phrases keep me and my clients on track."

You may think these suggestions are unduly harsh. By all means, if you have T.I.M.E. to spare, relax these rules. Go ahead and talk story to your head and heart's content. Most of us simply have too much to do to engage in long, leisurely conversations. We don't want to be unfriendly and focus only on business, but we can't afford unfocused conversations that take up a disproportionate amount of our workday. Our solution is to be efficiently friendly.

Technique 3. Diplomatically Deflect Lower Priorities

I can't give you the formula for success. I can for failure. Try to please everyone.
—Bill Cosby

Would you like to know what to say when people want you to ConZentrate on their priority, and it's not your priority? Instead of abandoning what you're doing in an effort to please people, use the following steps to politely postpone lower-priority requests. From now on, when you're working and someone or something interrupts:

Step 1. Ask yourself, "Is what they want more important than what I'm doing? Is this person's request or need a higher priority than my current project?"

Step 2. Yes? If it is, write a key word of what you were going to do or say next *before* you switch your attention. The few seconds this takes will help you regain your train of thought when you return. When you come back to your original project, you won't have to stare blankly at the page or person and wonder, "What were we talking about?" "What was I going to say?" Your note will trigger your memory and you'll reestablish that precious mental momentum. Plus, writing the key word down means you're now free to temporarily forget what you were working on. You don't have to keep your mental place, so you can give undivided attention to this new priority.

Step 3. No? If it's not, have the courage to reschedule this lower priority to a more appropriate time. Yes, it's important to be accessible, but at what cost? If we consistently honor other people's needs before our own, our ConZentration will suffer the consequences. If what this person wants is not the best use of our

T.I.M.E. right now, use the following positive phrasing to respect-fully let them know you have prior commitments you need to attend to first.

A. Express your intention to deal with their situation. Say "I **want** to discuss this with you" or **"I realize you need an answer to this."** You're acknowledging the importance of their request instead of brushing them off with "This will have to wait" or "I'm too busy to talk to you right now."

B. Explain your previous commitment, using the word "and." The word "but" creates conflicts because it's argumentative. Imag-ine if someone told you, "I realize this is urgent, *but* . . . " Hear the difference if he or she said, "I realize this is urgent, **and** I promised Mrs. Murphy I'd call back with . . . " See how the word "and" con-nects what's being said instead of canceling it out?

C. Ask, "Could we get together as soon as the meeting's over?" or "**Can I** call you right after . . . ?" Posing a question is a way to give the other person some control in the situation. *Ordering* some-one— "You'll have to come back later"—or *telling* him what you're going to do— "I'll call you when I'm finished with this"—is a unilateral action and people may feel they're being bossed around.

D. Close congenially by using her name and expressing your appreciation for her understanding: "Thanks, Sue. I appreciate you giving me a few minutes to wrap this up."

One seminar participant came up with a visual variation on this idea. She said, "I was promoted up through the ranks, and vowed that when I became a supervisor I wouldn't turn my back on my for-mer peers. I instituted an open-door policy so my staff would feel comfortable coming in and talking to me. Boy, did they feel com-fortable coming in and talking to me! My plan to be accessible backfired because I had a steady stream of employees coming in and dumping their troubles on my lap.

"I talked with my dad about this, and he gave me a great sug-gestion. He said, 'From now on, see yourself as an air traffic con-troller. Your desk is your runway and your phone is your airspace. From now on, *you* decide who lands on your desk, who enters your air space, and how long they stay there. If you've got a little Cessna who wants to land, and you've got a 747 sitting on your runway, wave that Cessna off and stack him up in the proper order. If you've got several planes who all want to land at the same time, determine who has priority status. Then bring them in one at a time, but let them know they need to clear the runway quickly because other planes are waiting.'" She said, "This visual metaphor helps me stay in control. Instead of letting whoever or whatever land on my desk and enter my airspace whenever they want, *I* decide who has priority."

Action Plan 13. Make Communication T.I.M.E. Sensitive

I haven't spoken to my wife in years. I didn't want to interrupt her.

—Rodney Dangerfield

From now on, remember it's not impolite to interrupt nonstop talkers, it's appropriate. It's not discourteous to defer requests for our T.I.M.E., it's necessary if we want to control whom and what we give our attention to, when, and for how long. Remember, the key to ConZentration is having the courage to courteously impose on time, people, and events *our* decision as to what's important and what must come first. Starting today, limit the length of your conversations by using Tactful Termination and Diplomatic Deflection. They'll help you balance your people and procedural needs so you can be suitably sociable and efficiently friendly.

Confusion	ConZentration
Suffer in silence when people hold us spielbound	*Speak up when people hold us spielbound*
"I can't believe she's droned on for half an hour without taking a breath."	"Myrtle, I wish I could hear the rest of that story, and it's time to pick up my kids from school."

Confusion

Feel it's rude to interrupt other people
"She'll get mad if I cut her off."

Needs out of balance, serving one person
"Doesn't he understand I have other phone calls to make?"

Endure overlong conversations
"That's the third time he's said that. How much longer is he going to keep me on the phone?"

Deluged with lower priorities
"So we're out of paper clips and we need legal-sized paper" (while you're thinking, "This is going to make me miss this deadline").

Wrapped up in other people's monologues
"Is she going to show me a picture of every single grandchild? I've got other people waiting in line."

ConZentration

Understand it can be right to interrupt other people
"Rita, I need to . . . "

Needs in balance, serving many people
"Roy, I'll look forward to continuing this tomorrow. I need to make some other calls now."

End overlong conversations
"Ben, I've made a note of that, and I'll bring it up at the staff meeting. Thanks for the call."

Defer lower priorities
"Thanks for telling me we need supplies. I'll stop by your desk after I finish this report and get a complete list of what we need."

Wrap up other people's monologues
"Louise, I wish I could see all your snapshots, and I need to check these customers out."

WAY 14

◉

Don't Agonize, Organize

One of the advantages of being disorderly is that one is constantly making exciting discoveries.

—A. A. Milne

A re you constantly calling out, "Eureka!" as you locate long-lost items? The disadvantage of making exciting discoveries is they're often of tasks we should have handled days (weeks?) ago. Your may have even seen the often-quoted factoid from a survey done by Dr. Richard A. Swenson that says an average American spends one year of his/her lifetime searching for misplaced objects.

The key to organizing can be summed up in one word—systems. William Blake said, "I must create a System or be enslaved by another man's." Systems help us turn repetitive tasks into routines so we don't have to reinvent the wheel every time we want to work. The following six organizational systems help us organize our work efforts so we can ConZentrate efficiently instead of putting out fires right and left.

Organizational System 1. Maintain One Master List

If you can keep your head when all about you are losing theirs,
it's just possible you haven't grasped the situation.
—Jean Kerr

Maybe the reason you're keeping your head is because you keep one master list instead of scribbling obligations on scraps of paper that are easily lost.

There are several important words within this suggestion. Some of us are diligent about writing reminder notes to ourselves. Unfortunately we write these notes on the backs of envelopes, napkins, and any spare piece of paper that happens to be handy . . . never to be seen again.

That's why I suggest we keep one master list that contains *both* our personal and our professional obligations. This can help us avoid those dreaded double-booked situations where we've scheduled ourselves to be two places at once (if you've figured out how to do that, please let me know). It also prevents the equally awful experience of having the phone ring and hearing a loved one say, "Weren't you supposed to pick me up an hour ago?"

Master list means we record every commitment we can think of. Why? Because if we don't write down that we need to "pick up a birthday card for Mom," "call for those concert tickets," or "corner Bill at the staff meeting," either we'll forget (which is not good) or we'll remember (which can also be not good). How so? Remembering mental messages makes our brain feel like a bulletin board with a whole bunch of those yellow sticky notes pasted on it. We're trying to ConZentrate and our mind is piping up: "Don't forget that birthday card!" "Remember to call for those tickets." "Be sure to talk to Bill at the staff meeting."

No wonder we can't get anything done. Our mind is going nutso with dozens of distracting mental memos. From now on, *write tasks on the master list the second we think of them.* That way, our mind can let the task go and give full attention to what it's supposed to be doing.

Be sure to put your master list in its place. Beryl Pfizer said, "I write down everything I want to remember. That way, instead of spending a lot of time trying to remember what it is I wrote down, I spend the time looking for the paper I wrote it down on." Pfizer's comment is a reminder of why we want to keep that master list in the *same* place all the time. It's also smart to have your list within reach, but out of sight. That way, you can jot down chores as they occur to you, but the list won't be visible, where it could jam your mental circuits and needlessly overwhelm you with all that remains to be done.

Organizational System 2. Work From a To-Do-Today List

> A schedule defends from chaos and whim. It is a net for catch-
> ing days ... A schedule is a mock-up of reason and order—
> willed, faked, and so brought into being.
> —Annie Dillard

Get each morning off to a good head start by extracting the *seven* most important items from your master list that need to be done *that* day.

Why only seven? Seven is the number of items we can keep in short-term memory. Plus, power is defined as "the ability to get things done." When we look at a long laundry list of obligations, we feel power*less* ("I'll never get all that finished!"). Looking at seven items makes us feel power*ful*—"I can handle that."

Furthermore, seven leaves room for changes in plan. It builds in time for the emergencies that will crop up during the day. As Dillard pointed out, a schedule imposes a sense of order on the day so we can proceed with reason instead of confusion. It defends us from reacting willy-nilly to chaos and whimsically ConZentrating on whatever happens to catch our attention.

Why list only jobs that need to be done that day? ConZentration is defined as focusing on a chosen project and ignoring irrelevant matters. Wouldn't you agree that tasks that don't need to be done until next week are irrelevant matters? "One never notices what has been done," observed Marie Curie, "one can only see what remains to be done." As Curie pointed out, why distract and depress ourselves thinking about undone projects ... especially when they don't need to be handled until later?

List the seven tasks in order of importance. Doing this means that every time you look at your list, you'll have a sense of clarity, not confusion. This organized to-do-today list visually reinforces your mental marching orders so you know exactly what needs to be done and in what order.

Dr. Hans Selye (sometimes called the father of stress management) said, "Trying to remember too many things is certainly one of the major sources of psychological stress. I make a conscious effort to forget immediately all that is unimportant and to jot down data of possible value . . . This technique can help anyone accomplish the greatest simplicity compatible with the degree of complexity of his intellectual life." A manageable to-do-today list with seven tasks listed in order of importance is a tangible way to simplify a complicated work life.

Organizational System 3. Ask, "What Do I Do Next?"

Have a purpose in life, and having it throw into your work such strength of mind and muscle as God has given you.
—Thomas Carlyle

Each time we finish a task, we have a choice. Julie Signore, a friend of mine who is a professional organizer, says it is the most important choice we make all day—and we make this choice dozens of times each day. The choice is what to do next. If we always proceed to our next highest priority after finishing tasks, we'll operate optimally no matter how many changes of plan we make. Consciously ConZentrating on what's most important each time we make the transition to a new project is the key to being effective.

Effectiveness is doing the right thing. Efficiency is doing things right. We can do both as long as we ConZentrate on the next highest priority each time we finish something, and as long as we give that new priority our undivided attention.

A woman named Tess said, "This was a real eye-opener for me. I realized that what I did next was often a matter of convenience. I like to check e-mail as soon as I get to the office. Some of the messages need an immediate response, but most of them can wait. I'm on a lot of joke lists, and I really enjoy sharing the funniest ones with my friends. I realize now that instead of taking an hour out of my morning to forward these jokes all around the country, I should discipline myself to ask 'What's the best use of my T.I.M.E. right now?' and do that next."

I was glad Tess brought up this sensitive issue. It's tempting to focus on what's fun and interesting instead of turning our attention to hard work. Unfortunately, hard work doesn't go away when we postpone it, it just accumulates. We can motivate ourselves to ConZentrate on what's most important by asking ourselves, "Do I have to do this? Do I want to have it done? Will it be any easier later?" This Face the Music Philosophy (covered in Way 9) can help us focus on what we're supposed to do next, instead of giving in to the temptation to focus on what we *feel* like doing next.

Organizational System 4. Purge Paper

We can lick gravity, but sometimes the paperwork is
overwhelming.
—Wernher von Braun

Are you drowning in paperwork? Have you fallen into the same trap as movie mogul Samuel Goldwyn? An efficiency expert suggested Goldwyn clean his cluttered office by throwing away all the old bills, letters, and invoices. Goldwyn reluctantly agreed but then nervously added, "Go ahead . . . but first make copies."

Chances are you've attended seminars on time management, so I won't go into the A, B, C classification system that is a hallmark of almost every program. I will share one favorite tip that can keep paperwork from piling up.

From now on, remember it's not the *paper* we need, it's the *information* on it. If you can access the data that's on a piece of paper elsewhere, *don't keep a copy of it in your office.* The goal is to drastically reduce the time it takes to handle, store, search for, and retrieve paper. Every moment spent filing and finding a piece of paper is a moment taken away from productivity. I know, the pack rat in you protests, "But the second I throw it away, I'll need it!" That's why I suggest you toss only papers that have info that can be found elsewhere. Novelist Isaac Bashevis Singer said, "The wastepaper basket is a writer's best friend." It can be ours, too. As long as you can locate the needed facts and figures, that paper doesn't need to be wasting your T.I.M.E. and overwhelming your mind.

Organizational System 5. Batch and Match

Wisdom is knowing what to do next.
—Herbert Hoover

Wisdom is also knowing what to do *together*. One of the most useful time-saving techniques I learned as a waitress was "Never make a run empty-handed." Food servers are the ultimate multitaskers. If they don't learn to batch tasks, they triple their mileage by making dozens of easily avoided extra trips. If they head to the kitchen to pick up an order for table 2, they grab the butter for table 4, the salt for table 6, and the check for table 7 while they're at it.

We'd be smart to follow their example. We can use a variation of this same concept to capitalize on our ConZentration. Group similar tasks and process them at the same time to get your mind in a groove. It will operate optimally because it doesn't have to stop, start, and switch gears. This is the mental equivalent of cruising in overdrive on an expressway as opposed to accelerating, braking, switching lanes, changing gears, and making little or no headway because we keep detouring. Scheduling phone hours, correspondence hours, and batching "same-same" tasks will increase efficiency because you're facilitating work *flow*.

Organizational System 6. Eliminate T.I.M.E. Wasters

Man is not the creature of circumstances. Circumstances are the creatures of man.
—Benjamin Disraeli

Workshop participants frequently tell me they can't ConZentrate because of one circumstance or another. A goal of the program is for them to understand they can change most circumstances for the better instead of continuing to allow these circumstances to compromise their productivity. The following tips can help you prevent unnecessary activities that take up precious T.I.M.E.

- **Leave complete phone messages to prevent telephone tag.** A travel agent said, "I always leave the purpose of my call and explain they can leave a full response on my voice mail if I'm out when they return my call. That way I can find out what I need in two phone calls without ever even having talked to the person. This is particularly important because many special fares only last a short time. My clients would miss out on these discount rates if I had to wait to book them until we talked in person. I also have fewer incoming and outgoing calls, which frees up time to process more tickets."
- **Call ahead.** A traveling salesman said, "After spending hours in airports waiting for canceled or delayed flights, I've learned to always call before leaving home to see if my plane's on time. I also call doctors, clients, just about everybody I have an appointment with to see if they're on schedule. If they're running behind, I either reschedule, leave later, or take work with me. Instead of cooling my heels in their office, I put that T.I.M.E. to good use."
- **Reduce "face time" by faxing and e-mailing messages.** A Realtor said, "I used to work seven days a week, year-round. I made tons of money, but I also ended up flat on my back in bed with chronic fatigue syndrome. When I returned to work, I had to force myself to cut down on face time. As much as I enjoy people, it exhausted me to be around them all day long. Now, instead of calling clients or talking to coworkers (even when they're in the same office twenty feet away), I e-mail or fax them. This not only drastically reduces the time it takes to do business, it gives me a written record of transactions, which prevents a lot of misunderstandings. I don't go overboard. The personal touch is still important, but putting things in writing means I work eight to ten hours a day max, instead of the twelve I used to."
- **Use your head . . . set.** A dental assistant said outfitting key staff members with headsets has been the single best thing they've ever done to improve efficiency. "We have two dentists, two assistants, a hygienist, an office manager,

and two receptionist/schedulers. Before, if we had a question for one of the doctors, we'd have to track him down. If we had a question for the hygienist, we'd have to go find her. If we needed to check a patient record, we had to stop what we were doing and go retrieve it. Our headsets have eliminated all that wasted running around. Now when we have a question, it doesn't matter where the person is. We click on and we've got the answer or information we need in five seconds instead of five minutes. That may not sound like much, but it adds up!"

Action Plan 14. Don't Agonize, Organize

Organization is what you do before you do something, so that when you do it, it doesn't get all messed up.

—Christopher Robin in *The House at Pooh Corner*

What are you going to do to organize your office so your ConZentration doesn't get all messed up? Are you going to work from a to-do-today list so you don't needlessly distract yourself by thinking about tasks that don't have to be done until next week? Are you going to write down tasks on your one master list as soon as you think of them, so your mind doesn't have to act as a mental switchboard? Are you going to eliminate T.I.M.E. wasters to free up focus for more important matters? Put some time into designing your own personalized organizational systems and you can improve your ability to ConZentrate when you want, the way you want.

Confusion	ConZentration
A lot of lists	*One master list*
"I know I wrote that down somewhere. Now, where did I put that?"	"I'll make a note of that on my master list so I remember."

Confusion	ConZentration
Remember everything we're supposed to do . . . in our mind "I can't forget to take Fido in for his shots . . . and I should stop by the hardware store on the way . . . "	*Record everything we're supposed to do . . . on paper* "Let me put this on my to-do-today list . . . Fido, Hardware. Now, my attention back to. . . . "
To-do list with too many tasks "I'll never get caught up. I'm so far behind it's hopeless."	*To-do-today list with seven tasks* "I'll list these seven tasks in order of importance so I have clarity."
"What do I want to do now?" "Look what came in the mail—my favorite magazine."	*"What needs to be done next?"* "I'll read that later. Back to that budget report."
Keep every piece of paper "This place is a pigsty. I could get lost in here and no one would find me for days."	*Keep access to the information* "I don't have to print up those e-mails . . . I can retrieve them if I need to."
Stop-and-start work pattern "Let's see, I'll fax this, and then go to that meeting, and then input some of that data, and make some calls."	*Process similar tasks at same time* "I'll walk that agenda over to Pam's office and pick up supplies on the way."
Telephone tag "This is the third time we've missed each other. I can't proceed until she signs off on this."	*Telephone takes messages* "Oh, good. Bev's message says she approves, and to go ahead with this project."

PART 5

ConZonetration

I'd liken it to a sense of reverie—not a dreamlike state, but the somehow insulated state that a great musician achieves in a great performance. He's aware of where he is and what he's doing, but his mind is on the playing of his instrument with an internal sense of rightness. It is not merely mechanical, it is not only spiritual; it is something of both, on a different plane and a more remote one.

—Arnold Palmer

WAY 15

◉

Let It Flow, Let It Flow, Let It Flow

> When it happens, I want to stop the match and shout,
> "That's what it's all about!" Because it is. It's not the big
> prize I'm going to win at the end of the match or anything
> else. It's just having done something that's totally pure and
> having experienced the perfect emotion.
>
> **—Billie Jean King**

Have you ever experienced the blissful flow state? Maybe you're an athlete who had one of those exquisite days where everything went right. Perhaps you got caught up in your hobby and hours went by without you even noticing. Maybe you're a dancer who lost yourself while moving to music and you weren't even aware of who or what was around you.

The good news is, *flow can be facilitated.* It can't be forced, but there are certain strategies you can use to increase the likelihood you'll play "out of your head." These ConZonetration techniques work for sports and performance arts (acting, dancing, singing, speaking) and in a variety of creative endeavors (painting, writing, sculpting, and drawing.) Whether you're a weekend warrior or serious competitor, you can use these steps to set up and sustain the zone.

First, it's important to clarify what F.L.O.W. is. It is a mental state that is the result and combination of being:

Fascinated with what we're doing
Lost in what we're doing
One with what we're doing
Wholly involved in what we're doing

If you've experienced this sublime state, you can identify with Arnold Palmer's description of it. He's right. When we're in this euphoric state, we're on a different plane field.

Entrainment

Whenever this feel comes, you just cherish it. What it feels like is you're out there by yourself. When I got in that rhythm, it was like a . . . a force.
—Michael Jordan

Years ago I read an article that described this force that Michael described. The article explained something I'd never heard of until then—a marvelous phenomenon called entrainment. Entrainment was first discovered by a Swiss physicist who noticed that the pendulums of two grandfather clocks placed side by side contrived, over time, to defy the laws of physics and synchronize their swings. Intrigued, he studied other forces of nature and realized this is a visceral yearning—to experience that ethereal fusion when hearts, minds, and bodies operate in unison.

If you're fortunate, you've experienced this transcendent state in which you forget yourself and become one with what you're doing. Musicians swinging together in an impromptu jam session are intimately familiar with this un-self-conscious state. In fact, jazz great Miles Davis once quipped, "I think, therefore I don't jam."

When we emerge from this reverie we usually feel a combination of feelings. Gratitude, wonder, and . . . a reluctant withdrawal. One hates to leave this peak experience because it is what we *all* seek: the experience of being swept up in something bigger than ourselves, and for that moment, life is everything we know it can be.

Throughout history, gifted individuals have tried to articulate their experience of this positive state. Sometimes—in fact, most times—words are inadequate. As Mark Twain said, "Ecstasy is a thing that will not go into words; it feels like music." Language can't do justice to something beyond description. Occasionally someone comes close. They do their best to explain what it was like, and we sigh, "Yes, I've experienced that," and yearn for it all over again.

When has this happened to you? Perhaps in a moment of divine inspiration, you painted a picture, the brush seeming to move of its own volition in your hand. When it was finished, you stood back in awe, knowing what you'd created was better than anything you could have done on your own. You emerged, blinking, suddenly aware that you had been unaware of anything else for that time being. The world slipped away and you were oblivious to your surroundings and the passage of time.

Play Out of Your Head

Wipe everything out of your mind but the ball. Glue your eyes to it. Marry it. Never mind your opponent, the weather, or anything. Make that ball an obsession. If you can get yourself into that trance, pressure won't intrude. It's just you and the ball.
—tennis Grand Slam winner Rod Laver

My own peak experience? The morning I had the Mauni Lani golf course on the big Island of Hawaii all to myself. I had presented a program for a convention group the evening before. There wasn't a flight back to Maui until late in the afternoon, so I treated myself to a round of golf at one of the world's premier courses. I rented a set of clubs and set out for an adventure. Little did I know what was in store for me. The starter said, "There's a twosome in front of you. If you hurry, you can catch them." I got to the first tee, looked in front of me, and then looked behind me. No one. A little voice in my head said, "Why catch up?"

I gave the couple ahead a few minutes lead time and then had the entire course to play at my leisure. I disappeared into Arnie's reverie. I was aware of my surroundings, but I wasn't. Each ball I hit was as sweet as I could possibly hit it. My drives sailed straight down the fairway. My three woods arced up cleanly off the grass. My irons lofted up over the sand traps and onto the green.

My putts? Well, my putts were the pits; but the beauty of hitting those long shots better than I knew how was inexpressibly fine. I was lost in a world of quiet, me, my clubs, and the course. I was vaguely aware of the sound of the ocean and somewhat conscious of the birds in the trees, but nothing broke the flow.

A hole on the back nine will be etched in my memory for the rest of my life. The 180-yard three par consisted almost entirely of a mammoth lava boulder that completely blocked the view of the green. I told myself I should drive up to peek around the towering stone so I would know where the pin placement was. Nope. I smiled and decided to hit it blind. I visualized driving the ball high over the rock and plopping it down in the center of the green. I stepped up to the ball, eased into my back swing, and lifted the ball off the tee up over the rock. I had no idea where it landed, but it felt goooood. I got in the cart, drove around the corner . . . and there was my ball sitting two feet from the hole. Jubilation.

To top it off, I actually sank the putt and birdied the hole. Probably the first and only birdie of my life. Perfection. I raised my club in triumph and looked around to share this great moment with someone, anyone. No one there. That didn't detract from the experience. I knew, somewhere deep down inside me, this was the way it was supposed to be. It was a gift. Of course there wasn't anyone around. I wouldn't have had this experience if there had been. This was between me and the course. Gift accepted. Absorbed. Appreciated.

That's ConZonetration. This section discusses how we can give ourselves more of these go-with-the-flow moments. As stated before, we can't command that they show up, but we can create circumstances that make it more likely.

Action Plan 15. Let It Flow, Let It Flow, Let It Flow

Inspiration may be a form of super consciousness, or perhaps of subconsciousness—I wouldn't know. But I am sure it is the antithesis of self-consciousness.

—composer Aaron Copland

The inspirational state of Con*Zone*tration is also the antithesis of self-consciousness. When have you experienced peak performance? Opera singer Luciano Pavarotti said, "On the day I'm performing, I don't hear anything anyone says to me." When was a time you were so caught up in an activity, you were unconscious of your surroundings? The rest of this section shares specific ways you can re-create that experience and facilitate F.L.O.W. by becoming **F**ascinated with what you're doing, **L**ost in what you're doing, **O**ne with what you're doing, and **W**holly involved in what you're doing.

Confusion	ConZentration
In our head	*Out of our head*
"Everyone is counting on me. I hope I don't walk this batter. I don't want to let my team down."	"Me and the catcher. See it in the glove. See it in the glove."
Aware	*Unaware*
"That college scout is in the stands watching me. If I blow it, I'll never get a scholarship."	"My fastball's humming. Okay, this one's going to nick the inside corner of the plate."
Self-conscious	*Swept away*
"I can't keep this up. I've got a no-hitter going. I always choke under pressure."	"I can get him out on a slider. Put it across the plate and he'll swing and miss."

Confusion	ConZentration
Reality	**Reverie**
"This is the final game of the season. This is my last chance to improve my stats. I've got to get my ERA down."	"I'm having a wonderful time. Every pitch is going right where I want it."
Imperfect experience	**Peak experience**
"Darn. That wasn't the pitch I wanted to throw. There goes the game. Coach is probably going to take me out now."	"This is my day. Everything is effortless. I feel like I can do anything."

WAY 16

◉

Practice Picture-Perfect Performance

You play the way you practice.

—Pop Warner

If we practice sloppy, we perform sloppy. Practice is not preparation for the real thing, it *is* the real thing. If, in our mind, practice doesn't count, we've diminished its potential benefit. Only when we invest it with our full intention and attention will we acquire the quality of ConZentration we want to be able to call upon during competition.

My sons had a soccer coach who insisted his players warm up before every game with precisely coordinated exercises and demanding drills. When a team member complained, the coach said, "You can't dog it in practice and expect excellence to magically appear a minute later." Smart man. The following eight steps help us P.R.A.C.T.I.C.E. as perfectly *as possible* so we are more likely to produce peak performance.

P.R.A.C.T.I.C.E. = Picture Your Desired Performance

The soul never thinks without a mental picture.
—Aristotle

The body never performs without a mental picture. Yet some of us start an activity "cold" without any mental preparation and then wonder why we're performing poorly. From now on, never engage in an activity without first painting a precise mental picture of exactly what you want to happen. As golfer Tom Weiskopf says, "You can't just hit and hope."

You've probably heard a lot about visualization and may already use it in your life. That's good, because constructive visualization *is* ConZonetration. (Destructive visualization is worry, but we'll explore that in Way 29.) Think about it. When we're visualizing, we're disciplining ourselves to focus on our chosen project while ignoring irrelevant matters. We're making wise use of our T.I.M.E. (thoughts, interest, moments, emotions) and putting our interest in action by immersing ourselves in our object of attention.

Previewing your hoped-for performance is a direct precursor to confidence. How so? Confidence (defined in two words as a feeling of "I can") is a result of recent, frequent, successful experience. Think about it. When we're familiar with a situation—when we've done an activity well, done it a lot, and done it recently—we can walk into that situation with assurance. We trust we can perform well because we've been there, done that.

On the other hand, we are anxious (defined as "not knowing") in new situations. When we're in unfamiliar settings, our body naturally produces adrenaline so we are prepared for fight or flight. We can't focus fully on what we're doing because we're preoccupied by our strange surroundings.

What does this have to do with ConZonetration? You've probably heard about and may have experienced the home-court advantage. Visualizing is a way to mentally familiarize ourselves with a situation so we feel at home when we get into it. It's a way of picturing the real-life situation and putting ourselves there in our mind. If you can't physically go there in advance to erase pre-game jitters, you can still get to know the place by vividly imagining every detail of what it will sound, look, and feel like.

Internationally ranked athletes prepare for meets in other countries by watching videos of competitions held at that arena, court, or field so they are familiar with the location even though they've never been there before. Equestriennes wouldn't think of jumping a course they hadn't "ridden" in their mind a dozen times. The goal is to thoroughly acclimate yourself to the conditions *in advance* so you feel at home instead of out of place. You've just given yourself the home-court ConZonetration edge.

Creative artists can remember what Vincent van Gogh said: "I dream my painting and then I paint my dream." Mentally paint your portraits or performances first. See them in your mind. Then produce what you've pictured.

P.R.A.C.T.I.C.E. = Rehearse Sequentially

> My thoughts before a big race are usually pretty simple. I tell myself, "Get out of the block, run your race, stay relaxed. If you run your race, you'll win. Channel your energy. Focus."
> **—Olympic runner Carl Lewis**

Did you notice Lewis mentally rehearsed his hoped-for performance from beginning to end?

Mentally rehearsing an event in sequence increases the likelihood our event will unfold as we envision it . . . *if* we take it one step at a time. It's important not to get ahead of ourselves. You've probably seen interviews with athletes in early rounds of a tournament where they're asked by a reporter to project their chances of winning. Smart athletes refuse to jump ahead and discuss whom they might face in the finals. They know that they've got to win *this* match first and that it would be foolish to spend any T.I.M.E. talking or thinking about the championship round before they get there.

Picturing our performance out of order doesn't duplicate how we want events to evolve on the big day. In fact, hit-or-miss mental rehearsal actually imprints a discordant feeling of being out of sorts. Only by preprogramming ourselves to do each segment in the proper sequence can we establish that rhythmic feeling of flow. This is key if we want to be able to switch to automatic pilot at game time.

Have you ever had a bad day in which you couldn't do anything right? Perhaps you were preparing a meal for a dinner party you were hosting. You were dropping pans, spilling ingredients, forgetting to turn on the oven, realizing you'd left a bag of ice in the trunk of the car, discovering the glasses had spots on them, and so forth. The question is, did you give your brain a blueprint before you started? We can't expect our bio-computer (brain) to perform optimally unless we program it with explicit instructions *in advance*. If we try to make it up as we go along, we better expect to make lots of mistakes.

From now on, take the time to physically or mentally map out a sequential step-by-step strategy. Write down what needs to be done and in what order *before* you start an activity so you can proceed smoothly and confidently. Instead of being flustered and worrying what else we forgot, we can efficiently follow the task itinerary we created so everything goes right, right on schedule.

Imagine you're a ballroom dancer competing for the right to represent your club at the regional finals. You can work yourself into a frazzle watching and comparing yourself to the other couples . . . or you can spend those moments mentally rehearsing every step, spin, and dip of your routine. Which do you think will be most helpful?

P.R.**A**.C.T.I.C.E. = Anticipate Your Worst Nightmare

The future is the past in preparation.
—Pierre Dac

Prepare for the unexpected so if your worst-case scenario materializes, you've already planned how to handle it with poise, not panic. Politicians wouldn't dream of walking into a press conference without first preparing for questions they dread hearing. They don't want to risk getting caught off guard and losing their composure, and neither do we. Anticipate what could go wrong and build mental backup plans so you can stay in the zone—no matter what. What if your mind goes blank in a presentation? Have options in mind so you can keep your mental cool instead of going up in mental flames.

You may be thinking, "Doesn't this advice fly in the face of everything you've taught us? Doesn't picturing our worst nightmare increase the likelihood it will happen?" It would if we just dwelled on all the things that could go wrong, but that's not what I'm suggesting. I'm proposing we prepare contingency plans so we can continue to ConZentrate without a hitch. If you lose your train of thought, wink at the audience and say with a twinkle in your eye, "That silence you just heard was me speaking my mind." The goal is to have a clear game plan for what you're going to do if something goes wrong so you can continue ConZentrating instead of going brain dead.

My sister Cheri used to be a piano teacher. She always made a point of teaching her students how to recover smoothly and seamlessly if they lost their place or misplayed a note. Instead of "awfulizing" their error and losing their cool, Cheri showed them how to stay calm and continue playing (without missing a beat). When recital time rolled around, Cheri's students always played with poise because they had learned how to keep composed in the face of calamity. Could you do the same? Could you anticipate what you hope won't happen and prepare a response; then if it does occur, you're ready to handle it with panache.

P.R.A.C.T.I.C.E = Compartmentalize Other Concerns

If you start worrying about the people in the stands, before too long you're in the stands with them.
—baseball manager Tommy Lasorda

Lasorda is right. We need to compartmentalize (separate and/or set aside into isolated categories) other concerns so we can pay complete attention to our upcoming performance. Unless we put other matters on our mental back burner for the duration, they'll distract us.

We can "unconcern" ourselves with worries or responsibilities by making a mental contract to address them at a prescribed (later) time. For example, you can jot down: "I will think about the job interview while driving home from this game. For now I will ConZentrate completely on playing as well as I can."

Remember, don't order yourself *not* to think about something that's distracting you. Tell your mind it *can* think about this other issue *after* you give your undivided attention to this current priority. And then fill your mind with a detail that keeps your mind in the present moment. Golfer Hal Sutton copes with pressure by "concentrating very intensely on a single blade of grass. It helps me block out the crowd and all other distractions." What's a detail you could focus on?

A woman who is active in community theater says she uses this idea to immerse herself in her roles: "When we have performances scheduled for Thursday and Friday night, I often come straight from my real job. I barely have enough time to go through wardrobe and get made up before it's curtain time."

Pat continued, "Sometimes I'd be a little frazzled and blow a few lines before I got into my part. Now, I go in a corner backstage for a few minutes and study my costume while rehearsing my first few lines. Really looking at what I'm wearing, whether it's a ball gown or street rags, gets me into character. Instead of thinking about what happened at work that day or wondering which of my friends might be in the audience, I'm totally focused on being who I'm playing."

P.R.A.C.T.I.C.E. = Transition

> If I can get that feeling of quiet and obliviousness within
> myself, I feel I can't lose.
> —Jane Blalock

How does golfer Jane Blalock get that feeling of invincibility? Before every tournament, she goes into the locker room and sits in a corner by herself for a few minutes of private transition.

You've probably heard the phrase "We don't get a second chance to make a good first impression." We also don't get a second chance to make a fully focused start. It's imperative to be at our best from the get-go. If we are tentative or preoccupied in the beginning, thinks will only get worse.

You've probably seen Olympic ice skaters giving themselves a secluded transition time in the wings before their turn. We want to do the same. Give yourself at least five minutes alone so you can steep your mind in a step-by-step preview of how you want to perform. Plot your first move so you start strong. Don't allow anyone to disturb your reverie. If someone wants your attention during this pivotal time, tell them you're mentally preparing and will be available afterwards.

If you're thinking, "I don't have the option of physically going off by myself," then *mentally* isolate yourself. Maui Masters swim coach and competitor Janet Renner can be found sitting Buddha-like in the moments before a meet. She's perfectly at peace even though the surrounding pool deck is bustling with activity. She says, "Instead of getting all tense and uptight about the upcoming race, I stay loose by taking a mental retreat."

Janet continues, "This isn't always easy because I taper off my training for big races. About three to four weeks before a championship meet, I gradually back off my workouts so I'll have power to spare on the big day. The thing is, your body has accumulated so much energy at that point, it craves working out. It's important to not let all that pent-up energy make you too hyper, so I always spend the last ten minutes before a race meditating. It helps me achieve an altered state of relaxed focus where I feel supercharged, yet self-contained and serene at the same time."

From now on, instead of planning to arrive on time, do yourself a favor by always planning to arrive early. The frenetic state that is a by-product of running late is the antithesis of the calm, focused state that is a prerequisite for ConZonetration. I remember a teacher telling me a sad story about her prize student losing in the first round of the state spelling bee. She had been convinced this bright young man could go all the way and had spent hours coaching him. Unfortunately, on the day of the contest, his mother got lost and couldn't find the school where the competition was being held. After being given wrong directions from three different people, the two arrived seconds before the contest was to begin. The boy never had a chance to regain his composure. He made a careless error on his second word and was out of the contest.

From now on, do yourself a favor by factoring in a cushion for Murphy's Law. Centering yourself in the moments before your competition or performance with a focused transition will help you get off on the right mental footing.

P.R.A.C.T.I.C.E. = Imagine What You Will

Imagination is the beginning of creation. You imagine what
you desire; you will what you imagine; and at last you create
what you will.
—George Bernard Shaw

A fellow author/speaker was asked to be a guest on Oprah Winfrey's
show to talk about her specialty, customers from hell. Rebecca Morgan was excited about this chance of a lifetime, but also was a little
intimidated about the prospect of being on national TV. Rebecca
did all the above steps so she could be the picture of ConZentration.
Instead of focusing on her fear of making a fool of herself in front of
fifty million people, Rebecca concentrated on developing interesting and useful tips she could share with the audience. She prepared
for her worst-case scenario by coming up with some clever come-
backs, so if an audience member asked an off-the-wall question, she
could smoothly segue into a helpful suggestion.

In the final hours before the show, Rebecca mentally rehearsed the
different scenarios she'd discussed with the program producer so she
felt completely comfortable with the material. She gave herself some
private time in the green room so she could collect her thoughts and
make sure she was 100 percent present when she walked on stage.
She filled herself with her mission to serve, not shine; inform, not
impress; make a difference, not make a name for herself.

And finally, and perhaps most important, she imagined herself
having fun. Instead of psyching herself out by thinking her professional future hinged on how well she did in this "career maker," she
decided to be grateful for the opportunity and enjoy every minute.
She wisely realized that while she couldn't control how the show
unfolded, she could control whether or not she had a good time. As
a result, Rebecca was able to speak her mind and present a valuable
segment that was enjoyed by all.

P.R.A.C.T.I.C.E. = Catch and Correct

Boy, was that a wrong mistake.
—Yogi Berra

Professionals know that one hour of ConZentrated practice is better than three hours of goofing around. Focused practice means upholding standards and holding ourselves accountable for performing and playing "right." If we perform a skill wrong, we should *immediately* correct it. Why is this so important? When acquiring new skills, we train new neural pathways and motor responses. Every time we use the same neural pathway and motor response, we stabilize and reinforce it whether it's right or not. If you're hitting a bucket of balls at the driving range and hook one, STOP! Figure out what you did wrong and make sure to do the next one *differently*. Change your motion, grip, or stance so the next one goes straight. If you mindlessly hit a hundred balls here, there, and everywhere, you are imprinting inconsistency and teaching yourself to spray them all over the place. Take a mini-break after each practice swing and evaluate what went well and what didn't. Then make a concerted effort to continue what was done well and reverse what was done wrong. Contrary to what Yogi Berra said, the only wrong mistake is one we don't learn from. If we catch and correct errors (instead of continuing them), each practice can produce improvement.

A workshop participant said, "I wish I'd known this stuff when I was sixteen!" She said, "I realize my practices have been kind of hit-and-miss. I never had anyone teach me these specific steps to setting up peak performance. I think how much better I could have been if I had used a system like this. I'm going to go home and share these ConZentration ideas with my kids so they can benefit from them. The least I can do is try to teach them what I wish someone had shown me long ago."

P.R.A.C.T.I.C.E. = Enjoy

> I first realized how much I loved the game of basketball when I began to look forward to practices. I mean, I enjoy the practices as much as the games.
> —Michael Jordan

That's the ideal! As basketball great Michael Jordan discovered, one secret to playing well is to enjoy practice and engage our emotions instead of simply going through the motions. Basketball great Kareem Abdul-Jabbar said, "Don't ever forget that you play with your soul as well as your body." ConZonetration almost always involves getting our mind off the intellectual level and into the essence of the experience. When we play out of our head, it's often because we're playing with our heart. Instead of trying too hard and forcing it, we're having fun. If we fill our mind with how fortunate we are to be healthy, physically active, and engaged in something we love, we set up the prerequisites for flow.

I've been lucky to take tennis lessons from a fit, active octogenarian named Tony Van Steen. Once I was having one of those Murphy's Law days where everything that could go wrong was. After I had missed three easy set-ups in a row, Tony motioned it was time to take a break. I moodily plopped down on his bench and stewed over my bad day. Tony sipped his water and wisely, patiently waited for me to get out of my funk. A few minutes later I started noticing the red cardinals trilling from their perches on Tony's colorful, bougainvillea-laden fence. Another couple of minutes and I, literally and figuratively, cooled down in the sunny Maui air and started noticing the spectacular day around me.

Aaahh, that was better. All of a sudden, I was out of my head and into nature. Instead of senselessly getting wrapped around the axle, I was wrapped up in a sense-filled appreciation of my surroundings. A few minutes later, I was back in the zone, stroking them back and forth with Tony, lost in the joy of moving and grooving on the court. As Tony had silently pointed out, there's no such thing as a bad day when we're healthy, outside, and grateful for the miracle of being alive.

Comedian Lily Tomlin has a wonderful line: "Did you ever wonder why no one ever tries softer?" Trying hard means excessive effort, which means tension and tightness—the opposite of the relaxed flow state. Instead of bearing down, ease up. We want a fluid focus, not a rigid intensity. Turn off your head and turn on your senses so the activity becomes a no-brainer. Note the smell of the nearby pine trees, feel the breeze on your skin, breathe in a deep draught of clean air to help you regain an experiential state instead of an intellectual state. Reconnect with the *essence* of what you're doing and you'll soon find yourself in a state of flow instead of taking every think so seriously.

You've heard the saying "Time flies when you're having fun"? It doesn't just fly, it *disappears*. When we're in this altered mental state, there is a tremendous sense of effortlessness. You can increase the likelihood of this happening by purposely "in-joying" yourself. C. G. Jung said, "The creative mind plays with the object it loves." The ConZentrated mind loves the activity it plays.

◉

Action Plan 16. Practice Picture-Perfect Performance

When I'm in this state of flow, everything is pure, vividly clear. I'm in a cocoon of concentration. I'm absolutely engaged, involved in what I'm doing. It comes and it goes, and the fact that you are out on the first tee of a tournament and say, "I must concentrate today," is no good. It won't work.

—golfer Tony Jacklin

Jacklin's quote begs the question "What *will* work?" What works is to use these eight **P.R.A.C.T.I.C.E.** steps to set up this dream-like trance where we're wrapped up in our performance, impervious to pressure and other people's attempts to psyche us out. What is an in-the-near-future situation where you'd like to be the picture of ConZonetration? How much time do you have between now and then? Are you going to spend that T.I.M.E. worrying or rehearsing?

Former tennis champion Ivan Lendl expressed it eloquently: "If I don't practice the way I should, then I don't play the way I can." Vow to picture your desired performance and put the minutes before "show time" to good use. Instead of randomly thinking about whatever comes to mind, rehearse in precise detail how you want your performance to unfold.

Confusion	ConZentration
Picture what we don't want "I've spent hundreds of hours studying for this exam. What if I don't pass? It will all be for nothing."	*Picture what we do want* "I'm going to keep cool and calm while taking the test. I will remember what I studied."
Rehearse—sloppy "There's just too much information here. No one could remember all this."	*Rehearse sequentially* "I'll quiz myself on these multiple-choice questions first."
Fear your worst nightmare "I hope they don't ask much about torts. That's my weakest area."	*Anticipate your worst-case scenario* "I'm going to study torts some more so I'm better prepared."
Stressed out about other concerns "I wonder if I put enough money in the parking meter."	*Compartmentalize other concerns* "I'm going to focus all my attention on this test right now."
Start immediately "Here goes nothing. I'm just not in the mood to do this."	*Transition* "I want to apply myself 100 percent so I can do my best."
Intimidated "I've heard that it's a zoo. You can hear the sweat drop."	*Imagine what you will* "I will walk in, take my seat, and get right to work."
Continue errors "Oh, no. I was supposed to do this in pencil. It's too late to do anything about it now."	*Catch and correct errors* "Let me read the instructions before I start. I'm glad I read this part about using a pencil."
Uptight "I'm so afraid I'll fail. My parents will be so mad at me. I knew I should have gone to bed early last night."	*Enjoy* "I've studied for this, my brain knows the answers. I'm going to let it do its work."

WAY 17

◉

Develop a W.I.N.N.E.R.'s Mentality

A competitor will find a way to win. Quitters take bad breaks
and use them as reasons to give up. Competitors take
bad breaks and use them to drive themselves just
that much harder.

—golfer Nancy Lopez

Lopez is a wonderful example of a winner. A time-honored truth
is that the top ten competitors in almost any field have a similar level of athletic ability. What determines who wins is who has
the *mental edge* that particular day. Who is able to maintain their
confidence if something goes wrong? Who is able to perform under
pressure?

My high school swim coach had her own version of Lopez's philosophy. She used to tell us, "Champions rise to the challenge.
Chokers run from it. Which would you rather be?"

Winning Is Not a Dirty Word

If winning isn't important, why do they keep score?
—basketball coach Adolph Rupp

In today's society, many people have adopted Grantland Rice's
timeless philosophy: "It's not whether you win or lose, it's how you
play the game."

As a parent of two sons who have grown up playing sports, I've certainly uttered that phrase hundreds of times myself (usually when we ended up on the short end of the score). I do agree with the essence of Rice's belief. We don't have to beat our opponent and come out on top to be a winner. I believe winners are people who perform their best and make the most of their talent, skills, and knowledge . . . regardless of the outcome.

I've also come to believe the "It's not whether you win or lose, it's how you play the game" concept (like most thinks in life) is not an either-or situation . . . it's *both*. It's important to be a good sport, give our all, and play our best, *and* it's also deeply satisfying and a whole lot of fun to win. I'll never forget the pure joy on my sons' faces the day they finally won a thrilling seesaw soccer match. Kids and parents alike celebrated this rare win as if they had won the World Cup.

I don't believe in winning at any cost, and I don't believe winning is the end-all. Baseball manager Leo Durocher obviously doesn't agree with this. He once said, " 'How you play the game' is for college boys. When you're playing for money, winning is the only thing that matters. Show me a good loser in professional sports, and I'll show you a player I'm looking to trade to Oakland." Most of us aren't professionals playing for money, so it's more appropriate for us to grasp that winning is *not* all that matters. There is value and honor to be had in participating, acquiring and improving skills, and putting our talent on the line. Our goal is to balance our competitive drive to win with a commitment to act with class. We want to focus on the process *and* the prize, not one to the exclusion of the other.

This chapter explains how we can use the following seven Con-Zonetration techniques to improve our chances of winning externally (on the scoreboard) and internally (having the satisfaction of knowing we played our hearts and heads out).

W.I.N.N.E.R. = Watch the Best

The best and fastest way to learn a sport is to watch and imitate
a champion.
—skier Jean-Claude Killy

We learn skills in one of two ways. We break the skill into its basic components and practice them repeatedly until we can perform them smoothly, or we watch a pro and follow his or her example. We can take ski lessons and learn about knees, ski edges, and weight distribution; or we can trail an expert skier down a beginner's slope and mimic his or her motions.

Yogi Berra (again!) said, "We can observe a lot just by watching." We can *learn* a lot by watching champions and adopting their winning ways. The first time I played golf, I played far beyond what I should have been able to do. Why? At the time, I was privileged to be working at the Rod Laver–Roy Emerson Tennis Facility on Hilton Head Island, South Carolina. Some days for lunch, I sat at the window of the clubhouse overlooking the golf driving range and watched touring pro Johnny Miller and teaching professional Bob Toski hit one perfect ball after another. That first day on the course, I knew nothing of the mechanics (which is sometimes a blessing!). I just stepped up to my ball and tried to mimic the drives, woods, irons, and chip shots I had seen hundreds of times before.

We can accelerate improvement by studying and adopting the proven style of someone who's more talented. Holding the picture in our mind of someone's perfect performance helps us come closer to duplicating it. If you're trying to learn a difficult figure-skating jump, watch videotapes of Tara Lipinski and learn from her impressive example. If you're working on your jumper, hold the timeless image of Michael Jordan freezing his follow-through on the last shot of his last game . . . and then do the same. It's a way to literally and figuratively "play out of your head" because you're no longer you anymore; you're playing as if you were this talented mentor.

I once consulted with members of a women's tennis team who were headed to regionals after winning their local league. These players were talented, but felt they lacked the killer instinct. We explored their reluctance to close out matches and realized the women didn't want to be perceived as being cut-throat. They sought advice because they knew they couldn't afford to let up on their ConZentration at this level of play or they'd let their opponents back in the match.

I told them the key to resolving this conundrum was finding a female athlete who is a role model of *both* compassion and competitiveness. If they could identify someone who exhibited both characteristics, they would have proof these qualities aren't mutually exclusive. They found their role model in Chris Evert. Here was someone who was a closer on the court and a kind person off the court. The women could now eliminate those limiting beliefs and feel free to finish their matches *and* be fair-minded.

What quality would you like to have? Who serves as a role model for those characteristics? Could you fast-forward to your desired skill level by adopting this pro's example? If you're up against an intimidating opponent and you're thinking, "I can't beat this guy," ask yourself "Who can?" and then play as that person would. Adopt their winning strategy so you play above yourself and surpass your self-imposed limitations.

W.I.N.N.E.R. = Invent Pavlovian Prompts for Pivotal Moments

I just kept my thoughts real simple. "Strong edge on outside ski and hands forward."
—Olympic gold medal skier Tommy Moe

Tommy Moe had never won a World Cup event in his career until he was the surprise winner at the men's downhill alpine ski racing competition at the Winter Olympic Games in Lillehammer. Asked after the race to comment on his strategy, Moe said, "I knew if I concentrated on those two things, I would ski fast. That's all I wanted to do."

Smart man. Instead of buying into the pressure of the moment and focusing on the fact he'd never beaten his competitors, Moe focused on the two fundamentals that would help him blast down the course as quickly as possible.

One day I was playing eighteen holes with a scratch golfer (I'm a century golfer) and couldn't keep the ball in the fairway. It was classic infantry golf, "right, left, right left." In exasperation I said, "This is embarrassing. I might as well pick up." Barry looked at me and said gently, "You can pick up, or you can hang in there and turn it around."

My not-very-gracious response was, "That's easy to say. How am

I supposed to *do* it?" He explained, "Pinpoint the pivotal part of your game and then concentrate all your attention on doing that one thing right. For some people, it's taking their club straight back. For others, it's keeping their head down and still. For others, it's keeping a steady one, two, three tempo. Focus on doing that part as perfectly as possible, and it will act like a lead domino. Everything else will fall in place." I've applied Barry's advice many times since then and found his advice sound.

What is the pivotal part of your performance? A bowler said releasing the ball at the same time every time is his key to throwing strikes. A baseball player thinks "smooth connect," which helps him get clean hits instead of wildly hacking at the ball. A sprinter may focus on high knees or driving arms to help him maintain his fastest form.

Understand that unless you *intentionally* fill your mind with a one-word prompt at pivotal moments, you will entertain any and every thought that comes to mind. Hockey goalie Patrick Roy once said, "My concentration was at such a high level. My mind was right there. It felt fresh, like I could stop everything." The key to clicking on a faucet of focus is to say key words at crucial moments.

Remember Pavlov's dog who salivated at the sound of the bell? Our goal is to do a constructive version of that mental conditioning. The first step is to develop a mental trigger (our version of the bell). For athletes, this means developing a succinct, meaningful command for each part of our performance. Since tennis is my game, I've developed the following commands: "shoulder" for backhand, "racket back" for forehand, "umbrella" for overhead, "eyes up" for serve, and "front" for volley.

How did I arrive at these particular prompts? By following Barry's advice and picking the key aspect of my form for each stroke. To hit a good backhand, I've got to turn my shoulder to the net. To stroke a decent forehand, I need to have my racket back so I'm balanced to step into the ball. The term "umbrella" reminds me to hold my racket high over my head. The key to getting my first serve in is to keep my eyes up. And if I want to volley crisply, I've got to punch the ball in front of me.

The second part of our Pavlovian training is to repeatedly, silently bark that command in the second(s) prior to performing that skill. It is a clear way to instruct our mind at pivotal moments to produce our preferred performance.

This may seem obvious, but most players don't have commands, which relegates us to a wait-and-react mode. Imagine we're waiting for our opponent to serve. Random thoughts race through our mind. "I hope she doesn't serve wide to my backhand. That's my weakness. Oh, no, here it comes. I'll never be able to return this . . ." and so on. Imagine how much better we'd play if we fill our mind with a command that directs our body to perform the way we want (for example, "Toes, toes" which reminds us to stay light on our feet so as not to get caught flat-footed).

Devise your own commands to say at critical moments. If you play soccer, your prompt for a throw-in may be "drag" so you don't lift your foot off the ground. When you go for a goal, you may want to say "smooth" so you have a sure kick instead of blasting the ball and missing it.

Golfer Gary McCord calls this "your brain giving your body a chance." He notes, "If you say to yourself, 'Whatever you do, don't hit it left,' guess where your ball is heading? Dead left most of the time. If you say, 'Okay, let's just start it out to the right and try to draw it back into the green,' bingo!" Next time you're at the tee on a par three that features a huge pond protecting the green, *don't* think, "Please *don't* hit in the water" or "Hit it over the water." Don't even use the word "water" or you'll be planting that image in your mind and planting your ball in the drink. Instead, use a one-word prompt that focuses on what you want: "flag." See the shape of your shot. Picture your ball flying high and plopping on the green by the flag. Hold that image in your mind and hit the ball so it does just that.

My son Andrew profited from this idea. Last year he was at the free-throw line with three seconds left in a tied-score basketball game. His command for free throws, one he's practiced thousands of times with the hoop in our driveway, is "swish." You can probably guess, as Paul Harvey would say, the rest of the story. Andrew sunk the shot, much to his and his teammates' delight. I'm convinced he was able to come through in the clutch because instead of begging himself not to miss, he pictured and imagined "swish."

W.I.N.N.E.R. = Next Time

Golfer Craig Stadler was asked why he was using a new put-
ter for the U.S. Open. Stadler's answer? "The old one didn't
float too well."

I guess we'd call that pique performance, huh? What do you do
when something goes wrong? Do you lose your cool and start tossing clubs? Or do you put your anger to work for you and ConZentrate on getting it back?

Remember the two words "next time." They're the key to keeping our cool, confidence, and ConZentration when we get upset.
Every time we commit an error, we have a choice. We can punish
the past or prepare for the future. The second we tell ourselves what
we should or should not have done—our performance will deterio-
rate because there's no way we can play optimally right now when
we're preoccupied with what happened minutes ago.

D. H. Lawrence noted, "If only one could have two lives: the
first in which to make one's mistakes . . . and the second in which
to profit by them." We don't need a second life to profit from mistakes. We can profit from errors the instant they occur if we immediately focus on how we can do it right next time instead of getting
mad because we did it wrong this time. We will make mistakes, but
they won't *stay* mistakes unless we persist in second-guessing ourselves.

Use the catch-and-correct method to focus on the future
instead of the failure. When you catch yourself making a mistake,
correct it with phrasing that paints mental pictures of what you
want rather than what you don't want. "I've got to stop hitting off
my back foot" will unintentionally imprint and perpetuate the
behavior that's causing our poor performance. "I'm not going to
sing so loud and overpower the rest of the quartet" is a prescription for disaster. We would continue to hit off our back foot and
drown out our singing partners, because that is what our mind is
focused on. Instead, tell yourself to step into the ball and sing low
and in harmony, so you're turning mistakes into lessons instead of
failures.

W.I.N.N.E.R. = Never Compare

The 49'er football player Jerry Rice was repeatedly being asked by reporters if he felt he was the top receiver in the NFL. He finally said, tongue-in-cheek, "I feel like I'm the best, but you're not going to get me to say that."

What if we're not the best? Even if we are hopelessly outclassed by our competition, what will help is to set a reasonable goal of planning to play *our* best even if we're not *the* best. We can't control our opponent's skill or performance, but we can our own. What matters is pledging to play at the top of our game, so we feel good about ourselves regardless of the final score. This way, our ConZentration isn't dependent on winning and it doesn't disappear if we're losing—our efforts are independent of the results.

Basketball player Scott Hastings once claimed, "I'm often mentioned in the same sentence as Michael Jordan. You know, 'That Scottie Hastings, he's no Michael Jordan.'" Clever man. If we're faced with a mismatch, we can get uptight about it or we can make light of it. We can marvel at someone's superlative skills without ridiculing our own. We can acknowledge their accomplishments and then get on with the business of accomplishing our own.

The key is to remember our choice: We can psych ourselves *out* or we can psych ourselves *up*. As soon as we believe that someone is better than us, we feel inferior and prematurely defeated. "Why should I even try? There's no way I can beat her." If our mind concludes this is a losing cause, it figures, "Why give my all? It won't make any difference anyway." The essence of ConZonetration is understanding that giving our all every time out *will* make a difference.

I was playing a college tennis match when my doubles partner took one look at our impressive (ranked number one in our league) opponents and pronounced, "I can't imagine us ever beating them." At that moment, I knew we were sunk unless I could turn around my teammate's mindset. If she couldn't see us winning in her mind, it wasn't going to happen in real life. I didn't succeed, and it was game, (mind) set, and match . . . to the other team.

There is another reason comparison ruins ConZonetration. One of the hallmarks of the zone is lack of self-awareness. When we're totally immersed in what we're doing, we have no thoughts of how we're stacking up against others. The minute we start wondering how we're measuring up, we are no longer in that flow state. We can't control whether we come out on top; we can give our top effort.

A fellow tennis player said he was cured of tanking by a college coach who gave him a lecture after he petulantly gave up when it was clear he was going to lose. His college coach sat him down and gave him a talking-to Rob remembers to this day. His coach told him, "Throwing in the towel is a coward's way of trying to save self-esteem. Tanking provides us with a ready-made excuse: 'I lost because I didn't try, not because I don't have the talent.'" Rob said his coach told him, in no uncertain terms, that if he wanted to stay on the team he better be prepared to play his heart out even if it was 0–6, 0–5, and the final point of the match.

A Hindu proverb says, "There is nothing noble about being superior to some other man. The nobility is being superior to your previous self." If your opponent is better than you, see them as a teacher. Appreciate this chance to "play up" and elevate your own game. Instead of being intimidated by someone's superior expertise or embarrassed by the lack of your own, see it as an opportunity to learn from their excellent example. Turn experts into allies by asking for advice, "Wow, you got twelve rebounds today. How did you learn to position yourself so you always seem to be under the basket at the right place and time?" Take advantage of their experience by adding it to your own.

W.I.N.N.E.R. = Encourage Yourself

When I am right, no one remembers. When I am wrong,
no one forgets.
—baseball umpire Doug Harvey

It's bad enough when other people overlook what we do well and focus only on what we do wrong. It's worse when we do it to ourselves. Would you agree that sports is a game of momentum?

Players talk about gaining momentum. Announcers observe a switch in momentum. Coaches sometimes claim their team lost momentum.

Momentum is interdependent with morale. When we feel good about our game, we play with confidence, and vice versa. If we were fortunate, we'd have cheerleaders on the sideline of every performance, saying, "You can do it. We believe in you. GO!" Their enthusiasm, support, and conviction would contribute to the high level of self-esteem that produces peak performance.

Realistically, we won't have fans following us from performance to performance, so we've got to become our own head cheerleader. From now on, we are going to give ourselves the encouragement fans would every time we win a point. We are going to do mental cartwheels when we block a shot, score a goal, or make an out. From now on, pump yourself up (e.g., "Great shot!" "Perfect pass!" "That's the way!") so you maintain morale and momentum.

We are also going to keep our spirits high when things are not going our way. Instead of panicking if the other player is on a roll, tell yourself, "Stay in the game. I can turn this around!" Jimmy Connors was a master at being his own head cheerleader. He kept himself from getting uptight by making light of his on-court mishaps. If he was aced, he would wave a white towel in mock surrender. He chased a ball into the stands one time, perched on an astonished woman's lap, playfully put his arm around her shoulder, and had a sip of her soda. The audience laughed, his opponent did too, and suddenly Jimbo was back in charge, with the crowd *and* the momentum on his side.

What can you do to be your own cheering squad? Make sure your body language projects confidence. Sports psychologists agree it's smart to never let the other side see you sweat. How you act and speak governs not only how *you* feel, but how your *opponent* feels. If you lose a few points and allow your head and shoulders to sag, your opponent's confidence will soar. If you visibly get down on yourself, the other player will quickly take advantage and seize control.

That's why it's crucial to pump your arm (à la Macaulay Culkin in *Home Alone*) when you pull off a great shot. Jog purposefully on and off the field so you look and feel on top of your game. If you're tired, dance on your toes in between points. You can trick your body into feeling more energetic, and your opponent won't get the psychological boost of noticing that you're dragging. If you blow an easy shot, literally and figuratively shrug it off. If you get a bad line call, physically and mentally shake it off, smile, and think to yourself, "Next one's mine."

W.I.N.N.E.R. = Rhythmic Rituals

> I used to have a hundred swing thoughts. Now I try
> not to have any.
> **—golfer Davis Love III**

Rhythm is defined as "movement marked by regular recurrence of elements." Flow is defined as "to proceed smoothly, to have uninterrupted continuity."

What an interesting insight. Rhythm and flow are inextricably connected. If we want to set up a state of flow, we need to establish a rhythm; and if we want to stay in flow, we need to maintain that rhythm. Our goal, then, is to create a smooth recurrence of elements and to avoid interruptions so we keep the current going. Sounds complex, but the following **Three Rules of Rhythm** make it straightforward (so to speak). These three rules can help us create, maintain, and regain rhythm.

Rule 1. To *create* rhythm, warm up physically and mentally with drills that have a cadence. Do stretches or calisthenics to a beat, and then progress to skill routines done with a sense of ticktock timing. Basketball teams commonly practice lay-up drills that feature a continuous, coordinated movement of players going to the basket. Baseball players warm up by rhythmically playing catch. As a tennis player, I can vouch for the exhilaration of trading rapid-fire volleys. Starting at the net (or the intense equivalent of any other sport or performance) is a great way to set up the flow state. When you stand close together and start rat-tat-tatting balls back and forth, it's happening so fast you *don't have time to think*. That's the idea. We want to warm up with a drill that expedites the reflex state, where we're simply doing it, not thinking about it.

Speed chess players experience a similar rush as they race

through moves trying to beat the clock. There's no time to ponder; they're thinking by the seat of their pants. Hockey goalies often have teammates fire slap shots at them, one after another, so they get accustomed to reacting viscerally. Violinists may play challenging sections of music to limber up their fingers and mind. The point is to make sure your preparation has a purposeful pace rather than letting it lag into haphazard and half-hearted efforts. A seminar attendee with a sense of humor quipped, "So what you're trying to tell us, Sam, is if we don't have rhythm, we'll be blue." Right!

Rule 2. The second part of this equation is to *maintain* rhythm by employing rituals during downtime. What do I mean by ritual? A prearranged physical routine we purposely repeat to stay focused. The zone state is most vulnerable during pauses, intermissions, and halftime. When we're playing a point, our mind is on the move and fully occupied. It is when the action stops *between* points, games, and sets that our mind puts the doormat out for distractions. Volleyball players rarely have to struggle to stay focused while they are on the court. It is when they have to sit on the bench for minutes at a time that the mental momentum comes to a screeching halt.

That's why you often see gymnasts walking themselves through their routine while awaiting their turn. Divers may be keeping warm in the Jacuzzi, but they don't talk with their fellow competitors. They stay focused by mentally rehearsing their next dive, seeing themselves taking their prescribed steps to the end of the board, springing into the air, and flipping, somersaulting, and twisting the precise number of revolutions before knifing into the water without a splash. Field-goal kickers can be viewed practicing their step, step, step, BOOM on the sidelines.

If you can't physically keep the rhythm going (perhaps you need to rest, there's an injury time-out, or it's between sets), at least keep your head in the game by keeping your eyes in your head. Remember when we discussed earlier that our attention is where our eyes are? If we allow our eyes to scan the sidelines, our mind may be thinking more about that cute guy/gal in the stands than about our game plan for the second half. That's why many professional athletes cover their face with a towel during time-outs, intermissions, or changeovers. They want to shut out the outside world and stay in the trance-like flow state where nothing exists but the game.

Rule 3. The third rule deals with how to *regain* rhythm once we've lost it. It is unrealistic for golfers (or anyone) to sustain continuous ConZentration for eighteen holes (which often takes four to five hours). It *is* realistic to ask our mind to focus intensely, rest, and then reapply itself.

The challenge, of course, is how can we maintain ConZentration during start-and-stop activities? By definition, taking a break breaks the flow; so how do we get it back? We re-establish rhythm by mentally and/or physically performing a prescribed number of ritualistic swings or skill rehearsals.

If we repeat the same pre-shot routine every time we want to click on our ConZentration, in time, performing that ritual will produce ConZentration. The routine becomes a signal to the brain: "Stop messing around. It's time to focus." The physical and mental ritual triggers your muscle memory and you drop into the automatic behavior that has followed the ritual hundreds of times before.

Have you ever watched Lee Trevino play golf? He's amazing. He can be joking and laughing with members of the gallery, and then, seconds later, place his drive two hundred plus yards straight down the fairway. How does he do that? He ConZentrates on doing the same pre-shot routine every single time. He stands behind the ball and studies the shot; takes three steps to move into his address position, places the clubhead down behind the ball, looks at his target, adjusts his distance, waggles the clubhead, looks at the target and adjusts his distance a second time, settles into his stance, waggles the club one last time, then hits the ball. This finely honed habit is his time-honored cue to pay attention.

Tennis players may argue with the chair umpire and then come back and ace the next point or rifle a winning return of serve. How do they do it? They go into their traditional "rocking back and forth, bounce the ball four times" service motion or their return-of-serve "dancing feet" routine. Those motions, repeated thousands of times over the years, enable them to make the transition from being angry at a line call to being all business.

Yogi Berra asked rhetorically, "How can you hit and think at the same time?" We can't, which is why it's important to design our own "go-to" routine we perform every single time we want to stop thinking and start doing. We're not *trying* to regain rhythm or *thinking* about regaining rhythm; we *are* regaining rhythm. Our ritual jump-starts the peak performance state.

Another way to stay wrapped in our ConZentration Cocoon is not to talk or think about it while it's happening. Establish a "don't interrupt the reverie" agreement with teammates. A perfect example of this happened in 1998 when pitcher David Wells of the New York Yankees pitched a perfect game. While this rare athletic accomplishment unfolded and the tension mounted, the sports announcer described some of the unwritten rules surrounding such a feat—teammates stayed away from Wells in the dugout and gave him plenty of physical and psychic space so he could stay unconscious. They didn't even *look* in his direction for the last several innings and were very careful not to do or say anything that would yank him out of his reverie.

W.I.N.N.E.R. = Ready to Improve

A glorious thing when one has not unlearned
what it means to begin.
—Martin Buber

It's when we think we know it all that our troubles begin. I remember being surprised to see a professional golfer on the practice tee of the Harbour Town Golf Links the day after he won the Heritage Golf Classic. He had won the event by several strokes, and I thought he'd be basking in his victory. Instead, here he was, pounding out drives by the bucket. When I asked how he felt he could improve on his winning game, he said with a twinkle in his eye, "You don't have to be sick to get better." He knew that even though he was at the top of his sport that week, he still had things to learn.

Growth is proof of life. Some of the most glorious champions of the last fifty years are role models for *kaizen* (a Japanese word meaning "continual improvement") and what Zen practitioners call a beginner's brain. Michael Jordan and Larry Bird traditionally arrived early to practice shots—even when they were world champions. Mark McGwire worked with a batting coach to improve his swing—the year *after* he broke the record for most home runs in a season. They realized that there's always room for improvement and that the day they stop getting better was the day their skills started to stagnate.

Today's assignment is to identify some aspect of your ability you'd like to improve. Perhaps you could ask the best bowler in the league to show you a new way to deliver the ball. Maybe you could sign up for a lesson from a voice coach even if you've been singing professionally for twenty years. Experiment with that new potting wheel at the art studio. And remember, when it feels awkward and uncomfortable, don't denounce the experience as a failure and quit. You know what they say: "If at first you don't succeed, you're doing it wrong." (Sorry, couldn't resist.) Remind yourself that it's normal to feel awkward when attempting something new and different. That doesn't mean give up. It means persist through that initial awkward stage so you can add to your talents instead of resting on your laurels and sticking with the status quo.

Are You a Coach or a Critic?

> That's our mother-in-law strategy—constant nagging and harassment.
> **Celtic basketball coach Rick Pitino**

Pitino was actually describing a defensive play, but he could have just as easily been describing the communication style of some coaches. If you're a coach, vow to help your athletes become W.I.N.N.E.R.s by keeping these coaching tips in mind (and mouth) when managing your players.

Tip 1. "Don't find fault, find a remedy," wisely advised Henry Ford. If players are physically or mentally benched for making mistakes, they soon become terrified of making them, and that's all they'll think about. Of course, the more afraid they are of making mistakes, the more likely they are to make them. Vow to be a teacher, not a tyrant, by *suggesting*, not "shoulding." Telling players what they should have done will only make them feel worse and cause them to resent you because they can't undo what's been done. No matter how tempted you are to lash into a player if they make a dumb mistake, remember that criticizing serves no good purpose. "Shoulding" ("You should have thrown to home plate; you just cost us a run") keeps players' thoughts on what they did wrong and does not teach them how to do it right. Instead of scolding mistakes, communicate how this maneuver can be done *correctly* . . . from now on.

My son's Little League coach found this to be a revelation. "This is so obvious, Sam. Why don't more people practice it?" I agree that this idea is common sense. Unfortunately, it's not common practice. Even some professional coaches seem to feel that making their players feel bad will somehow motivate them to play better. I think the key to steady progress (and isn't that a coach's goal?) is to help each player improve his or her performance and play at his or her best. You may not have been blessed with the best team, but that's out of your control. What is in your control is to lead, teach, and guide each team member so he/she is inspired and enabled to fulfill his/her potential and make the most of the talent they do have.

Tip 2. Coaches, also remember the "not, not" idea. Avoid using ghost words in orders to your team: for example, "Don't quit now." "We're not beat yet." "Don't let them mess with your minds." These will come back to haunt you. More helpful suggestions would be: "We can win this." "Keep your heads up." "Play proud."

We're in the countdown to the '99 Super Bowl as I write this, and today's Media Day interviews (conducted the Wednesday before the biggest sports event of the year) were full of players and coaches saying, "We can't afford to commit any turnovers." "Our special teams can't make any mistakes." "The key to the game is no interceptions and no fumbles." Arrgghh. They're focusing on the very think they don't want to do! Be sure to keep your attention and your team's attention on what you want, not what you don't want. ("We're going to control the ball.")

Tip 3. Teach the mental game. Remember earlier in this book, I mentioned that hardly anyone teaches us this all-important skill of ConZentration? Be the exception to the rule. Instead of spending all your time helping team members develop physical prowess, do them a favor by sharing these techniques so they can also acquire the mental edge. Encourage them to develop individualized pre-game and pre-shot rituals. Have them identify pivotal aspects of their game and pick Pavlovian prompts so they can consistently produce peak performance under pressure. Ask who their role model is, why, and how they intend to adopt a W.I.N.N.E.R.'s mentality. Start each practice with five minutes dedicated to mental preparation. Share the team's game plan and have each player state a specific individual goal so everyone is clear, committed, and ConZentrated on playing their best.

Action Plan 17. Develop a W.I.N.N.E.R.'s Mentality

Your mind is only as strong as your weakest think.

—Graffiti

Our flow stays only as long as we *don't* think. As soon as we entertain one "I can't keep this up" or "she's cleaning my clock," we plummet back into a state of self-conscious performance—the antithesis of the non-thinking zone state.

What's a competitive situation in your near future that you'd like to win internally and externally? Whom are you going to watch and model yourself after? How can you be your own head cheerleader and maintain your morale and momentum? What pivotal aspect of your stroke can you ConZentrate on to set up "lead domino" performance? How are you going to stay focused on doing your best instead of worrying about who's best? How are you going to remind yourself (and your fellow players) to turn mistakes into lessons? Take these steps and you'll be a winner regardless of the outcome on the scoreboard.

Confusion	ConZentration
Choker	*Champion*
"They've been the state debate champs for the last five years. We'll never win."	"We've spent weeks preparing. Let's show what we can do."
Wonder how to win	*Watch how a pro wins*
"Every one of them is a National Merit scholar. We don't stand a chance."	"Let's go early and watch them debate South High. We can analyze their strengths."
Already know it all	*Interested in improving*
"I'm going to drop out of the debate. This is no fun."	"Back to the drawing board. We can put this to good use."
Should be a critic	*Next time, be a coach*
"Sharon, you shouldn't have lost your cool. It made us look bad."	"We'll all going to stay calm and composed, okay?"
Compare and want to be the best	*Never compare, strive to do our best*
"If we don't come in first, this whole thing will be a waste."	"Let's conduct ourselves in a quality way so we can be proud."
Get down on ourselves	*Encourage ourselves*
"What were we thinking of? We could never beat a powerhouse like them."	"Aaron, you did a great job. Bill, we believe in you. Go get 'em."
No routines	*Rhythmic rituals*
"Wow, they're even better than I thought. Oh my gosh . . . it's my turn!"	"Karen and Wes, when you're not speaking, be sure to take notes so you can stay focused."

PART 6

Make Your Home Your Castle (Not Your Hassle)

To be happy at home is the
ultimate result of all ambition.

—Samuel Johnson

WAY 18

◉

Fun H.O.U.S.E.

Other people have analysis. I have Utah.

—Robert Redford

T hat was Robert Redford's succinct response when asked how he
kept his sanity in the high-pressure world of showbiz. Where or
what is your Utah?

Demanding schedules, multiple responsibilities, and pressing
deadlines require us to ConZentrate almost around the clock. Our
tired bodies and brains need a break from that killer mental pace.
We all need someplace private we can go to rest, relax, and be ourselves. For some people, that is no longer home. Far from being an
oasis, their home has become an extension of the office. Instead of
being a source of comfort, it is more of the same—a never-ending
list of obligations and hassles.

Do you relate to this? Has your home become, as Victor Borge
expressed it, "a place to hang your head"? Or the cyber version of
that: "Home is where you hang your @"?

Would you like to learn how to make your home a place to *rest*
your head? Face it, if we can't find comfort there, where can we find
it? The following steps can help us turn a madhouse into a fun
H.O.U.S.E. These tips can help us take much-needed mental vacations without ever having to leave home.

H.O.U.S.E. = Hold the Phone

The telephone is an invention of the devil which abrogates
some of the advantages of making a disagreeable person keep
his distance.
—Ambrose Bierce

Does the name Pavlov ring a bell? Repeat after me: "Just because a phone rings doesn't mean I have to answer it." Say it again: "Just because a phone rings doesn't mean I have to answer it." Some of us are conditioned to pick up the phone whenever it rings. I suggest we designate a phone-free hour each night. During that time period, no one picks up the phone. No one. Not to talk to a boyfriend calling for a date, a coach calling about tomorrow's game, a relative calling to catch up. Unless it's an emergency, it can wait for an hour. This is a statement you're making to your family: "We deserve and need an hour in which being together is our top priority." If you live alone, it is a statement to yourself: "I need and deserve an hour of privacy during which I tell the world to keep its distance."

A woman said, "With three teenagers, and with my husband and me active in our church, we never got through dinner without us popping up and down like toast. I finally laid down your law. No phone calls during supper. Breakfast is on the run; my husband's out the door by six A.M. to beat the traffic, my kids are on two different bus schedules, and I drive a car pool. Dinner is the *only* time of day we're together. I agree that the unspoken message when we leave the table to take calls is that everyone else is more important than our own family. Putting the answering machine on is a way of, for an hour a day, putting each other first."

H.O.U.S.E. = Order

The only thing I can't stand is discomfort.
—Gloria Steinem

When we say, "I want to get my life in order," we mean just that. The need for order is primal; it gives us a visceral feeling of security to know everything is where it should be. As Steinem pointed out, we feel out of sorts when things are out of place.

This was demonstrated rather dramatically when Hurricane Iniki swept through the Hawaiian Islands in 1992. Kauai was especially hard hit. You may have seen the dramatic TV footage of roofs being blown off houses, waves flooding beachfront properties, and palm trees bent almost to the ground and stripped of their foliage by the gale-force winds. Luckily, there were few injuries and no fatalities, but some residents' homes and workplaces were devastated.

A week after the hurricane I received a phone call from a long-time friend, Dianne Gerard, a psychologist on Kauai. She rather sheepishly confessed she was calling from her car, where she had retreated to listen to the radio for news of the outside world. She reported she was a reluctant, albeit fascinated, subject of Maslow's hierarchy of needs—turned upside down. Dianne told me, "I am supposed to be in my office filling out insurance forms, but my mind simply refuses to concentrate." She admitted ruefully, "It's hard to keep your mind on paperwork when your world's been blown apart."

Bingo. Abraham Maslow created what he called a hierarchy of needs to explain, among other things, why certain people are engaged in certain levels of behavior. He theorized that human beings' first thoughts are of survival. Only after we obtain food, water, and shelter are we free to focus on the next level of needs, the desire to reproduce and to be part of a family and community. When those needs are fulfilled, we move on to self-esteem and self-actualization needs—improving ourselves, engaging in recreational activities, etc. Maslow postulated that once a need is met, we don't give it much thought because it's taken care of.

Iniki had thrust the people on Kauai back into a survival mode. Residents were scared and anxious because the world they had once trusted to be safe and secure no longer was. Food and water were available only at certain locations and residents had to wait in long lines for their share. No wonder Dianne's mind refused to focus on bureaucratic paperwork. She had more important thinks to attend to.

As a mental health professional, Dianne was asked to help up-rooted residents cope with this devastating event. Her first advice? *Re-establish routines.* These people needed to initiate activities they could count on in a world that had turned upside down. By establishing and adhering to a schedule, they at least knew what was going to happen next. By going to get water at the same time, going to bed at the same time, and so forth, they were getting their lives back in order.

Has a metaphorical hurricane just swept through your life? Has some bad news turned your world upside down? If so, one of the best things you can do to cope with this turmoil is get your life in order. You may not be able to control what happened to you; you can control aspects of your life by re-establishing routines so you have something to count on.

My sons and I just moved from a home we'd lived in for ten years. I'm embarrassed to say, a couple of days after arriving at our new home, I found myself yelling at Tom and Andrew. They had gotten into a fight because they couldn't find their school clothes. We were eating cereal for dinner because we hadn't unpacked the kitchen implements. We were sleeping on couches instead of our beds because boxes were piled so high we couldn't get into our rooms. Just looking at the mess was enough to send us into stress tailspins.

None of us liked how we were behaving, and we decided getting settled needed to be our top priority that weekend. We hired someone to help us and went through the house room by room, unpacking boxes, putting things away, and re-establishing order. We held a family meeting (another ritual we had abandoned during the transitional move) and recommitted to our routines. Within days, we had re-created the harmony we were all sorely missing. Our home was once again a haven where we feel safe, secure, and loved instead of being out of sorts and at odds with each other.

Is your home unsettled or in a state of turmoil? It's almost impossible to feel on top of thinks if your living space is in a state of chaos. Can you make it a family project this weekend to start with one room of the house and work your way through cleaning and organizing it so your home is no longer a mess? Could you re-establish rituals you can count on so you feel more in control of your life? The more you put your home in order, the more you'll get your life in order, and the freer you'll be to ConZentrate on higher-level thinks.

H.O.U.S.E. = Uncommon Courtesy

Life is not so short but that there is always time for courtesy.
—**Ralph Waldo Emerson**

Life is not so busy but that there is always time for courtesy . . . especially toward our loved ones. There are rules for almost every human activity. In boxing, you can't hit below the belt. In football, you can't tackle a player after the whistle. When driving, we obey traffic signs and keep to our side of the road.

Ironically, most homes have no rules. Most of us never sat down and agreed to common rules of courtesy so we can coexist cooperatively with a minimum of conflicts. Anything goes. We call each other names, mindlessly interrupt each other's ConZentration, and say insensitive things that hurt our loved ones' feelings.

Time after time, participants come up to me after a seminar to share a common concern. A nurse articulated this problem well: "I'm on my best behavior at work. All day long, I do everything I can to be kind and caring. By the time I get home, I'm emotionally exhausted. I use up all my patience at work and don't have any left for my family. I end up snapping at my kids and husband. I don't like doing this, but I'm all 'niced out.'"

Sound familiar? Do you suffer from "compassion fatigue"? Do your coworkers and customers get the best of you and your loved ones get the worst of you? Sit down this evening with your partner, roommate(s), or family and agree to common-courtesy rules. Agree to treat each other with the same respect you show coworkers, customers, and complete strangers throughout the day.

One way to do this is to establish a "moan and groan" moratorium. Where did we get the idea it's okay to vent frustrations on our family? From now on, before you tell your partner about the terrible day you had, stop and ask yourself, "What makes me think he/she wants to hear this?" Just because you had a miserable day doesn't mean you have the right to dump all your woes on your loved ones and make them feel miserable. Pouring out your soul may make you feel better, but it will probably make them feel worse. Is that fair?

What *is* fair is to design a "whine time" policy that lets us get things off our chest without ruining everyone else's mood. A good rule is that every person gets only fifteen minutes to gripe about the frustrations of the day. You can talk about the supervisor who criticized you in front of your peers, complain about the committee member who left town and didn't tell anyone, tell about the teacher who assigned you a term paper two weeks before the end of the semester. Everyone gets fifteen minutes of blame, and then that's it. No more. Time to turn your attention to better thinks.

Another way to hold ourselves accountable for being kind and caring with our loved ones is to vow to give five minutes a day of undivided attention to each loved one. We are often so preoccupied with our many obligations, we rarely give full attention to family members. They see a lot of glazed eyes and hear a lot of "Not now," "Keep it short," "Hurry up," and "Can't this wait?" The unspoken message that is being communicated is "I have more important things to think about than you."

I know you're busy, but wouldn't you agree that setting aside five minutes a day to give each loved one your undivided attention is T.I.M.E. well spent? When are you going to see your housemates next? Vow to sit with them one by one, put other thoughts aside, and for five minutes make this individual the most important think in your world. Everything else can wait. Say, "Tell me about your day." "How did that presentation go?" "What was your favorite part of the field trip?" And then, for those few moments, listen with your eyes and your ears to what they're saying.

Listening is the very essence of ConZentration. We're putting our interest in action. We're deciding this individual is our top priority and deserves to come first, and we're connecting with the object of our attention. And perhaps best of all, we're putting our mind where our mouth is and showing, not just saying, that we love this person and that he or she is important to us.

H.O.U.S.E. = Sound Advice

Take a music bath once or twice a week, and you will find that
it is to the soul what the water-bath is to the body.
—Oliver Wendell Holmes

I agree. Music has an amazing ability to elevate mood and evoke emotion. That's why it's smart to start your morning with pleasant music. Simply said, it's hard to be down when listening to upbeat music. Just as the soundtrack from the popular movie *Titanic* can make our spirits soar, the peaceful tones of instrumentals can soothe our soul and start our day with serenity.

The mood we wake up with is often the mood we maintain. People who don't like to get up in the morning often take their bad mood out on whoever happens to be sitting across the breakfast table. While we may wake up grumpy, it's almost impossible to stay that way when surrounded by gracious music. Pleasant music sets a positive precedent by enveloping us in an agreeable emotional environment.

Music can also work on a subliminal level when there's anger in the house. If you've had a disagreement and there's some lingering tension, put on some beautiful music. Save the hard rock for another time. You may enjoy its driving beat, but it is not congruent with peace of mind. Listening to lovely music can turn hostility into harmony (so to speak).

Don Campbell, the director of the Mozart Effect Resource Center in St. Louis, has collected startling research on the potent impact music can have on the mind, body, and spirit. He's found that music by Mozart invariably calms the listener's mind, promotes better communication of emotions, concepts, and thoughts, and stimulates the motivational regions of the brain.

Campbell particularly likes Mozart's violin concertos nos. 3 and 4 to enhance mental alertness, and also recommends Pachelbel's Canon to relieve anxiety, Beethoven's *Pastoral* symphony to boost your imagination, and the *Flashdance . . . What a Feeling* soundtrack to put you in an energetic mood.

Songbird Buffy Saint-Marie said, "You have to sniff out joy. Keep your nose to the joy trail." It behooves us to keep our *ears* to the joy trail. Stop by a music store today and invest in two CDs or tapes of joyous music. At the top of my list is *The Best of Enya*, a collection of ethereal music that lifts us out of our mental doldrums. I'm playing it right now because it provides an inspirational background for creative work. I often play Bach's *Goldberg Variations* and Handel's

Water Music when Tom and Andrew are doing homework because it keeps them energized and creates an atmosphere conducive to ConZentration.

Try it tomorrow. Instead of beginning your day with TV news or talk radio (and its horrifying reports of man's inhumanity to man), bathe your heart and mind with melodies that *soothe* rather than stress your soul and spirit.

H.O.U.S.E. = Escape

Where do you go to replenish yourself? This is not a luxury, it's a necessity if we don't want our energy to run dry. Somewhere in our lives, each of us needs a free place, a little psychic territory. Do you have yours?
—Gloria Steinem

You may have heard the grisly research about what happens to rats when they're crammed together in a tight place. People who live in, work in, and commute to cities often spend hours surrounded by fellow human beings. After a mentally exhausting day of serving everyone else's needs, you may find it more than you can handle to walk into a house full of chores and kids clamoring for your attention.

Starting today, gift yourself with a mini-vacation as soon as you walk in the door. A travel agent once told me, "The purpose of a vacation is to provide *contrast*. If you work in a sedentary job, you probably crave adventure. If you make decisions all day long, you probably yearn to go somewhere where the biggest decision you have to make is whether to have lunch by the pool or in your room."

If your day is usually jam-packed with people, obligations, and deadlines, you need and deserve a few minutes' contrast to that. Let your housemates know you're going to take a fifteen-minute retreat as soon as you get home so you can recharge your brain's batteries. Explain that you need (and deserve) some downtime.

Grant this privilege to anyone else in the house who wants it. If you live with others, greet each other and then take your favorite tea, book, or eye pillow and escape to your private place to "roominate." Orders are you're not to be disturbed unless it's an emergency.

Emerge fifteen minutes later, refreshed and ready to face the evening and your loved ones with a kind heart and replenished mind.

Home-Based Business Rules

> A man is not idle because he is absorbed in thought. There is
> a visible labor and an invisible labor.
> —Victor Hugo

Are you one of the millions of entrepreneurs operating a business from your home? Do your family members understand you're not being lazy when you're sitting on your bed in your bathrobe staring off into space? You could be deep in thought, conjuring up new marketing strategies.

It's important to devise rules so household members know when we're available and when we're to be left alone. Melodie Beattie said, "Why are you feeling ashamed? Whose rules are you breaking? Someone else's or your own?" Many of the home-based entrepreneurs I've met feel *conflicted*, not ashamed. They often feel torn because they're "ruleless," lacking operating procedures that clearly state, "This is my workplace and work time. Please respect it."

Martin Mull said, "Having kids is like having a bowling alley installed in your brain." If you are raising small children at home and trying at the same time to run a business, you may feel your office has turned into a bowling alley. It's in everyone's best interest to establish guidelines so you can act professionally—even when it's three P.M. and you're peeling and segmenting oranges for your daughter's soccer team while on the phone with an interstate conference call.

Set up your own personalized version of ConZentration Courtesy. If my sons want to talk to me during office hours, we have an agreement. They *don't* call out to me . . . I could be in a moment of divine inspiration. Instead, they walk upstairs and check to see if I'm intent on my work. If I am, they write a note with their request and put it in front of me. Sometimes their request requires a simple nod (for example, "Can we go to Hari's house? We'll be back by six P.M.") and they're off. Sometimes their question—"Can you drive us to baseball at four P.M.?"—needs to be discussed. If so, our deal is that as soon as

I'm finished with that particular task, they are my next priority. At that point, I call them or go to them, we talk about what needs to happen, and then I return to work and they proceed with their plans. This policy is a win-win system that lets me run an efficient home office while still being accessible to my sons.

Design your own policies and procedures for when you need a few more minutes of ConZentration. Agree to your own "home rules" so everyone honors each other's right to have physical and psychological space. Joseph Campbell said, "A sacred place is an absolute necessity for anybody today. You must have a room or a certain hour of the day when you have . . . creative incubation." What are you going to do to create your own sacred space and time at home?

Action Plan 18. Fun H.O.U.S.E.

They keep coming up with new things that nobody really wants. Cameras that talk and clocks that make coffee. You know what we really want? To lie down for a second.

—comedian Paul Reiser

Our home is one of the few places in our life where we can mentally lie down and not feel compelled to ConZentrate every waking minute. What can you do to create a home that re-energizes (versus de-energizes) your body, mind, and soul? Football coach George Allen said, "Leisure time is the five or six hours when you sleep at night." Hopefully, our home is more than simply a place to get our five (?!) hours of sleep. Which of these steps are you going to take tonight to make your home a "fun H.O.U.S.E." instead of a madhouse?

Confusion	ConZentration
Home is extension of office, a place to hang our head	*Home is an oasis, a place to rest our head*
"I can't believe my boss said that to me in front of everyone."	"Enough of that. I'm going to leave my boss at the office."

Confusion

ConZentration

Madhouse
"They were supposed to put me in charge of that project; instead they gave it to Carl. The nerve."

Fun house
"I'll talk to my supervisor about that tomorrow. Let's play some Ping-Pong."

Answer the phone all the time
"Jennie, it's for you. That's the third phone call in the last ten minutes. Are we ever going to finish this conversation?"

Hold the phone
"Let the answering machine handle that. So, how'd cheerleader practice go today?"

Chaos rules
"What a pigsty."

Order rules
"Pick up the living room."

Speak up whenever you want
"I don't care if Dad's on the phone. Steve has to know now if I can go with him to the park."

Uncommon courtesy
"I'll write a note asking Dad if I can go shoot hoops with Steve."

Moody
"Boy, did you get out of the wrong side of bed this morning. Why are you so grouchy?"

Sound advice
"I'll play some Mozart. That will get our day off to a good start."

Running on empty
"When am I going to get some peace and quiet?"

Escape to replenish ourselves
"I feel like a new person. That nap was just what I needed."

WAY 19

◉

Cleanliness Is Next to
. . . Impossible

Cleanliness is not next to godliness. It isn't even in the
same neighborhood. No one has ever gotten a religious
experience out of removing burned-on cheese from the
grill of the toaster oven.

—Erma Bombeck

Erma's right, there are parts of housework we won't enjoy no matter how much Zen we bring to the countertop. Doesn't it make
sense then, to eliminate as many of these unpleasant tasks as possible?
Dave Barry has a creative way of dispensing with onerous chores. He
suggests, "The best way to clean a frying pan that has burned food
cemented to the bottom is to let it soak in soapy water for several days
and then, when nobody is looking, throw it in the garbage."

You've heard the expression "killing time"? The goal of this
chapter is to share some ideas on how we can handle household
responsibilities without it killing our T.I.M.E. As Phyllis Diller said,
"Housework. I hate it. You make the beds, do the dishes . . . and
have to do them all over again six months later." We'll probably
have to attend to our chores more often than every six months, but
at least these tips can keep cleaning time to a minimum so we're
free to ConZentrate on higher priority projects. You've already
learned how to have a fun house. Now here are some tips on how
to take a bite out of grime and have a **C.L.E.A.N.** house.

C.L.E.A.N. = ConZentration Catch-22

One cannot collect all the beautiful shells on the beach.
—Anne Morrow Lindbergh

We should not even try. Yet we often get caught up in "acquisition fever" and end up with so much stuff we become shell-shocked.

I once saw a pillow in a knickknack shop that read: "First we own our possessions; then they own us." It's time to downsize our possessions. Why? Because one of the most important lessons I learned while studying this topic is that quantity and quality are often mutually exclusive. I call this **ConZentration Catch-22**. The more things we own, the less of our attention is available for what's really important.

We can increase the quality of our ConZentration by decreasing the quantity of belongings. Possessions don't just take up physical space; they take up mental space. A stuffed, crowded home produces a stuffed, crowded head. As Henry David Thoreau observed, "Our life is frittered away by detail. Simplify, simplify."

We can simplify our life by getting rid of everything in our home that is not beautiful or functional. I know, I know. It's one thing to *talk* about reducing our number of possessions, it's another thing to do it. Many of us have an ingrained objection to parting with property. There's always that nagging suspicion that the second we give something away, we'll need it—the next day. The following five options can help us S.T.U.F.F. possessions in satisfying ways so we don't regret parting with them.

S = Sell it. There's money sitting in them thar closets! Garage sales can generate some decent income out of items that are generating nothing but dust. Those records you never play could be a find for a record collector. That bike you never ride could be just what your neighbor is looking for. Make it a family project. The kids get to keep the revenue from everything they contribute. A day of preparation time and a Saturday of your weekend can produce up to a thousand dollars that can then be spent on something you really need or want.

T = Toss it.   Promise yourself you're going to toss five items every time you open one of those knickknack drawers that seem to attract loose items. Are you in the kitchen looking for the can opener in the odds-and-ends drawer? Instead of thinking, "What a mess!" and then closing the drawer and going about your business, stop and take out five mystery items. If you're in your closet rummaging around for a pair of boots and notice a box of old Christmas letters from five years ago, keep a couple for the family album and then take ten seconds to contribute the rest of them to the circular file cabinet (that's right, the trash basket).

U = Use it or lose it.   You know those "thin" clothes you have in the closet you're going to wear when you lose twenty pounds? How long have they been hanging in that closet? How about those electric hand warmers you won as a door prize that you wouldn't get caught dead in? Organizational experts tell us if we haven't worn or used something in the last year, we're probably never going to wear or use it. Pin a note to the item with a date six months from now. If we haven't worn or used it by then, there's someone out there who needs it more than we do.

F = Fix it or nix it.   Be honest with yourself. Sure you could sew a button on that blouse and it'd be just like new. But you're not a seamstress, and never will be. And you're not willing to go to a dry cleaners and pay to get the button reattached. So are you going to let that unworn shirt stay in your closet (causing you guilt every time you see it), or are you going to contribute it to Goodwill? What about that table with the broken leg that has been collecting dust in the corner of the garage for (ahem!) three years. Isn't it time to face the fact we're never going to have any spare time to fix it, and we might as well get a few dollars for that handyman's special?

F = F(ph)ilanthropize.   (Okay, okay, so I reached for this one.) Let the college kids know that if they really want their trophies from their T-ball team, they'd better come get them—or else they're going to be recycled to the local recreation department. Those books you've already read that you keep "just in case you want to read them again someday" get donated to the library where they'll do someone some good. Those Disney classic videos you can't bear to part with (because they bring back wonderful memories of watching them side by side with your kids) can be lent to a local day-care center, where they'll bring joy to a generation of new youngsters.

An author friend who proofed this manuscript calls this "take your treasures to town." She wrote a note in the margin that a trip to United Way, the hospice, or Big Brothers/Big Sisters not only clears away our clutter, it yields a tax deduction and the goodwill of giving back to our community by putting these unused items in the hands of people who need them more than our closets do. She noted that some nonprofit organizations will even pick up, sort, clean, and repair usable castoffs. All we have to do is make a phone call.

"It is preoccupation with possessions, more than anything else," thought Bertrand Russell, "that prevents us from living freely and nobly." Friends recently experienced the joy of S.T.U.F.F.ing it first-hand when they put their large house up for sale. After a walk-through, the real estate agent delicately suggested the house would show better if they made a clean sweep of it. She said it was tough for prospective buyers to visually put *their* possessions in the house when it was already packed to the gills with someone else's possessions. Our friends were ruthless. Their criteria were: (1) Did they use or wear it in the last six months? (2) Was it beautiful, functional, or personally meaningful? (3) Did it add value to their lives? If it didn't meet at least one of those criteria, out it went.

In the days afterward, they kept walking through the house exclaiming, "I like it so much better like this!" Their house felt so spacious, clean, and light. They no longer felt hemmed in and weighted down. They felt, as Russell had intuited, *free*. They understood what former Texas governor Ann Richards meant when she said, "When I don't live in the mansion anymore, I want to live in the smallest house I can find." Not only did they *not* miss their years of accumulated possessions, they wished they had never paid good money to acquire them in the first place.

In his book *The Importance of Living*, Lin Yutang said, "I do not think that any civilization can be called complete until it has progressed from sophistication to unsophistication, and made a conscious return to simplicity of thinking and living." The trite adage "You can't take it with you" is true. The question is, Should we even have it now? What purpose is it serving? Are these possessions adding value or pulling us away from our values? Are they taking T.I.M.E. and requiring ConZentration we could use better elsewhere? If so, resolve to clean house this weekend. As Ann Landers is fond of saying, "The most important things in life aren't things." Cleanse your life of meaningless things this weekend. I've never met a single person who regretted simplifying. I've met only people who regretted not doing it sooner.

C.L.E.A.N. = Leverage T.I.M.E. with the QTC Triangle

> Everything in your house calls to you. There isn't an item in your house that isn't saying, "clean me, read me, fold me, finish me, take me to Aunt Jane's house, answer me, write me." It's a din. You have to get that racket down to a murmur.
> —Barbara Sher

We have a limited supply of time, energy, and attention. We don't want to dissipate that supply by spreading it too thin on too many split ends. A tool that can help us see if we're handling our housework as efficiently as possible is called the QTC (quality, time, cost) Triangle. The idea is based on the premise that we can trade off any two variables to give ourselves more of the third. Figure out which aspect of the triangle is most important to you. If you're willing to sacrifice or compromise on the other two, you'll end up with more of what you really care about.

I was introduced to this concept years ago at a small-business conference. A fellow panel member shared his observation that a disproportionate percentage of first-time entrepreneurs fail because they try to do it all themselves. Their reluctance to delegate (or outsource, as it is called now) means it's only a matter of time before they burn out. He felt the key to success was allocating our limited resources wisely so we're always ConZentrating on what we love most or do best. He agreed with management guru Peter Drucker, who believes that "the success of any business is determined by whether work is being done at the lowest possible organizational level."

He illustrated his point by saying that many small-business owners choose to do their own accounting. Unless they're financial wizards, this can be a big mistake. They may be saving C (money) by managing their own finances, but their unfamiliarity with payroll procedures and tax laws may triple the T (time) it takes to keep updated records, and they may be making mistakes Q (quality) that are going to come back and haunt them if the IRS conducts an audit. This consultant theorized it was wiser for entrepreneurs to pick quality and time as their priority and hire a professional bookkeeper. It would cost some cash, but it would free them up to ConZentrate on other aspects of the business only they could do and it would assure that their finances would be error free.

How does this principle apply to housekeeping? It's a given that most of us are busy. It makes sense, then, to outsource some of our chores (even though we may have to sacrifice in quality and cough up some money) so we have more of what we really need—precious time.

You may be thinking, "But I can hardly pay the bills I've got." There are other options. Could some of those chores not get done as often or as well as you think they should? One self-confessed perfectionist said, "It finally came down to this. I could ConZentrate on getting the mildew out of the corners of the showers, the dustballs out from behind the refrigerator, and the smudge marks off the windows—or I could ConZentrate on my kids. I realized every hour spent maintaining my *Good Housekeeping* standards was an hour taken away from my eight-year-old son and my six-year-old daughter. I'm no longer willing to slave away to have the house look perfect. I figure years from now the kids won't remember or care whether their sheets matched their curtains or if we had a spotless carpet—but they will remember our visits to the zoo, our hikes on the hill behind our house, and flying kites at the reservoir."

Erma Bombeck echoed this sentiment when she said, "If I had my life to live over again, I would have waxed less and listened more." This week, take one household chore you would normally do and substitute T.I.M.E. with a loved one. And when you're with that person, give them the attention you otherwise would have given to that linoleum.

C.L.E.A.N. = Engage

When I dance, I dance, when I sleep, I sleep; yes, and when I walk alone in a beautiful orchard, if my thoughts drift to far-off matters for some part of the time, for some other part I lead them back again to the walk, the orchard, to the sweetness of this solitude, to myself.
—Montaigne

One of the fundamental concepts of Zen is there are no menial tasks, only menial attitudes of people who have not yet realized that the simplest activities can bring enlightenment. Stories abound of Zen students traveling to expensive retreats only to find themselves scrubbing dishes and mopping floors—the better to learn this lesson. The Japanese tea ceremony, in which the tea is slowly and reverently prepared, served, and sipped, is an example of immersing ourselves totally in what we're doing so the act becomes a sacred experience.

Thich Nhat Hanh said, "If I am incapable of washing the dishes joyfully, if I want to finish them quickly so I can go and have dessert, I will be equally incapable of enjoying my dessert. With my fork in hand, I will be thinking about what to do next, and the texture and flavor of the dessert, together with the pleasure of eating it, will be lost. I will always be dragged into the future, never able to live in the present moment."

Today, we are going to "now" ourselves by selecting a household chore and engaging in it as fully and reverently as possible. The task we choose is not as important as how we choose to approach it. What we want is to simply do what we're doing . . . with complete, caring attention.

You can choose to give your dog a bath . . . just make this the most thorough and loving bath your pet has ever had. Mentally apply yourself so that your whole world becomes the sink, the dog, the shampoo, and you. Lather him up, scrub him all over, and rinse, rinse, rinse. Think of it as a massage with soap and water for your loyal pet.

"The essential achievement of free will," thought William James, "is to attend to a difficult object and hold it fast before the mind." I like to modify this quote by saying the essential experience of free will is to attend to a *delightful* object and hold it *slow* with the mind. You may choose to prune your rosebushes. Stand back and look at one bush as a bonsai artist might. Pick out the perfect shape, the form it wants to take. Carefully trim away superfluous branches that detract from its ideal contour. Select several buds that are just on the verge of opening. Reverently snip the flowers, take them into your house, and arrange them artistically in a lovely vase so they're pleasing to the eye and spirit.

You can even make cleaning the refrigerator a religious experience. I know, you think I'm off my rocker . . . but the point is, almost anything can become a fulfilling experience if we choose to lose ourselves in it. Tossing out food that isn't fresh, disinfecting the shelves until they gleam, gazing with a feeling of gratitude at the many culinary delights available at our fingertips. A mundane chore can be transformed into an interesting experience if we give it our all.

A man reported, "Every night I drove into (squeezed into!) my garage and looked at the mountains of junk crowding every available corner, I'd tell myself I had to do something about it. I work six days a week, though, and the last thing I wanted to do on my one day off was tackle that mess. Your comments about how much messes bother us on a subliminal level really got to me, so I decided to stop procrastinating and clean the garage. I told myself I might as well enjoy it, so I brought out my *American Graffiti* tapes and organized, threw away, boxed, and swept to oldies but goodies like

'Peppermint Twist,' 'Good Time Sally,' and 'Chantilly Lace.' I made like Robin Williams in the movie *Mrs. Doubtfire* and boogied my way through the piles. Instead of it being the god-awful experience I'd been dreading, I actually had a pretty good time. It convinced me I can have fun doing almost anything—if I get engaged."

Chances are you've heard the cliché that we're supposed to be human *beings*, not human *doings*. What you may not have realized is the way to be is to do what you do. One wag called this the Frank Sinatra philosophy. (Hum the words "Do be do be do" to the first few bars of the song "Strangers in the Night" and you'll understand what he meant.)

Vow today to select a specific task and give it your complete ConZentration. Invest 100 percent of your attention and discover for yourself the satisfaction that comes from a job well done. One workshop participant decided to polish the family silver. Ruth said, "Thanksgiving was a couple of weeks away and, for the first time, we were hosting the traditional turkey dinner at our house. I decided to do it up right. I was going to use our grandmother's lace tablecloth, get out all our old family recipes for stuffing, gravy, overnight salad, yams, and vegetable casserole, and use our heirloom china and silver. The silver was tarnished, so I decided cleaning it was going to be my 'do be do be do' task.

I put on the first Christmas music of the season to get me in a holiday mood and started lovingly polishing each fork, spoon, and knife. As I cleaned each piece of silverware, I remembered our first family holiday meal and thought back through the years, remembering whose house we'd been in, who'd been there, and what had happened. That could have been a task I handled mindlessly while watching a talk show. Instead, it turned into a precious hour time-traveling through some of my favorite family memories. I've decided to make that an annual ritual. I will never mindlessly polish silver again. I'll always use it as an opportunity to prepare for our holiday meal in the proper spirit."

You've probably heard the words "halfhearted" and "wholehearted"? The "I'm engaged!" exercise is a way of being "wholeheaded." It may sound highfalutin, but we can find the mystical in the most mundane household chores and experience a rapturous feeling of being alive if we devote our undivided attention to doing what we're doing.

C.L.E.A.N. = Assign and Share Chores

When men do the dishes, it's called helping. When women do the dishes, it is called life.
—Anna Quindlen

Another way to keep a moderately clean house without it consuming all our T.I.M.E. is to understand housekeeping and family time are not mutually exclusive. The goal is to be a mother, not a martyr. Assigning chores to kids not only relieves us of some of the burden, it is one of the best things we can do to help our children grow into good citizens. Chores teach responsibility, self-discipline, time management, and a variety of other values.

Parenting Power columnist John Rosemond said, "When children are allowed to take from the family more than they contribute, they become parasitic, self-centered, and believe something can be had for nothing. Study after study has shown that early success at small chores produces adults who are healthier, happier, and more successful. This result is true regardless of ethnicity, income, education, background, or family circumstances."

When is a chore not a chore? When it is shared. A coffee-mug equivalent of Anna Quindlen's humorous(?) insight is "So much work to do, so few women to do it." From now on, set aside a time when *everyone* in the house has a responsibility. Don't ask others to help you or help out. At some level, they'll perceive they're doing you a favor. Ask them to pitch in and do their fair share. That way they shoulder some of the responsibility instead of feeling it's your job.

A fellow Little League parent agreed with this idea. Lisa said, "Some of our best times have been when we were all busily occupied doing something around the house. Doing chores side by side can be a fun family time *if* everyone is given a function and works in unison. There is a shared glow and satisfaction that results from tidying up our home together."

C.L.E.A.N. = No Muss, No Fuss

> I never get tired of housework, I don't do any. When guests
> come to visit, I just put out drop cloths and say we're painting.
> —Joan Rivers

One way to have less housework is not to make messes in the first
place. I'm not pulling a Pollyanna here. My sons and I have agreed
that we would rather keep things picked up as we go than spend half
our Saturday plowing through piles that have accumulated through
the week. The day after reading this timeless proverb (found in
Sarah Ban Breathnach's inspirational book *Simple Abundance*) I
gave Tom, Andrew, and myself an index card and we each wrote it
out in our best handwriting:

> If you take it out, put it back.
> If you open it, close it.
> If you throw it down, pick it up.

I then posted Tom's card on the TV, Andrew's on the refrigerator, and mine on the dining room table. Do these visual reminders
work all the time? No. Is our house spotless? No. Does our vow to
pick it up and put it back work *some* of the time? Yes. Is our house
neater and more of a joy to live in? Yes. And when Saturday rolls
around, we clean house in a couple of hours and are then free to
spend our precious weekend T.I.M.E. however we want.

A single mom spoke up at a seminar and said she had read an
article that said messiness was contagious. She said, "This article
described a study of college roommates where the research found
that if *one* roommate was chronically sloppy, it was only a matter
of time before the other person succumbed to the mess and
slacked off on her standards." Alice said, "I really related to this
because our home was starting to look like a disaster zone. You
know the old line 'My kids don't have stress, they're carriers'?
Well, it didn't bother my two teenagers in the slightest that our
house looked like a disaster zone, but I couldn't live that way anymore.

"I sat my girls on the couch and instituted the following policy: They could leave their rooms any way they wanted and it was all right with me, but the common areas had to be picked up on a daily basis. I told them any possessions I found in a common area after six P.M. were *mine*. If they wanted them back, it was going to cost a buck an item. After a few weeks of spending their entire allowance to buy back their shoes, backpacks, and textbooks, they quickly learned to take a few seconds to put things away instead of dumping them whenever and wherever they wanted."

Action Plan 19. Cleanliness Is Next to . . . Impossible

My mother used to say, "You can eat off my floor." You can eat off my floor, too. There's thousands of things down there.

—Elayne Boosler

So what are you going to do to create a clean enough home that leaves enough energy for you to ConZentrate on higher priorities? The most important use of our T.I.M.E. isn't to fill our days with cleaning, sweeping, dusting, vacuuming, washing, ironing, scrubbing, and mopping. Rose Macaulay said, "A house unkempt cannot be so distressing as a life unlived." Have the courage to downsize the stuff that's been causing a ConZentration Catch-22 and you'll find there's no place like www.home.com.

Confusion	ConZentration
Life frittered away by stuff	*Life freed up from stuff*
"It's going to take the whole weekend to clean this mess."	"I can sell it, toss, it, use it, fix it, or farm it out."

Confusion	ConZentration
ConZentrate on acquiring, more is better "Look at those neat knickknacks. And they're 25 percent off. Let's get several."	*ConZentration Catch-22, less is better* "Do I need them? Are they beautiful and functional?"
Lose time by trying to do it all "I've got a college degree and I'm on my hands and knees scrubbing tubs."	*Leverage time with the QTC Triangle* "I can have a cleaning service come in twice a month and keep these bathrooms spotless."
Do chores mindlessly "I could be outside having a good time, and instead I'm stuck inside vacuuming."	*Engage and do chores mindfully* "I'm going to put on my old disco album and dance while I'm vacuuming."
Insist on doing it ourselves "I can't trust anyone to clean as thoroughly as I can. They just do the surface stuff."	*Assign it to someone else* "The boys are old enough to start doing their own laundry. We can fold clothes together."
Nothing gets picked up "Look at this place. We clean it, and half an hour later, it's a mess again."	*No muss, no fuss* "If you open it, close it. If you drop it, pick it up."

PART 7

Now and Zen

We are here and it is now.
Further than that, all human
knowledge is moonshine.

—H. L. Mencken

WAY 20

◉

Don't Hurry, Be Happy

"Now thyself" is more important than "Know thyself."

—Mel Brooks

Here, here! If you learn one thing from this book, it is this lesson. The happiness we seek, the contentment we yearn for, the quality of life we crave is available to us anytime, anywhere . . . if we bring our mind into the present moment and experience it fully.

The question, of course, is how do we do that? That's what this section is about. We'll discuss different ways you can center yourself in the midst of stressful surroundings. You'll learn how to establish ConZentration—the ability to maintain peace of mind despite the pressure, multiple priorities, and mad pace of today's society.

Blaise Pascal said, "Most of the evils in life arise from man's being unable to sit still in a room." Hurrying and unhappiness are like the chicken and the egg. Are we unhappy because we're rushing here and there, or are we rushing here and there because we're unhappy? No matter. The key is to slow down long enough to find our way.

A well-known Zen saying is "We are like a man standing in a clear stream while dying of thirst." Philosophers shake their heads at our frantic attempts to find happiness in outer circumstances. In this we are, as the Polynesians say, "standing on a whale fishing for minnows." Contentment can't be acquired by outer means. Peace of mind is an inside job. It is there waiting for us; all we have to do to give it a chance to emerge is to trying the following four **Now and Zen** ways.

Now and Zen Way 1. Sit and Do Nothing

> If they try to rush me, I always say, "I've only got one other speed—and it's slower."
> —actor Glenn Ford

For many people, the only other speed they have is faster. As one mother of three said, "I can't slow down. I have too much to do as it is. If I don't go at top speed, I'll get so far behind I'll never get caught up." If we stop to think about it (so to speak), we realize the only way to catch up to ourselves is to stop rushing. That's not asking much, is it? Actually, for many of us, it is.

When was the last time you sat down and did nothing? You may have sat down to read the paper or have a meal, but then, many of us don't even do that anymore. We wolf down breakfast while watching the morning news, munch our lunch while looking through a magazine, and eat dinner in the car while driving home from work. I even saw an article in the December 27, 1998, issue of *Parade* magazine describing a Burger King in Manhattan that features a wall of computers for its customers so they can surf the Net while chewing their cheeseburger.

We rarely do one thing anymore, much less no-thing. So much to do, so little time—so we do two or three things at once, and then wonder why we feel stressed.

The key to counteracting such behavior is to do the exact opposite. Today, set aside a time to set aside your mind. Leo Tolstoy said, "If you want to be happy, be." The goal is to sit quietly with no assignment you are supposed to do, feel, think, or experience. That's the point. For five minutes, your head is free to be. It is released from the pressure to perform or produce. It can do what it wants without the fear of being chastised. Anything and everything it cares to do or not do is perfectly okay. Your mind is liberated to exist however it pleases.

Your mind will cautiously peek out, not believing its good luck. When it's clear that it won't get scolded for doing something wrong, it will slowly venture out and stretch like a cat in the sun. It will expand with its newfound freedom. It will relax in a way not possible in the other waking hours. The rest of the day the mind is tightly controlled—constantly told what to do, think, and say. Only for these few blissful moments does it get to be unrestrained. If you let your mind off its leash, it will relax, roam free, and return refreshed and re-energized, ready to go back to work.

William Penn said, "In the rush and noise of life, as you have intervals, step within yourselves and be still." Don't wait for those intervals to occur naturally. Give yourself a five-minute sit-and-do-nothing interval each morning so you can start the day Zentered. Satchel Paige said, "Sometimes I sits and thinks, and sometimes I just sits." Today, take a few minutes to just sits.

Now and Zen Way 2. Be Where You Are Instead of Hurrying to Be Somewhere Else

> No man (woman) who is in a hurry is quite civilized.
> —**Will Durant**

Perhaps you've seen the BMW ad that says, "If you can't buy happiness, lease it." We don't have to sit still to get a new lease on life. We can reframe hurriedness into happiness wherever we happen to be.

I was in a checkout line at the grocery store today, and there was an older woman in front of me slowly taking items out of her shopping cart and placing them one by one on the conveyor belt, all the while exchanging pleasantries with the cashier. I had somewhere I needed to be and was exasperated with her for taking so long. I was, as Oscar Levant once described, "a study of a person in chaos in search of frenzy."

Then I stepped outside myself and realized I was getting uptight with a seventy-five-year-old woman for taking an extra two or three minutes. What a complete lack of empathy and compassion!

Instead of standing behind her and doing a slow burn, I offered to help out. This lady was someone's grandmother. Who knows? She could have been moving slowly because she had arthritis or wasn't feeling well. An excursion to buy groceries may be the only opportunity for socialization she gets. Or she could be a master teacher there to remind me that hurrying is a waste of mind.

Vern McClellan said, "Ambition is a get-ahead-ache." I had been so caught up in my compulsive urge to get ahead, I didn't see what a kind person she was. Obviously, the only place I needed to be was right were I was. As Buddha so simply and eloquently suggested, "As you walk, eat, and travel, be where you are. Otherwise, you will miss your life."

Now and Zen Way 3. Give Yourself a "Stopwatch"

> Dogs lead a nice life. You never see a dog with a wristwatch.
> —George Carlin

The more we look at our watch, the more wound up we get. Most of us live by our watches; we have to get up at this time, be out the door by this time, be at work before this time, and so on throughout the day. This scheduled-to-the-minute mentality may be a necessity most of the time, but we need an occasional vacation from being, as Golda Meir said, "governed by the clock."

Pick a day this weekend and plan on taking your watch off and turning your clocks around so they're facing the wall. Resolve to live by your senses and biological rhythms instead of the artificial application of hours. Get up when you wake up. Eat when you feel like it. Go the store when you're ready. Give yourself a nice life for a day by getting rid of that wristwatch and freeing yourself from the tyranny of arbitrary time.

I imagine you're saying, "There's no way I could do that. I've got so many things to do, I'm running from the moment I get up until the moment I go to bed." That's the point. As Erich Fromm said, "We are so busy, we have so much on our minds that we don't feel anything anymore." When are we going to realize how much of a toll an on-the-run lifestyle takes on us? I know we have to be realistic; which is why I'm suggesting we put away our watches for a few hours, not throw them away. That's not asking too much. That's simply giving ourselves what we so desperately need—a "stopwatch."

Now and Zen Way 4: Calm to Your Senses

We have to lose our minds to come to our senses.
—Fritz Perls

You may find, when you first try to quiet your mind, that it fills with thoughts of what you ought to be doing. During this supposed downtime, your mind is actually up and racing with thoughts of whom you need to call, what you should be accomplishing, and where you ought to be. If that's the case, **calm to your senses.** Instead of trying to shut out the world, steep yourself in it.

You can do this right where you're sitting or you can go outside for a few minutes. After reading this paragraph, you're going to close your eyes to heighten your senses. We're going to do as Ram Dass suggested: "The quieter you become, the more you can hear." Is that a cardinal chirping outside? Is a dog barking? Can you hear leaves rustling on the trees? Next is feeling. Feel the air on your skin (even if it is from an air conditioner). Is it cool, warm, gentle, harsh, moist, dry? Can you feel a gentle breeze caressing your arms or face? Now, sniff the air. Can you detect some coffee being brewed? Is someone nearby wearing cologne? Can you smell the fragrance of fresh-cut grass? "Silence is wonderful to listen to," noted Thomas Hardy. It is, isn't it?

Did you notice that when you were experiencing those physical sensations, you weren't worrying about that sales presentation you have to give tomorrow? You weren't resenting the fact that your husband forgot your anniversary? You didn't give a moment's thought to that rude salesclerk who ignored you?

"You must learn to be still in the midst of activity," suggested Indira Gandhi, "and to be vibrantly alive in repose." The key to doing this is to sit quietly, with our senses on full alert, so the vibrancy of life has a chance to permeate our up-till-now maxed-out mind. We can **calm to our senses** any time we want by turning off our thoughts and tuning in to what we hear, see, feel, smell, and taste. Franz Kafka suggested, "You do not need to leave your room. Remain sitting at your table and listen. Do not even listen, simply wait. Do not even wait, be quite still and solitary. The world will freely offer itself to you to be unmasked. It has no choice, it will roll in ecstasy at your feet."

Isn't that a wonderful mental image? The world rolling in ecstasy at our feet? Actually, I think it rolls in ecstasy in our minds, and the way to make this happen is to, as soon as you finish reading the next paragraph, take Shakespeare's advice and "think with thine ears." Take five minutes to put this book down and employ your senses one by one.

Action Plan 21. Don't Hurry, Be Happy

It is an old and ironic habit of human beings to run faster when we have lost our way.

—Rollo May

How are you going to remind yourself to be "here, here" instead of "here, there, and everywhere"? If you find yourself doing a hundred things at once, and none of them well, stop. Turn your mind off and tune your senses in. Bid concerns bye-bye and choose to **sit still and do nothing, calm to your senses, be right where you are,** or **give yourself a stopwatch.**

Aaah, that's better. Bertolt Brecht likened moments of silent wonder to "lying in the meadow and dangling with my soul." Today, promise to get in touch with your own "mental meadow" and see if it isn't a marvelous way to put things in perspective. You'll discover for yourself that one way to achieve balance is to counterbalance your norm, and the norm for many of us is life on the run. What's the opposite of rushing around? Sitting restfully, serenely still. Author David Peterson said, "A young man fears that by going too slow he risks missing something. An older man knows that by going too fast he risks missing everything."

Confusion

Hurry
"Get moving! We should have left fifteen minutes ago. Why do you have to take so long?"

Race through our day
"I've got to go to the DMV to get my license renewed, stop by the drugstore, and pick up those photos."

Do everything
"I never have a moment to myself. This schedule is driving me crazy."

Be here, there, and everywhere
"Timmy, don't try to talk to me now. I've got too much on my mind. We'll discuss this at dinner."

Governed by the clock
"Let's be at the pool by ten A.M., stay an hour, go shopping from eleven to three, be home by three-thirty, and then drive . . . "

ConZentration

Happy
"Let me help carry that out to the car, hon. You look pretty in that new dress."

Relax during our day
"I'm going to give myself five minutes to have an iced tea, and then I'll finish the errands."

Do nothing
"Ahh. It feels good to let go of all those obligations for a minute. I feel better already."

Be where you are
"So, hon, tell me about the spelling bee. I want to hear how it went."

Give ourselves a stopwatch
"Let's have breakfast and then see if we feel like going for a swim, okay?"

WAY 21

◉

Oh, Say, Do You See?

The moment one gives close attention to anything, even a blade of grass, it becomes a mysterious, awesome, indescribably magnificent world in itself.

—Henry Miller

Remember the first words of the National Anthem? "Oh, say, can you see . . . " The real question is "Oh, say, *do* you see . . . ?" Our hectic lifestyles make it easy to overlook our surroundings. Betty Smith said, "Look at everything as though you were seeing it either for the first or the last time. Then your time on earth will be filled with glory."

Are you wondering, "And who's supposed to take care of my responsibilities while I'm filling my time on earth with glory?" You're right. We have to attend to the business of living, so our mind learns to ignore the everyday marvels that exist around us. The problem arises when we overlook these blessings so often we become oblivious to them.

Starting today, vow to set aside your mind and three minutes of your time to really *see* your surroundings. That female curmudgeon Fran Lebowitz said, "There's no such thing as inner peace. There is only nervousness and death." Surely she jests. We can give ourselves peace of mind any time we want by giving ourselves an eyeful. This chapter offers several ways we can "see" our way to ConZentration.

"I See"

Really seeing shakes us out of the ruts of ordinary perception,
and is an experience of inestimable value to everyone.
—Aldous Huxley

A fellow speaker once suggested I call this following exercise "eye
à la mode." He had a good point. We can *look* at things while we
are talking, while listening to the radio, or processing paperwork,
but we *see* things only when we give them our exclusive attention. Giving our eyes, mind, and undivided attention to a single
thing is a way to appreciate its essence. Furthermore, it is a positive form of ConZentration because we are focusing solely on a
single priority.

Artist Georgia O'Keeffe said, "Nobody sees a flower, really, it is
so small, we haven't time, and to see takes time." You've heard
the oft-repeated insight that our eyes are the windows to our soul.
The "I See" exercise below takes three minutes. Promise yourself
you'll take the time to do it as soon as you finish this section. It
can open our window on the world and remind us that we *have* a
soul.

**Step 1. Look around right now and let your eyes settle on one
specific thing. Make it for your eyes only.** Really look at the
chair in which you're sitting. Feel the fabric, bounce on the cushion, examine the construction. How many times have you sat on
this chair? How long have you owned it? Think of all the experiences you've had in that chair, the hours spent in it. What you
didn't even notice, seconds ago, has now become a source of fasci-
nation.

**Step 2. Gaze at something else in your vicinity and examine it
closely.** Is there a computer nearby? Chances are you boot it up and
use it without even stopping to think about the marvel of tapping
on some pieces of plastic and being able to instantly transmit a message to a friend thousands of miles away. Look at this inanimate
beige box plugged into the wall and realize what it's capable of. Let
your mind marvel at the emotions you've felt as a result of this

appliance: the laughs you've had as a result of reading funny e-mails; the ideas you've created that are now permanently recorded for posterity. It's almost impossible to take this device for granted after giving it just a minute of eye T.I.M.E.

Step 3. Move your eyes to another item in your area and see it for the first time. In less than three minutes this powerful exercise can turn apathy and unawareness into appreciation and awe. Gazing intently at one thing is a tangible way to get you out of the mental muck and into the moment.

A-ten-shun!

For lack of attention, a thousand forms of loveliness elude us every day.
—**Evelyn Underhill**

I relearn this lesson constantly. I give my sons a back massage as part of their bedtime ritual. It's an opportunity to have a few minutes together, wrap up the day, and say a pleasant good night. Sometimes, though, I'm tired by the time ten P.M. rolls around. One night last year while giving Tom and Andrew their back rub, I was preoccupied with a presentation I was scheduled to give the following day. I was wondering if I had packed my handouts, tucked the airline tickets in my purse, left an "I'll be away" message on my answering machine, and so forth. I was so distracted by my other obligations, I might as well have been in the next county.

Then my eyes happened to fall on the boys' faces and I awoke from my musing. I really *looked* at my sons and was immediately flooded with a sense of gratitude for these two marvelous young men. I studied their faces, ruffled their hair, and gloried at their good health, intelligence, curiosity, and youthful vitality. I felt enormously blessed to have them in my life. In an instant, an ordinary moment became extraordinary.

What was the difference between an experience that barely registered in my brain and one that resonated deep in my being? **I saw.**

I put my mind on hold and experienced with my eyes. As soon as I did that, my eyesight formed a bridge between us and we were connected. Moments before, I had been sitting inches from my sons, but might as well have been millions of miles away. Only when I saw with my mind's eye was I fully present.

Who is a loved one you haven't seen for a while? And I don't mean that relative who lives in another state, I mean one who lives in the same house. Could you gaze upon them anew today? When are you going to see them next? Could you put aside your other concerns for a moment and simply study their face and reawaken yourself to the miracle of this person?

Give Notice

Develop interest in life as you see it; in people, things, literature, music. The world is ... simply throbbing with rich treasure, beautiful souls, and fascinating people.
—Henry Miller

What Miller didn't explain is that the way to develop interest in life is to look upon it with our mind's eye. As soon as we do, even the most commonplace things are no longer commonplace. Exquisite moments are available any time we want ... for a *moment's notice*.

A government worker took this message to heart and posted a sign above her desk and on her refrigerator that said, "Life is postponed until further notice." She said, "I'm in a golden-handcuffs situation. I've worked for this agency for twenty-two years. I wanted to quit years ago, but couldn't find an equivalent job and paycheck. I've got to hang in there two more years until I can retire with a full pension, and then I'll be a free woman. Your ConZentration workshop reminded me there was a lot more to life than what happens from nine to five in my little cubicle. There's a whole world existing right outside my head that I've ignored for a long time. My sign reminds me that I'm not yet in a position to give notice to the state, but I sure can give notice to my surroundings. I can ConZentrate on how much I dislike my job, or I can ConZentrate on the many other things that make me happy." She smiled and said, "It all depends on how you look at it." Exactly! She had discovered a philosophy Abraham Lincoln espoused: "Most people are about as happy as they make up their minds to be."

Thinks Are Looking Up

When the eye wakes up to see again, it suddenly stops taking
anything for granted.
—Frederick Franck

Many times when we're feeling depressed, it's because our eyes are cast downward or inward. You've heard the expression "things are looking up"? That's not just an expression, it's a prescription. The way to lift your spirits is to lift your head. Elevate your mood by elevating your eyes. Simply said, it's hard to feel down when you're looking up.

A friend used a variation of this technique just the other day. We got together for a long-overdue lunch at a restaurant nestled at the foot of a magnificent pali (Hawaiian mountain range). Over our meal, she was telling me how sad she was about still being single in her forties. She said, "I always thought I'd meet the right guy someday, marry, and have a family. It looks like that's not going to happen, and there's nothing I can do about it. Any suggestions?"

I didn't want to trivialize her problem; however, I knew there was a lot right with her life that she was temporarily overlooking. I suggested, "Look up. Don't say anything. Just gaze around and take it all in."

She sat back in her chair and slowly swept the landscape with her eyes. After a moment she looked at me questioningly. I said, "Tell me what you just saw." She said, "Well, I saw the mountains." I interrupted, "Describe in detail what you just saw." This time she got it. "I saw purple, orange, and fuchsia bougainvillea bushes. I saw green pineapple fields extending up into the hills . . . " and she continued to recount what she'd just seen. I asked, "How do you feel now?" She thought about this for a moment and then smiled, "Better." Right.

Almost any time we're down in the dumps, we're usually hanging our head, standing or sitting in a slouched position, focusing inward on our bleak emotional landscape, and mentally talking ourselves into a state of despair. Try it today. If you're feeling down, look skyward. The mere raising of your eyes can help lift you out of the doldrums. It's a simple step that can make a big difference in how you feel and think at that moment.

Eye, Eye

Writing is the act of saying "I, I, I."
—Joan Didion

There's another way you can use your eyes to change your mood. When you stop to think about it, much of our unhappiness results from ConZentrating on "I, I, I." "*I* don't have anyone who loves me." "*I* am overweight." "*I* never do anything fun." We can get our mind off an unhealthy self-absorption by directing our eyes (and thus our mind) to something else. As soon as we do, we transform **"I, I"** into **"Eye, Eye."**

Simply said, it's hard to feel self-pity when we're "eye-eyeing" another person. As soon as we focus on others—"How are *they* feeling?" "What's on *their* mind?" "What would *they* like to talk about?"—we stop focusing on our troubles or insecurities. Eleanor Roosevelt said, "The essence of charm is the ability to lose ourselves in the other person." We lose our self-consciousness when we lose ourselves in someone else. Making someone else the most important thing in our world, for the moment, is not only the essence of charm, it is a healthy way to get our mind off ourselves.

Try this today. If you're in a gathering of people, and you're wrapped up in your own thoughts—"How do I look?" "What should I say?" "I feel so conspicuous"—simply transfer your wholehearted attention to the people you're talking with. Draw them out with genuine, open-ended questions that begin with the two words "Tell me." Get yourself out of your head and into theirs, and minutes later you can be enjoying yourself and having fun instead of obsessing about your discomfort.

Nurture Yourself in Nature

The clearest way into the universe is through a forest wilderness.
—John Muir

A student once asked a Zen master where she could enter Zen. "Hear that brook?" he asked her. "Yes." she replied. "Enter there," he told her.

What does that parable mean? For me, it means that a Zen consciousness is most easily accessed through nature. To observe nature is to drown ourselves in awareness and appreciation for its (our) existence. Nature doesn't have a point to prove. It doesn't worry what people think of it. Nature doesn't spend countless hours thinking, "Should I have done this or that?" "I can't believe this happened." It just is.

Philosophers from the beginning of time have talked about the power of nature to put thinks in proper perspective. Frank Lloyd Wright said, "I believe in God, only I spell it Nature." Saint Bernard said, "What I know of the divine science I learnt in woods and fields." Aldous Huxley commented that his father "considered a walk among the mountains as the equivalent of churchgoing." And Katherine Mansfield eloquently expressed a similar sentiment: "Wind moving through grass so that the grass quivers. This moves me with an emotion I don't even understand."

Some of us have become so "citified" our world consists of man-made structures: skyscrapers, subways, streets, and mini-malls. Maybe you agree with comedian Will Durst, who said, "I hate the outdoors. To me that's where the car is." For us to access the tranquil state of mind that is called ConZentration, we may need to get out of our concrete jungle one day this weekend and drive out into the country. Perhaps there, as Muir, Wright, Huxley, and the others suggest, where we are surrounded by the magnificence of nature, we'll be able to experience the complete peacefulness and sense of rightness that is a hallmark of ConZentration.

Teilhard de Chardin said, "The whole of life lies in the verb *seeing*." Every time I read this insight, something deep within me says, "Yes, yes, emphatically yes!" When we truly look at the wonders in our world, we can't help but experience a deep sense of gratitude. When we see the "nature" of things, we are re-minded that we are all companions striving to connect, wanting to love and be loved. Seeing fills us with a sense of unity rather than isolation. We can't help but smile at the simplicity of it all. If we will just look around, we will understand that everything we want is right here, right now. If we drink it in with our eyes, we can't help but savor the fact that we are alive, that we can feel, hear, smell, see, taste. It is enough. All else is beside the point.

Could you do yourself a favor this Saturday or Sunday and drive to a nearby seashore, mountain range, forest, lake, river valley, or nature reserve? Could you spend at least an hour not reading a book, not talking to anyone, and not thinking about your life back home? During that time, open your eyes, mind, and heart to what's around you, and if you're lucky, you might experience what Bernard Berenson did one summer day: "It was a morning in early summer. A silver haze shimmered and trembled over the lime trees. The air was laden with their fragrance. The temperature was like a caress. I remember—I need not recall—that I climbed up a tree stump and felt suddenly immersed in Itness. I did not call it by that name. I had no need for words. It and I were one."

Action Plan 21. Oh, Say, Do You See?

There's less here than meets the eye.

—actress Tallulah Bankhead's review of a Broadway play

Today, make sure that *more* meets your eye. Make a conscious effort to stop and really look around you. Vincent van Gogh said, "It is looking at things for a long time that ripens you and gives you a deeper understanding." How long is long enough? When you no longer take items around you for granted, when you're astounded by them—that's when gazing transcends into ConZentration.

"If you let yourself be absorbed completely," suggested Anne Morrow Lindbergh, "if you surrender completely to the moments as they pass, you live more richly those moments." If you're an Elvis fan, think of this as "returning to surrender." Set aside five minutes for the "I See," "Eye, Eye," "Give Notice," "A-ten-shun!" or "Thinks Are Looking Up" exercises today and surrender to your surroundings. See if these simple exercises don't have the power to turn mediocre moments into memorable ones by helping you see your world as if for the first time. Julius Caesar is famous for saying, "I came, I saw, I conquered." Hopefully, at the end of our life, we'll be able to say, "I came, I saw, I ConZentrated."

Confusion	ConZentration
Ignore surroundings "We've got three hours before our next plane? How boring."	*Acknowledge surroundings* "Well, we've got three hours. Why don't we go explore the rest of the airport?"
Overlook everyday marvels "This is such a waste of time just sitting and waiting."	*Appreciate everyday marvels* "I didn't know there was a flight museum in this terminal. Let's check it out."
Experience rages in our mind "I'm so mad at our travel agent for making these terrible connections."	*Experiences resonate in our soul* "Look, there's dozens of planes headed for destinations all around the world. What's someplace you'd like to visit?"
"I, I." "I can't stand all this sitting around. It's driving me crazy."	*"Eye, Eye."* "Look at that snow. It's beautiful, isn't it? Shall we go outside for a couple minutes to collect some?"
Never in nature "The only nature I ever see is that poor tree in the park everyone's carved their initials in."	*Nurture yourself in nature* "I forgot how marvelous it is to sit by a quiet stream and watch the water glide over rocks."

WAY 22

◉

Meditation—It's Not What You Think

Meditation is not a means to an end.
It is both the means and the end.

—Krishnamurti

The same is true of ConZentration. It is both a means to an end (focusing helps us achieve desired goals) and an end in itself (focusing is our desired goal).

Bishop Fulton Sheen said, "The word 'meditation' is rather an abused word . . . it would be much better to use the words 'quiet time,' in which a person shuts out the noise of the world and enters into himself." He's right. Meditation is not some New Age mumbo-jumbo; it is simply a way to counteract the mental clutter caused by a chaotic day and can be done (almost) anywhere, anytime, by anyone.

This chapter suggests several different types of meditation: breathing meditation; mantra meditation; and clearheaded meditation. These quiet times have different purposes, but they all will soothe and Zenter your spirit. Feel free to practice the one that is most meaningful for you, and/or the one that is most suitable for the situation you're in.

Belly-Breathing Meditation

> You should realize that your soul suffers if you live superfi-
> cially. People need times in which to concentrate, when
> they can search their inmost selves. Resolve to keep a quiet
> time. . . . Then your soul can speak to you without being
> drowned out by the hustle and bustle of everyday life.
> —Albert Schweitzer

Our brain suffers when we breathe superficially. When asked the
secret to life, actress Sophie Tucker said simply, "Keep breathing."
This may seem like a blazing attack of the obvious. After all, we
know how important it is to breathe; we do it all the time. Precisely.
Most of us have become inured to the power of breathing because
we do it automatically and *without thinking*. Today, instead of taking
this marvelous process for granted, we are going to give it the attention it deserves. Doing so will reconnect us with the essence of our
existence.

A friend gifted me with a certificate for a birthday massage. I
walked into the massage therapist's office; she took one look at me
and said, "I can tell you're not breathing." She went on to say. "The
opposite of breath is death. When we're not breathing fully, we're
not living fully. When we hold our breath, it's often because we're
holding back painful emotions. We don't breathe deeply because
we're afraid of feeling deeply. Breathing shallowly is a way to live on
the surface."

Amazed (I had come in for a back massage and I was getting psy-
choanalyzed), I asked her to continue. She said, "The opposite of
breathe is *seethe*. Exhaling is a way to release what's toxic and stale
inside of us. Inhaling is a way to bring in fresh air and fresh perspective. When we don't breathe, we're not letting go of perceived
slights. We're not airing out emotions. As a result, they accumulate
in our body and poison our mind and system."

This Merlin of a massage therapist said, "I'm going to give you a
massage, but the best thing you can do for yourself is to take a
deeeep breath—and to make a conscious effort to keep taking them
throughout the day." I did, and never could have guessed that such

a little thing could make such a big difference. I was a little late to discover what many philosophers, doctors, and poets have known for years. As Elizabeth Barrett Browning said, "He who breathes deepest lives most."

For many of us, our breathing follows our mental state. When we're resting, our breathing is slow and steady. When we're anxious, our breathing speeds up. Allowing our surroundings to dictate our breathing pattern poses a problem, because it means we're at the mercy of our circumstances. If things are going well, wonderful. But if things go wrong, our breathing quickens and becomes shallow; we feel short of breath. This reinforces our sense of risk, which adds to our panic, which makes our breathing even more rapid, and so on.

The goal of Belly-Breathing Meditation is to reverse this automatic process so our breathing *directs* our mental state instead of *reflects* it. In other words, we're going to learn to regulate our breathing so we can regulate our state of mind. By purposely breathing slowly and deeply, we can slow a racing mind and heart.

Most of us only use the top third of our lungs. Today, we are going to start using all three parts of our lungs. This Five-Minute Belly-Breathing Meditation will reacquaint you with how it feels to have a satisfyingly full exchange of oxygen and will also demonstrate the power you have to quiet your mind in even the most chaotic circumstances. Here's how it works.

Step 1. Sit tall on a firm, straight-backed chair (not a couch or lounge chair), or on the floor in a cross-legged position. Make sure your back is not arched, slouched, or leaning forward. Hold your head erect and facing forward. Relax your arms and rest your hands on your thighs. Close your eyes and tell your mind to ConZentrate solely on your breathing for the next five minutes. Think only about exchanging deep drafts of air.

Step 2. Inhale from the bottom up. Visualize your lungs as consisting of three parts: a lower space located in your abdomen, a middle space just about your navel, and an upper space higher in your chest. As you breathe in through your mouth, picture the lower space filling first. Then imagine your middle space filling with energy and air; feel your waistline expand. Finally, feel your chest and upper back open up as air enters the area. The inhalation should take about five counts (five seconds).

Note: It sometimes helps to place your palm on your abdomen so you can feel it expanding and contracting with each breath. Many of us have programmed ourselves to suck in our gut and keep our tummies tucked in. That's appropriate for other times, but not for this exercise. Go ahead and relax those tight muscles. It's even okay to pooch your tummy out. The focus, for the next few minutes, is on filling that area with air, not on maintaining a flat stomach.

Step 3. When your lungs feel comfortably full (don't force it), stop the intake of air. Then, exhale in a smooth, continuous movement (not a whoosh) with the air streaming steadily out of your mouth. Feel your chest and your stomach contract.

Step 4. Make five complete inhalations/exhalations in a minute, pausing only a second or two between breaths. You may want to help yourself stay focused by saying "one, two, three, four, five" as you inhale, "pause," and then "one, two, three, four, five" as you exhale.

Here's a standing version of the Belly-Breathing Meditation. Take a stance as if you were preparing to resist someone who's trying to push you off center. Stand straight and place your feet a shoulder-width apart. Position your chin so it's level, not tucked in or sticking out. Balance your weight evenly along the entire length of your foot, not just on your toes or on your heels, so you feel completely stable.

Visualize pulling your mind down until it is in your hara (your center of gravity in your lower gut). When I say "pull down," I mean picture your mind coming down through your neck and chest until it settles into your lower abdomen. Your life force (what martial artists call ki or chi, and what yoga practitioners call prana) emanates from this spot. Bringing your consciousness down to this mental middle ground helps you maintain mental equilibrium because you're no longer in your head.

Exhale through your mouth. Feel your body release its tension and feel your center of gravity move even lower in your body. Repeat this procedure five times and feel the anxiety leave your body as you breathe deeply. You will now feel more balanced and "grounded." Thinking and breathing from this centered source will keep you from losing your head and reacting impulsively to events. Fears, worries, and other people's opinions and expectations will no longer have as much power to pull you off center because you are aligned body, mind, and soul. You'll feel a solid rather than a situational sense of stability because you're rooted in reality.

A fellow speaker belly-breathes and grounds herself before every presentation. She says, "If I don't, I start out with this high, squeaky voice. That reminds me I'm thinking from the neck up, and I immediately take a deep breath and picture bringing my mind down into my gut. As soon as I do, my voice lowers and becomes warmer and more resonant. My neck relaxes and my shoulders unclench and settle into my body instead of hunching up. And I feel centered instead of feeling flighty and off balance."

Mantra Meditation

Man has made his bedlam. Let him lie in it.
—Fred Allen

We may have made our bedlam. Fortunately, we don't have to lie in it. Meditating on a mantra (a simple sound that is silently chanted) can help us turn mental bedlam into peace of mind. By giving the mind a soothing word stick to hold on to, meditation can hold off thoughts bent on destruction.

The mantra you select is up to you, although it works best if it's one syllable, pleasing to the ear, and personally meaningful. You can use the same word while breathing in and out, or you can use one word for the inhalation and one word for the exhalation. I like to pick a word that represents a characteristic I want to *own* on the inhalation, and a word that reflects a quality I want to *exude* on the exhalation. I particularly like to use the word "calm" because it has the traditional "om" sound and serves as an affirmation.

Try this where you're sitting as soon as you read the following directions. Blaise Pascal said, "The idea of calm exists in a sitting cat." You'll find it's almost impossible to feel scattered if you're sitting as still as a contented cat and quietly ConZentrating on the word "calm."

Step 1. Close your eyes and breathe in through your nose five counts while silently saying the word "calm." As with the the Belly-Breathing Meditation, breathe up from your gut.

Step 2. Breathe out through your nose five counts while thinking "calm."

Step 3. Repeat this process five times. Hold the thought "calm" in your "belly brain" as you inhale and exhale. In the beginning, you may feel self-conscious or silly because you'll be aware that you're watching your own mind. If you persist, though, there will be flashes where you're thinking of your breathing and your mantra and nothing else. You may even get to the point where you're no longer even saying "calm"; you're simply sitting there sublimely relaxed. Good for you. The point of meditation is to bring you into a restful and mindful state. Goal accomplished.

A stockbroker named Zoë attended one of my public seminars in New York and reported that this technique changed her life. "Before that class, the idea of calm didn't even exist in my life. I work on Wall Street. It's nonstop cacophony, with people pushing and shoving, bells clanging, and constant pressure to make the deal. It used to take me at least an hour to get to sleep at night because my mind was so wired."

Zoë went on, "On the way home from your seminar, I decided trying this 'calm' meditation couldn't hurt, and maybe it could help. I was surprised at what a difference it made. That night in bed, instead of lying there reliving the day and second-guessing what I should have said and done, I simply focused on breathing in 'let' and breathing out 'go.' Within a couple of minutes, I felt my mind unclench. The next thing I knew, it was morning. Saying that mantra relaxed me so much, I went to sleep! That's success." Zoë proved we don't have to lie in bedlam if we choose to meditate on a soothing mantra instead.

Another word to focus on is "home." Ram Dass tells a story about being homesick while he was on a speaking tour. Following a presentation, he returned by himself to his hotel room and sat there, feeling lost and lonely. In the midst of his misery, he experienced a mini-epiphany. He realized that wherever he was . . . was home. To playfully reinforce this image, he walked out of his hotel room, closed the door, and then re-entered, calling out, "I'm ho-ome!" Voilà! He had given himself a tangible way to feel at home anywhere, anytime.

What's this mean for you? If for some reason you're missing home, simply inhale while saying "home" and exhale thinking "home." Ah, there you are. You weren't lost, you'd just (temporarily) lost your way home. Author Jon Kabat-Zinn said, "When you are immersed in 'doing' without being centered, it feels like being away from home. And when you reconnect with 'being' even for a few moments, you can make yourself at home no matter where you are." From now on, make a home for yourself in your mind and heart by breathing in the words "calm," "soothe," "peace," and "love." They can become your own personal homing device.

Clearheaded Meditation

> When we are unable to find tranquillity within ourselves, it is useless to seek it elsewhere.
> —La Rochefoucauld

Yoga practitioners have found that many people favor one side of their nose when they breathe. This may happen because of a head cold, sinus problems, or simple clogging. Whatever the case, it creates an unbalanced and incomplete exchange of air.

Tweedledum in *Alice in Wonderland* said, "I'm very brave generally, only today I happen to have a headache." If you have a headache or if your mind is congested (as one woman put it), air out your brain with this exercise. It can help clear away mental fog so you're better able to ConZentrate.

(Note: please stop if at any time you feel dizzy or light-headed, and don't stand up until you feel steady on your feet.)

Step 1. Inhale and exhale through your left nostril. To do this, place your right thumb on your right nostril, your two middle fingers on your forehead above your nose, and your ring finger on your left nostril. Close the right nostril and inhale through your left nostril while picturing the air coming up under your fingers on your forehead and clearing your brain. Imagine the air sweeping around your head cleaning out the mental cobwebs. With the right nostril still closed, exhale through your left nostril, seeing the air empty out of your mind and taking all the tension with it.

Step 2. Next, inhale and exhale through your right nostril. Close the left nostril with your ring finger, and breathe in through your right nostril while imagining yourself bringing in revitalizing oxygen. With your left nostril still closed, breathe out your right nostril and breathe out all the accumulated concerns that were crowding your mind.

Step 3. Alternate back and forth for three minutes. Breathe rhythmically and comfortably—all the while visualizing your brain getting an oxygen bath. After three minutes, resume breathing in and out through both nostrils. You'll feel mentally refreshed, and you'll also find yourself thinking better because you've just unclogged your brain and given *both* sides a workout.

A fellow author was diagnosed with a deviated nasal septum during college but was told it was purely a cosmetic nuisance, so she didn't pay much attention to it. She said, "The first time I did this exercise I realized the left side of my nose was almost completely blocked . . . who knows for how long? This situation isn't life-threatening, but it means I've been breathing shallowly for years. I always do the Clearheaded Meditation just before I play sports and write so I'm oxygenating my brain and so I'm in my right (and left) mind."

The next time you need to be at your intellectual and creative best, take a few minutes to do this exercise and see if it doesn't clear thinks up.

C. S. Lewis had fallen on some hard times and was asked why he prayed since it seemed God wasn't listening and didn't care. "I don't pray to change God," Lewis replied, "I pray to change me." We don't meditate to change the world, we meditate to change ourselves so we can better deal with the world. The peace of mind that is a by-product of meditation can help us face each day more calmly and serenely, and can help us ConZentrate on the breath and gift of life.

Action Plan 22. Meditation—It's Not What You Think

I've taken up meditation. I like to have espresso first to make it more challenging.

—Betsy Salkind

If you want to make your life less challenging, vow to take up meditation today. If conflict starts swirling around you, sit as calm as a cat and ConZentrate on thinking and breathing the quality you want to exude. See yourself being the eye of the storm, the quiet center in the midst of cacophony. Evelyn Underhill said, "After all, it is those who have a deep and real inner life who are best able to deal with the irritating details of the outer life." Meditating for even five minutes a day is a way of getting in touch with our inner life so we have a way of coping with the sometimes "eat lunch or be lunch" outer life.

Confusion	ConZentration
Scattered thoughts	*Collect our thoughts*
"The first day on my new job. What if people snub me? I feel so out of place."	"I'm going to inhale 'peace' and exhale 'love.' "

Confusion	ConZentration
Nonstop activity	**Stop all activity**
"There's so much to learn. I'll never be able to remember all this. I'm overwhelmed."	"I'm going to take a couple minutes to Zenter myself so I stay cool and collected."
Crazy pace	**Calm place**
"That's the tenth new person I've met in the last hour. How am I supposed to remember their names?"	"Stacy, relax. Slow your breathing down. I can handle this if I stay calm."
Chaotic, off-center mind	**Quiet, middle mind**
"I saw the secretary looking at me funny. I feel so self-conscious. Maybe I should have worn a suit instead of this dress."	"Stacy, get out of your head and into your gut. Belly-breathe and focus on your mantra. That's better. I feel grounded."
Miss our home	**Make ourselves at home**
"Why did I accept this new position? What was I thinking? I should have stayed where I was."	"I'm going to relax and be myself. Think home, breathe home, feel at home."
Meditate to change the world	**Meditate to change ourselves**
"My new coworkers are really giving me the cold shoulder. They're completely ignoring me."	"I choose to be serene. I will remain loving and will ConZentrate on being kind."

PART 8

Does It All A.D.D. Up?

I'm getting so absent-minded and forgetful. Sometimes in the middle of a sentence, I . . .

—Milton Berle

WAY 23

◉

Stay O.N. T.A.S.K.

He's so poor he can't even pay attention.

—Damon Wayans

Some of us feel we're poor at ConZentrating because our mind is either a "million miles away" or constantly flitting from one think to another.

If inattentiveness or distractability are chronic for you, you may want to get tested by a qualified medical professional to see if you have attention deficit disorder. ADD is defined as a "disorder of the central nervous system ... characterized by disturbances in the areas of attention, impulsiveness, and hyperactivity." It's important to note that neuroscientists and experts within the field are increasingly dissatisfied with ADD being called a disorder. They prefer to see ADD as a distinctive type of brain organization, one that favors creativity and *simultaneous* multilevel processing over linear, detail-oriented thought. A growing faction characterize ADD as an alternate and perfectly natural way of brain wiring.

Unfortunately, ADD is sometimes still seen as a disadvantage and labeled as a learning disability in today's society, which favors structured thinking, rote learning, and systematized performance. It's important to understand that ADD is merely *different*, not deficient. People with ADD don't ask for it and can't "cure" it. They can learn how to deal with it so they can behave more appropriately in the different situations in which they find themselves.

Everywhere at Once

> There are people who want to be everywhere at once, and they seem to get nowhere.
> —Carl Sandburg

Most of us don't want to be everywhere at once. We don't like feeling that we're mentally going in circles and getting nowhere. The problem is, we haven't been taught how to keep our mind on the straight and narrow. The following insights can be used by *anyone* who would like to learn how to stay O.N. T.A.S.K.—regardless of whether we have ADD. These techniques can help us continue to ConZentrate when our brain has better thinks to do.

O.N. T.A.S.K. = Organize Needed Materials in Advance

> Order is power . . . man's greatest need and his true well-being.
> —Henry F. Amiel

It is to our benefit to "call thinks to order" before we start a project so we don't have any excuse to get up once we get to work. Talk yourself through the task to see what supplies should be on hand. Then sharpen those pencils, retrieve the dictionary, and grab plenty of paper *in advance*.

A friend said this simple suggestion really helped him. He said, "As long as I stay *seated*, I can stay focused. As soon as I stand up to fetch something, it's all over. I invariably find something infinitely more interesting than what I was working on, and my ConZentration goes out the window."

O.N. T.A.S.K. = No Competing Stimuli

The most effective act is once the mind is made up to go forward without looking backward.
—Zen master D. T. Suzuki

We will be more effective if we make our mind go forward without looking *around*. If we allow our eyes to wander, our mind will wander, and we'll end up thinking about everything but our original assignment. ADDers are particularly suspectible to being distracted by movement. All it takes is for someone to walk by or for something to catch their eye, and they're off on a mental flight of fancy.

A young man with ADHD (attention deficit hyperactive disorder) put it this way: "I went to the library so I could work on my homework. I saw a fellow student walking by, which reminded me of the class we take together, which made me think of a question the teacher wanted us to research for the next day, so I got up to ask the reference librarian where I could find the answer. She told me where to look, but on the way there, I passed the bestseller section and they had the newest novel by my favorite author. I took it back to my seat, and to make a long story short, I never did get back to my homework. That's typical."

So, what to do? There are several ways to keep our eyes and mind on the straight and narrow. We can:

1. Make sure our desk does not face a hallway. Our eyes will constantly monitor the foot traffic, and it will be almost impossible to maintain the work flow that is a result of uninterrupted effort. If we're afraid of offending people by having our back to the door, we can turn our desk so it faces the *side* of our cubicle. We'll be able to stay focused on what we're doing, yet still have an open posture so visitors don't perceive us as rude. If you study in an open space (cafeteria, dining room, study hall), face away from the action.

2. Move anything we're not working on (other books, correspondence, etc.) outside the periphery of our vision so it's

out of sight, out of mind. Keep the wall we face blank. If we post family photos, messages, appointment calendars, and other nonessential items, we'll get distracted every time we look up.

3. Remember the Focus Pocus technique? If it's impossible to physically move lower priority paperwork out of the way because your space is too crowded, block those other obligations out by using our hands as blinkers. A progressive school on Maui actually hands out three-sided cardboard cubbies the students can place on their desks to create their own private space.

I'm about to say something that may surprise you. While blocking out *visual* distractions can help, blocking out *sounds* can hurt. How can that be? Today's younger generation has become accustomed to cacophony. Street sounds, the screeching of brakes, trucks changing gears, and the wail of ambulances are their norm. For these people silence can actually be disconcerting because it's so unusual.

I'll always remember a parent who battled with his teenager about the issue of whether or not his son could do a quality job on his homework while listening to MTV. This conservative individual simply couldn't believe his son could ConZentrate with that "racket" on. I asked how his son was doing in school, and he admitted that his son was maintaining a 3.6 GPA and that his teachers consistently praised him on his report cards. I told the man that as long as his son seemed to be studying effectively, even with loud rock music on, to let him do his think.

Research has shown that people with ADHD actually need stimuli in order to focus. If the environment becomes dull, they will look for and create their own stimulation. If you're one of these people who works better when surrounded by stimuli, go ahead and leave the TV or radio playing *in the background.* That's the key phrase. If these programs are pulling your attention away and compromising your productivity, then they're sabotaging your efforts. If they simply provide a presence in the room that facilitates your focus because you don't feel alone, they're serving a good purpose.

Horizons Academy, a private school in Hawaii that has a number of students with ADD, has initiated several innovative policies to help kids ConZentrate. One is to allow them to bring portable CD players to school and listen to music through earphones while working on assignments. This may fly in the face of standard school policy, but students say the music helps them focus by filtering out the dozens of sounds they'd be hearing otherwise. Students are also allowed to chew gum during instructional classtime. Gum on campus is a public education no-no, but many ADDers say it helps neutralize motor overload. It gives them something to *do* and significantly increases their ability to stay on task and complete classwork.

Students at Horizon also have permission to remove themselves from an overstimulating environment. A friend who volunteers there told me, "I've seen kids pick up their books and papers and go out in the hall to study if it gets too noisy. If someone's causing a disturbance, they are free to go outside to regain control. The school also uses a positive behavior management program that provides clear expectations, frequent feedback, and reinforcement for appropriate on-task, attending behavior. This structured yet nurturing educational environment has worked wonders for many kids who had given up hope trying to fit in elsewhere."

O.N. T.A.S.K. = Transcend Frustration

> Perhaps the most valuable result of all education is the ability to make yourself do the thing you have to do, when it ought to be done, whether you like it or not. This is the first lesson to be learned.
> **—Thomas Huxley**

People with ADD can be quick to switch mental horses in midstream. Unfortunately, *not* finishing tasks wears us down because we're literally and figuratively coming undone. Furthermore, a propensity for abandoning projects midway means we rarely get to experience the feeling of competence that is closely allied with completion.

Jean-Jacques Rousseau said, "Perseverance is the first thing a child should learn—it is what he will have most need to know."

Perseverance is the first thing all of us should learn. We can have all the talent and intelligence in the world, and it won't matter if we habitually give up when the mental going gets tough.

The key is to develop the habit of reapplying our attention when we're frustrated, instead of throwing our hands up and mentally walking away. The way to do this is to adopt the **"Five More" Approach.** If you're writing a term paper and the words just aren't coming, make a deal with yourself: "*Five more minutes* and then I'll get up and stretch." If your child is working on math and angrily pushes away from the table, exclaiming, "I give up. I hate algebra," encourage him to finish *five more* problems and then take a break. If you're reading a complex technical manual and your mind just can't take it anymore, tell yourself: "*Five more* pages and then I can take a breather." The "Five More" Approach benefits us in several ways.

- We learn to keep going at the moment of frustration, instead of giving up at the moment of frustration. We are educating ourselves to do what we have to do when we have to do it, whether we feel like it or not. Frustration is often momentary. If we push through that momentary malaise, we can often re-establish momentum. Moments later we realize we're back in the flow of thinks, and our exasperation is a think of the past.
- Just as world-class marathoners can develop the physical endurance to run continuously for long distances, we can develop the mental endurance to ConZentrate for longer periods of time. Runners know that in a long race they'll reach a wall, a point when they will run out of energy and want to stop. If they consistently persevere through that temporary moment of despair, they can find their second wind. When working on a long or complicated project, we too can run into a wall. If we push through our temporary moment of despair, we can find our second mind.

By adding a small increment to our study or work time, we can condition our mind to maintain attention for extended periods of time without rest. We can gradually increase our mental stamina by starting with a reasonable study/work time and then adding five-minute increments every two to three days. Isaac Newton said, "If I have ever made any valuable discoveries, it has been owing more to patient attention than to any other talent." If we patiently increase the length of time we pay attention, we'll develop the ability to mentally go the distance.

O.N. T.A.S.K. = ADDitudes That Accentuate the Positive

Argue for your limitations, and sure enough, they're yours.
—Richard Bach

ADD is not caused by lack of moral character or discipline, but it can be tempting to use it as an excuse. Saying things like, "I'm always losing things because of my ADD" perpetuates the unhealthy impression that we're passive victims. It's crucial to take responsibility for our behavior. The following tips can help us develop **Can-Do ADDitudes** that help rather than hamper our ability to ConZentrate.

ADDitude 1. Set yourself up for success with an "I believe, I believe" approach. You may have heard the slogan "Success comes in cans." Well, failure comes in can'ts: "I *can't* stop fidgeting." "I *can't* keep my attention on anything for more than a few seconds." From now on, boost your perception of capability by saying, "I *can* sit quietly," "I *can* stay focused."

Norman Cousins said, "Everything begins with belief." Believe that you can be more effective, and your belief will help create that fact. There's a wonderful example of planting and presuming desired behavior in the basketball movie *Hoosiers*. The game is on the line in the final seconds with the score tied. The coach (Gene Hackman) gathers his players together in a huddle and, in the midst of the bedlam, says calmly, "*After* Steven makes these two shots, go into this . . . " His assumption that the player would sink both free throws eased doubts, eliminated fear, and imprinted confidence.

ADDitude 2. Seek out someone who supports you. In survey after survey, adult ADDers say *the* primary factor to their being able to maintain a healthy self-image was having at least one person (a parent, teacher, or favorite relative) who reassured them that they were okay.

Ideally, we would all be surrounded by supportive people who are this enlightened about ADD. That's not always the case. ADDers frequently hear only what they do "wrong." "Quit messing around." "Stop bothering me with all these questions." Henry Wadsworth Longfellow said, "Hard words bruise the heart of a child." Harsh words also bruise the *minds* of us all. That's why it's essential to find at least one benefactor who shores up your self-esteem and instills in you the conviction you *do* have something to offer.

ADDitude 3. Catch yourself doing something right so you per-petuate positive behavior. "I stayed calm when that lady bumped into me with her shopping cart instead of flying off the handle. That was good control." "I held my tongue instead of mouthing off to the teacher. That's progress." Put negative labels in the past by prefac-ing them with "I used to . . . " "I *used to* let my mind wander when people talked to me; and now I keep my eyes on their face so I can stay tuned." This is a way of shaping our behavior instead of sham-ing it so we feel encouraged rather than discouraged.

ADDitude 4. Educate yourself about ADD. The more you learn about how to deal with ADD's idiosyncrasies, the better you'll feel about yourself. A helpful resource is the book *Driven to Distraction* by Edward M. Hallowell, M.D., and John J. Ratey, M.D. You also may want to check the following websites for comprehensive information about diagnosis, treatment, medication, and professional counseling.

- ADDA (Attention Deficit Disorder Association) at http://www.azstarnet.com/~sled
- ADD on AOL at http://members.aol.com/JimAMS/ addonaol7.html
- ASK (Adults Seeking Knowledge) about ADD at http://www.azstarnet.com/!ask

ADDitude 5. Join a support group. Many ADDers have told me their involvement in these groups has been a godsend. Anyone who's gone through a tough time knows what a huge relief it is to connect with others who understand what we're experiencing. The universal, heartfelt feeling is, "It's so nice to know I'm not the only one who feels that way!" CHADD (Children and Adults with Attention Deficit Disorders) publishes a fascinating and fun newsletter called (what else?) *CHADDER Box.* Call them at 305-587-3700 for more information, and contact ADDA (800-487-2282) to receive a brochure about their annual convention.

O.N. T.A.S.K. = Systems, Systems, Systems

He who laughs last had a backup disc.
—**Internet joke**

A friend with an ADD son previewed this section of the manuscript and laughed out loud at the above quote. She said, "The only way we survive is with backup *lists.* We place reminder notes for Randy *everywhere.* We have a checklist on the bathroom mirror for personal hygiene chores. We have a checklist on the front door for school supplies. Randy has a checklist in his backpack for homework items to bring back on the bus. We have a chore chart and a message center on the refrigerator *and* on the TV so household responsibilities don't get left to chance.

"When we first started posting these notes, we had trial runs where we walked and talked through the routine countless times until it became a habit for him to check the door before he left, look in his backpack before he walked out of his classroom, etc. Placing reminders around the house stimulates his memory of his responsibilities and counteracts the spaciness of ADD. Structure and systems are our lifesaver."

A techie friend once told me tongue in cheek, "In my next life, I'm going to have more memory installed." Checklists are a tangible way of installing memories of what we're supposed to do, where we're supposed to be, whom we're supposed to meet, and when. The following systems can help us remember our responsibilities.

Same place system. Human beings are creatures of habits. Habits (good and bad) are patterns of behavior we repeat without thinking. If we always fix something to eat when we're in the kitchen, our mind starts thinking about food as soon as we walk by the refrigerator. If we always fall asleep watching the late news in our lounger, our eyelids will start getting heavy a few minutes into that broadcast.

Our goal is to repeat *positive* actions until they're automatic. By imprinting desired behaviors at the same time and place, again and again, we'll find that going to that place is enough to trigger our hoped-for habitual behavior. If we follow our systems consistently, these activities become ingrained and we do them without thinking *despite* our preoccupation, inattentiveness, or exhaustion.

For example, if we *always* leave our keys on the key ring by the front door and if we do it without fail for several weeks, then our hand will automatically reach to place the keys on the hook as we walk in, even if we're not thinking about it. If we always put our electronic calendar back in the zippered compartment of our briefcase, we'll never have a panic attack worrying where we left it. Best of all, we'll save the hours of lost time searching for mislaid items.

Same time system. We do ourselves a huge favor by establishing designated times for required tasks, and doing them at that time without fail. It's a variation of the "If it's Tuesday, it must be Belgium" theory. Our mind says, "If it's seven P.M. on a weeknight, it must be time to do homework." "It's the first of the month, must be time to pay bills." "If it's Sunday evening, it must be time to call my folks." If we establish these rituals and adhere to them religiously, we can counteract chronic forgetfulness.

Same work space system. The drawback of using the kitchen table for studying is it triggers thought patterns contrary to our purpose. We sit down to study, and all we can think about is fixing ourselves a snack. We share the dining room table with our siblings and homework hour ends up being a social hour. Efficiency experts suggest our desk be kept sacrosanct and that we don't do anything there but produce and process work requirements. Want a cup of coffee? Go somewhere else. Want to talk with a coworker? Take it to the conference room. Our spouse wants to discuss weekend plans? Get up and go into the living room. This may seem extreme, but keeping this commitment lets us know, on a visceral level, that whenever we're at our desk, we're there to work or study.

O.N. T.A.S.K. = Know Your Style

I would go without shirt or shoe . . . sooner than lose for a
minute the two separate sides of my head.
—Rudyard Kipling

Do you know what your preferred learning style is? People prefer to process information with a favorite sense. An easy way to figure out what your style is is to identify how you greet and say good-bye to people. What do you say? "Nice to *see* you again." "Good to *hear* your voice." "Let's keep in *touch*." "You're *looking* good."

If you agree with what someone says, how do you respond? "I *hear* what you mean." "*Sounds* good to me." These are auditory styles. "I *see* what you're saying." "*Looks* like this will work." These are visual preferences. "*Feels* right." "I *sense* this will work out." Those are a kinesthetic style.

This is a simplistic explanation of preferred learning styles, but the point is to introduce you to the concept so you can, to the degree possible, match and maximize your work/learning efforts. If you have an auditory preference, you are quick to get ideas simply by listening to them. You may want to tape meetings, presentations, or classroom lectures so you can review them while commuting. Some ADDers with a visual style find it almost impossible to learn from talking heads. They need to see problems graphically worked out on a chalkboard, or have material illustrated with visual aids before ideas click for them. Tactile people often do well in hands-on workshops and labs, where they can be physically involved taking notes or conducting experiments.

Most people, especially ADDers, operate best in an active mode where they *have* to think on their feet and seat. It's too easy for us to daydream if we're left in a passive mode. That's why I suggest you jot notes to yourself in the margin of this book when you read ideas that are particularly timely or relevant. We pay attention best when our mind is actively thinking about what we're reading instead of just silently observing or absorbing it.

I still smile at the memory of what happened at the closing keynote of a national conference. As frequently happens in the final general session, a number of attendees had already left for the airport and the room was less than half full. The speaker was directing her comments to about fifty people seated in the front of the huge, almost empty ballroom. A man wandered in and sat in back. After a few minutes he called out, "Speak up, I can't hear you." The keynoter looked at the man, paused, and said simply, "Move closer."

What's this mean for us? It's important to take responsibility for our own learning. "Circumstances?" sniffed Napoleon Bonaparte. "I *make* circumstances!" Instead of blaming circumstances for blocking our ability to ConZentrate, we need to make circumstances conducive to ConZentration. Initiate on your own behalf and take the necessary steps to facilitate your focus. If you're in study hall and want to study the inside of your eyelids more than the book in front of you, start taking notes. Sit up close in presentations so you can't hide out in back. If you have chatty neighbors, change seats so you can focus on the professor instead of their small talk.

A manager said, "My problem isn't that I *can't* ConZentrate. I ConZentrate all too well. In fact, I become so intent on what I'm doing, I often space out appointments. I've learned to use the alarm feature on my electronic calendar and laptop computer to remind me of meetings. By setting my beeper to go off ten minutes before I need to be somewhere, I can go ahead and get engrossed in what I'm doing without having to worry that I won't show up where I'm supposed to be." This smart man made accommodations for his style. How can you make accommodations for your learning/working style so you set yourself up for success?

Empathy for Hyperactive Individuals

The task of the educator lies in seeing that the child does not confound good with immobility, and evil with activity.
—Maria Montessori

Sometimes Maria Montessori's insight is easier to read about than to emulate. A teacher took my workshop because she was exasperated with three ADHD children who were in her class of thirty (?!) third graders. Sandy said, "I'm not a teacher, I'm a warden. These kids have the attention span of a gnat. It's almost impossible to accomplish anything because I spend all my time trying to keep these three from destroying the classroom. I'm exhausted by the first recess and these kids still have energy to spare at the end of the day."

What can we do when we're haggard and the people we're dealing with are hyper? This teacher was able to turn her antipathy into empathy by watching a video called *Fat City* (produced by the Public Broadcasting System and available at 800-344-3337). This video was filmed from the perspective of someone with ADD and shows what it's like to have a brain that's always on the go. "It was an eye-opening experience getting inside the head of someone with ADD. The crazy camera angles, blurry focus, and constant switching from object to object made me dizzy. I told Brandon, one of my ADD kids, that I was exhausted just *watching* the video. He looked at me in astonishment and exclaimed, 'Now you know what it's like for me. That's how I feel *all the time!*'"

Sandy continued, "I'm not as impatient with these kids as I used to be. After experiencing their life for twenty minutes, I have a profound empathy for them. I can't even imagine what it's like having a mind that's rapid-firing every minute of the day. I'm a lot more compassionate now because I remind myself what it's like for them. I've made my teaching style more hands-on so they can learn by doing instead of having to sit still for hours on end. And I've seated my three ADDers in the front row corner. If they're physically distant from me, they'll be mentally distant, too. I understand now it's almost impossible for them to ConZentrate on the chalkboard when they're in the back row. By placing them close by, I can walk over and command their attention with my proximity."

To Medicate or Not to Medicate?
That Is the Question

One is always seeking the touchstone that will dissolve one's deficiencies as a person and as a craftsman, and one is always bumping up against the fact that there is none except hard work, concentration, and continued application.

—Paul Gallico

Upon hearing Gallico's quote, a student said, "Uh-oh. You mean there's no magic pill. I've got to work at this?" Yup, we've got to work at it. The good news is that there are some pills that have worked magic for ADDers.

Please note. I am *not* a doctor, so I am not recommending medication. I *am* recommending that if you (or a loved one) have been correctly diagnosed with ADD by a physician, you talk with him/her to discuss prescription drugs such as Ritalin (generic name methylphenidate), Dexedrine (dextroamphetamine), Cylert (pemoline), Norpramin (desipramine).

Finding the right medication and dosage can take several months of trial and error, but if it proves effective for you, it can help you ConZentrate for longer periods of time, reduce irritability and mood swings, and improve impulse control. One young girl at Horizons Academy described it this way: "I feel like I'm going to *explode* if I don't take my meds. I'm just bursting with energy. They don't work that way for my best friend, though. They make him too dizzy."

Medication works wonders for some people and doesn't work at all for others. It is not a panacea. As *Time* magazine said in a cover story about "The Age of Ritalin," "Even doctors who have seen Ritalin's positive, sometimes miraculous effects warn that the drug is not a substitute for better schools, creative teaching and parents' spending more time with their kids. Unless a child acquires coping skills, the benefits of medication are gone as soon as it wears off."

Inspiring Words About ADD

I felt a cleaving in my mind—as if my brain had split.
I tried to match it—seam by seam—but could not make
    them fit.
The thought behind—I strove to join—unto the thought
    before.
But sequence ravelled out of sound—like balls upon a floor.

—Emily Dickinson

Wow. Emily Dickinson wrote the previous poem in 1864, yet many ADDers relate to it more than a hundred years later. A seminar participant said, after hearing Dickinson's poem, "She said it much more eloquently than I ever could; but that's what having ADD is like. I feel my mind is trying to juggle a dozen different balls in the air, and I'm dropping every single one of them."

If you ever get discouraged, think of Benjamin Franklin and Albert Einstein, both incredibly capable individuals who probably would have been diagnosed with ADD today. They certainly achieved great thinks, and so can you. It's important not to view ADD as a curse. Although he was not labeled as ADD (there was no such diagnosis back then), Thomas Edison felt that his inability to stick to one task was the source of his creative efforts. Like many people called geniuses later in life, Edison had difficulty in school. He dropped out early and bounced from one dead-end job to another until he created a career (inventor) that matched his mental style. By 1877, he was working on forty different inventions *at the same time.* He kept his own hours, worked on what he wanted when he wanted for as long as he wanted, and led an incredibly productive and rewarding life.

Former Vice President Dan Quayle once made a memorable blooper when speaking at a banquet honoring the United Negro College Fund. You may be familiar with their slogan: "A mind is a terrible thing to waste." Quayle mixed up the words and said instead, "What a waste it is to lose one's mind, or not to have a mind. How true that is." Commit to using these six O.N. T.A.S.K. steps and they can help you use more of (versus lose) the mind you have.

Action Plan 23. Stay O.N. T.A.S.K.

**Many people with ADD are "Equal Opportunity Attenders."
They give everything and anything the opportunity to
grab their attention.**

—Kate Kelly and Peggy Ramundo,
You Mean I'm Not Lazy, Stupid, or Crazy?!

How do you plan to turn ADD into an ADDvantage instead of a disADDvantage? Could you do a mental trial run of your project so you collect needed supplies beforehand? Could you remove visual alternatives so your mind isn't tempted to take off on flights of fancy? Could you use the "Five More" Approach to stretch your attention span? Could you believe in yourself and focus on what you can do instead of what you can't? Are you going to set up some systems to help you remember your responsibilities?

George Bernard Shaw said: "Progress is impossible without change; and he who cannot change his mind cannot change anything." You can change your mind and improve your ability to stay O.N. T.A.S.K. if you choose to use these steps.

Confusion	ConZentration
Any excuse to get up	*Organized so won't get up*
"Doing the annual budget report is my least favorite activity. Oh, I forgot to get the income figures. Oh, hi, Jan. How are you?"	"Let me make sure I have everything. Okay, I have the expense sheets, income figures. I'm all set to get started."
Lots of competing stimuli	*No competing stimuli*
"That copier makes so much noise. How is anyone supposed to get work done with the racket?"	"I'm going to work in the conference room. I can spread out and no one's using it."

Confusion

Give in to frustration
"English is my worst subject. I'm terrible at these essay questions. I'm just going to turn this in as it is."

ADDitudes that hurt
"This is hopeless. I might as well give up right now."

No systems
"I'd rather play video games. I'll study on the bus on the way to school."

No style preference
"I've been reading for a half hour, and I can't remember a single thing."

ConZentration

Transcend frustration
"Okay, five more minutes and then I can take a break. I'll finish the rest after dinner."

ADDitudes that help
"I know I can stay focused if I put my mind to it."

Systems
"It's seven P.M. Time to study."

Know your style preference
"I'm going to take notes so I'll remember what I'm reading."

WAY 24

◉

Mind Your Manners

It's not that I don't want to listen to people. I very much want to listen to people, I just can't hear them over my talking.

—Paula Poundstone

Sound familiar? "There are two distinct classes of thought," mused Thomas Paine, "those we produce in ourselves by reflection . . . and those that bolt into the mind of their own accord."

People in my ConZentration workshops are quick to tell me that thoughts bolt into their mind on a constant basis. Unfortunately, the thoughts that bolt into their mind often tend to bolt out their mouth . . . creating social faux pas that cost them friendships. Sufferers from the "I should have said" or the "I can't believe I said that" syndrome sometimes unintentionally hurt peoples' feelings by blurting out what's on their mind without first evaluating it to see if it's appropriate.

A complicating factor is a disproportionate mind-capacity/task-simplicity ratio. Our mind can process information at an amazingly fast rate (approximately 1,200 words per minute). Unfortunately, we often find ourselves in situations where information is being delivered at a painfully s-l-o-w rate. That's why our mind wants to wander or rush ahead when we're listening to a boring speaker or a slow-talking individual. Our mind is capable of so much more, it's tough to stay tuned to people who are waxing not-so-eloquent.

The good news is, people with a short attention span can turn social gaffes into social graces if they'll **L.I.S.T.E.N.** up. The following six tips can help us interact in sensitive, balanced ways so our relationships thrive.

L.I.S.T.E.N. = Learn to Think First, Talk Later

Tact is thinking all you say without saying all you think.
—Leo Rosten

Many of us do the opposite of this. Our mind is racing with ideas and we just have to share them. Or our quick brain knows what someone is going to say and we can't help but jump ahead and finish their sentence for them. We strongly disagree with an individual's opinion, and the next think we know, our mouth blurts out, "That's not what happened." Then we're off and verbally running.

A famous anecdote about George S. Kaufman has him listening (and listening) to a dinner guest drone on and on about her life. Toward the end of the meal, Kaufman couldn't contain himself any longer. He turned to her and asked, "Do you have *any* unexpressed thoughts?" Good point. Just because we want to say something doesn't mean we have the right to say it.

Repeat the mental mantra **"think first"** on your way to meetings, social events, and business get-togethers. Promise to practice social discipline. *Before* speaking up, ask yourself, "Is this sensitive? Is this timely? Is this appropriate? Will it add value?" If the answers are yes, your contribution will be tactful and deserves to be contributed. If not, keep the thought to yourself so you don't get caught in your own mouth-trap.

L.I.S.T.E.N. = Interpret and Use Body Language

A yawn is a silent shout.
—G. K. Chesterton

People may not be comfortable *telling* us we're coming on too strong, but they don't have to because their body will. We want to train ourselves to watch other people's eyes, expressions, and posture for signs that we may be stepping on their mental toes.

In addition to interpreting other people's body language, we're going to monitor ours to make sure we're communicating appropriately. If individuals in our conversational circle are yawning, it's their polite way of saying, "Enough already." If people's eyes are flitting around, they may be looking for a way to escape. If someone is staring at us wide-eyed, perhaps, in our passion, we said something offensive. If people are backing up or turning away from us, they're trying to break the connection and distance themselves. Time to courteously bring the conversation to a close.

"Look at me when I talk to you" is an admonition some of us have heard before. Elbert Hubbard said, "Eyes are the spectacles of the brain; the peephole of the consciousness." Simply said, if we're not looking at someone, we're not listening to them. The way to pay attention and preclude preoccupation is to give people **L**. These four steps activate interest and direct it *off* ourselves and *on* the object of our attention. The next time you want or need to give someone your ear, give 'em **L**.

L = Look the person in the eye. Noticing the color of the person's eyes ensures that you're really looking at him or her.

L = Lean *slightly* forward. The word "slightly" is important, since some ADDers, in their intensity, get too close and come across as intimidating.

L = Lift your eyebrows. Try it. It's impossible to be lethargic with your eyebrows lifted.

L = Level your attention. This is especially important with children. Kneeling down so we're the same height creates rapport because we're now seeing thinks eye to eye. They'll now believe we understand how they feel because we're on the same level.

How many times have you asked someone, "Are you listening to me?" Even though it's obvious they're not, they still say yes. From now on, if you want a distracted child to give you his/her attention, say, "Give me your eyes." Then *wait* until they face you squarely and look at you with *both* eyes. If their body is slanted away, or if they're looking at you out of the corner of their eyes, they'll be only half there.

And if you need to communicate with someone who's in another part of the house, office, or room, go to them or ask them to come to you so you can eyeball each other while you are talking.

L.I.S.T.E.N. = Script Important Conversations

I'm going to speak my mind, because I have nothing to lose.
—S. I. Hayakawa

Oops. Former college president Hayakawa just proved otherwise with this opening remark.

I suggest we write what we think and wish to speak, so we can say what we mean. I am not suggesting we become mechanical robots reading from prepared texts. I am suggesting we prepare succinct, socially acceptable responses to frequently asked questions and commonly encountered situations so we can handle them with assurance instead of anxiety.

For example, what do you say when people ask the ubiquitous conversational opener "What do you do?" Can you respond to that with a compelling sound bite that gives people a hook on which to hang a conversation? Do you have a repertoire of generic questions you use to keep conversations rolling? "Tell me more. . . . " "What is your favorite . . . ?" "How did you get into this line of work?" are *talk tools* you can use to avoid being tongue-tied if your mind goes blank. And if that happens, use a line that speakers trot out: "That silence you just heard was me speaking my mind."

I strongly recommend we think ahead and rehearse gracious openings so we can get first meetings off to a good start. "Thank you for inviting me. I'm looking forward to getting to know your friends." "Feel free to put me to work." "What can I do to help out?" Keep in mind several all-purpose phrases you can say to handle those often awkward first few minutes smoothly and graciously. "This is my first time here. Any suggestions?" "I'm new to town. What are some activities you recommend?"

L.I.S.T.E.N. = Tongue in Check

Spilling your guts is just exactly as charming as it sounds.
—Fran Lebowitz

Conversations are supposed to be dialogues, not intersecting monologues, as Rebecca West once pessimistically pointed out. Instead of being a competitive exercise in which the first person to take a breath is considered the listener, they are supposed to be a balanced alternating of expression and absorption.

An ADDer once introduced himself in a seminar by saying, "I have a problem with impulse control. I don't have any." The question is, how can we curb our impulsivity so we can communicate more sensitively? We tell ourselves to *take turns* and to keep our tongue in check. One man I know gives himself a one-minute time limit. It may sound unnecessarily strict, but he claims if he didn't keep his mouth on a tight leash, it would run away with him and chase away potential friends. His self-imposed rule is to talk for a minute and then ask a related question of the other person. There are times this self-described motormouth goes over his minute, but watching his watch keeps him mindful and prevents him from monopolizing conversations.

Another thing this man learned to do is to ask open-ended questions—"What do you like to do when you're not working?"—instead of close-ended questions—"Do you like living in Seattle?" Close-ended questions already have the answer in them and relegate the other person to grunting yes or no. They bring conversations to a crashing halt. Open-ended questions seek in-depth answers that move conversations past platitudes and shallow chitchat.

L.I.S.T.E.N. = Enlist a Friend to Catch You in the Act

I don't pay any attention to him. I don't even ignore him.
—**Samuel Goldwyn**

When we tune others out, we're usually not ignoring them on purpose. Our inattentiveness isn't intended to make a statement; it's just that our butterfly brain is engaged elsewhere. If you are staring off into space or suffering from foot-in-mouth disease, arrange with an associate to give you a gentle elbow in the ribs (wives have been using this technique for years!).

Some of us have what's called *disinhibition*. We get so caught up in what we're thinking or saying, we forget to self-monitor. We have a tough time blocking inappropriate thoughts and are apt to react without considering the consequences. That's why it helps to have some help. Ask a partner or friend to politely police you and give a prearranged signal if you start rambling, dominating a discussion, or coming on too strong.

Some of us have the opposite problem. Instead of overwhelming people with intensity, we are more apt to be in our own world woolgathering. Comedian Steven Wright described this condition when he said, "This morning I woke up out of a dream and went right into a daydream." If you're lost in thought when you should be listening, have a pal pull you out of your reverie so you can pay attention to the person talking.

L.I.S.T.E.N. = No Crossing Boundaries

Who needs a book of etiquette? Everyone does . . . for we must all learn the socially acceptable ways of living.
—**Amy Vanderbilt**

People with ADD often feel things passionately and express thinks intensely. The combination can be intimidating. People shrink back from over-the-top energy levels and tend to avoid bulldozer personality types. We can throttle down intensity by speaking "low and slow." Talking fast revs up our energy, which increases our volume, which causes us to speak more rapidly, and the cycle escalates—while the people nearby plan their getaway. Hold the thought **"low and slow"** in your mind and it will help you speak at a pace and volume that are more pleasing to the ear and psyche.

In their excellent book *You Mean I'm Not Lazy, Stupid, or Crazy?!* authors Kate Kelly and Peggy Ramundo suggest we visualize a hula hoop (remember those?) surrounding each person. Vow not to violate that person's space. This is not a petty issue. We want to avoid invading people's comfort zone (about an arm's length on all sides). Hold the thought **"give 'em some space"** and take a step back so we're respecting people's need for elbow room.

Action Plan 24. Mind Your Manners

**I have mental joys and mental health,
Mental friends and mental wealth.**

—William Blake

Shirley Maclaine said, "Fear makes strangers of people who could be friends." Strangers can be quick to interpret inattentiveness as rudeness, disinterest, or lack of respect. That's why it's important for all of us to L.I.S.T.E.N. up. By interacting mindfully (versus mindlessly) with everyone we meet, we can make and keep more friends.

What mental sticks are you going to use to remind yourself to mind your manners? Are you going to "think first," speak "low and slow," and "give 'em some space"? Are you going to prepare several gracious questions to kick off conversations and keep them going? Are you going to observe body talk or enlist an associate to give you the high sign if you start crowding someone's comfort zone? Resolve to do even one of these ideas and people will notice and appreciate your uncommon courtesy.

Confusion

ConZentration

Talk first, think later
"Wow, you've really put on some weight. I thought you were on a diet. What happened?"

Learn to think first, talk later
"Patty's probably already self-conscious about her weight gain. I won't mention it."

Ignore body language
"Don't go yet. I'm not finished. I wanted to tell you about the time . . . "

Interpret body language
"Oops, I'm sorry. I think I got carried away with that story."

Feel awkward, don't know what to say
"Uh, am I the first one here? Aren't there other people coming? I hope I'm not the only one."

Script conversations, know what to say
"Hi, Katy. It's good to see you. Is there something I can do to help out?"

Tongue runs wild
"And then I let him know exactly what I thought of his behavior. I'll tell you what I told him. I said . . . "

Tongue in check
"What would you have said in that situation, Mike? Was there a better way to handle it?"

Alienate a friend
"I can't believe he's wearing that outfit. I wouldn't get caught dead in a leisure suit."

Enlist a friend
"Look at what Ralph is wea—Hey, they're about to open the buffet. Let's go."

No observing of boundaries
"IT WAS SUCH A GREAT CATCH! HERE, PUT YOUR HANDS OUT AND I'LL SHOW YOU HOW HE DID IT."

No crossing boundaries
"Here, I'll back up a little and demonstrate the unbelievable reception he made."

PART 9

Head Master

A good education should leave
much to be desired.

—Alan Gregg

WAY 25

◉

S.T.U.D.Y. Do Right

All some students want out of school is themselves.

—classroom poster

A re you thinking, "I'm not in school right now, so this section doesn't apply to me?" Perhaps you share Groucho Marx's attitude. When his mom found out he'd been cutting classes, she asked, "Don't you want to get an education?" "Not if I have to go to school to get it," he quipped.

For many of us, *life* has become our classroom. We have homework even though we're not in school. We may read technical journals to keep up with trends in our industry. Perhaps we study procedural manuals to learn how to use new computer software. Doctors, nurses, teachers, engineers, auto mechanics, Realtors, and many other professionals keep continuing education credits current by attending conferences to update industry-specific knowledge and skills. Maybe your company wants to send you to an intensive management training program.

Learning on Purpose

Studying without a liking for it spoils the memory, and it retains nothing it takes in.
—Leonardo da Vinci

And if you *are* going to school? What are you trying to achieve by studying? If you don't know or if you're studying just because you have to, your mind will not apply itself. Why should it? It has no good reason to.

It's said, "Activity without purpose is meaningless." Every time we study, whether it's for the SATs or a spelling bee, we need to clarify what we're trying to accomplish and why it's worth our while. Contrary to the popular proverb, ours *is* to reason why! It's imperative to come up with a motive to learn, or we won't.

The following S.T.U.D.Y. techniques can help us "live and learn" and become students of life. Whether we're preparing for the bar exam, a flight test, or whatever, these steps can help us make the most of our studying so it's T.I.M.E. well spent.

S.T.U.D.Y. = Schedule Topics Using Difficulty, Environment, and Energy

> My grades were four Fs and a D. My tutor suggested I was
> spending too much time on one subject.
> **—comedian Shelby Metcalf**

Since many of us don't look forward to studying, it's vital to set up homework time to make the most of our limited motivation. We can do that by taking into account the comparative difficulty of the subjects we need to study, the condusiveness of our environment to studying, and the amount of mental energy we have. From now on, figure out how much time to spend on each subject and in what order by **scheduling topics using:**

Difficulty. Rank your homework topics in descending order of how demanding they are. Imagine you need to study English, history, and math. You love English and tonight you simply need to read a five-page story. You're mildly interested in history and all you have to do is research some dates on the Civil War, which will take about half an hour. You hate math and your teacher was mad at the class for goofing off, so he assigned thirty complex problems that will take at least an hour to figure out. If you take these factors into account, it appears that English is your easiest assignment, history is second easiest, and math is your toughest.

Environment. Evaluate the setting in which you'll be studying. Are you in a college dorm or studying at home on the kitchen table with younger siblings? Will it be noisy, quiet, crowded, or private during the hours you'll be hitting the books? Obviously, it's in your best interest to study where there are as few distractions as possible . . . but that can't always happen.

Energy. Estimate how long it will take to complete your studies and what your vitality level will be over the course of that time. Take into account your energy patterns. Maybe you're a night owl who doesn't kick into gear until after nine P.M. Perhaps you're the proverbial early bird who's up at the crack of dawn raring to go, but is ready to call it a night by nine P.M.

Now, combine all these factors so you are studying your *hardest* topic when your energy is *highest* and the environment is most *helpful* to studying. Imagine you've decided it will take about two hours to finish your assignments, and you plan to study from seven to nine P.M. You know it's noisy around the house early in the evening because of your younger sisters and brothers; things start to quiet down about eight when they go to bed, and your energy will be flagging by eight-thirty.

Taking those variables into account, it'd be wise to tackle history first when you're fresh but your surroundings are a bit chaotic. Next, you might want to work on that challenging math assignment when you have more peace and quiet and your energy has kicked into gear. It's probably smart to leave English for last when your mind is tired but the topic isn't as tough.

This S.T.U.D.E.E. (Schedule Topics Using Difficulty, Environment, and Energy) method is designed to help us tackle homework *strategically*. If we just dive in and hit the books, chances are we'll hit a blank wall. This approach can help us allocate our energy so we're ConZentrating on the right topics at the right time.

My son Tom learned, the hard way, to use these S.T.U.D.E.E.

ideas. Like many left-brained individuals, he doesn't get poetry. He's a whiz at math, science, and similar subjects; but when it comes time to interpret what authors really mean, his head says "Huh?"

One fateful evening, Tom saved language arts for last. By the time he tackled "The Funeral," his brain was burned out. He sat there, pencil in hand, and stared at the poem for twenty minutes without one thought coming to mind. The more upset he got for not getting the assignment, the more blocked he became. He finally decided to get up early the next day and tackle the assignment when he was rested. The next morning, his mind was more prepared to cooperate and take a stab at what the poet was really saying. Now, Tom plans what he's going to study, when, and how, and it's helped him avoid late-night exercises in frustration.

S.T.U.D.Y. = Time Out

No sinner was ever saved after the first twenty minutes of
the sermon.
—Mark Twain

Twain knew what he was talking about. Unless we're fascinated with what we're doing, our attention gradually deteriorates after approximately twenty minutes because of the law of diminishing returns. After that time period, we cease giving pure attention and become partially preoccupied. Less than 100 percent focus means we're comprehending and retaining less, and it also means we're more likely to make mistakes because we're not as attentive to detail.

Leonardo da Vinci suggested, "Every now and then go away. Have a little relaxation; since to remain constantly at work will cause you to lose power of judgment." To remain constantly at (home)work will cause us to lose our power of ConZentration. I remember the time my son Andrew slammed his math book shut and stood up from his desk saying, "I quit!" I asked why he was giving up and he said simply, "My mind is full!"

The way to maintain attention for a long time, therefore, is not to try to maintain attention for a long time. It is far more effective to apply ourselves, take a mental breather, apply ourselves, take a mental breather . . . than to try to focus nonstop for hours on end. Time-outs are not a cop-out, they're a necessity if we want to avoid mental meltdown. The following points can help us rest and refresh our brain *before* it reaches the breaking point.

Tip 1. Take a five-minute break each hour. Time breaks give us a chance to recharge our mental batteries. Our mind uses this downtime to rest, absorb, and assimilate what was just learned. It will bounce back refreshed and ready to reapply itself. Obviously, don't take a break if you've achieved the optimal learning state of ConZentration. You wouldn't want to arbitrarily disrupt your mental momentum and take a chance of not being able to regain it, so *go with the flow.*

Tip 2. Take a five-minute break when transitioning from one topic to the next. Topic breaks are a way to literally and figuratively close the books on one subject before starting another. If we wrap up one homework assignment and immediately start another, the mind has no opportunity to switch mental gears.

Topic breaks are particularly important when moving from a left-brained subject to a right-brained one. Psychobiologist Roger W. Sperry received the Nobel Prize in 1981 for his innovative studies, first published in 1968, which revealed the dual nature of human thinking. Sperry postulated that verbal, analytic thinking is mainly located in the left hemisphere, and visual, perceptual thinking is mainly located in the right hemisphere. It's important to give the brain a *tangible* transition when changing from linear thinking (i.e., rote memorization of science tables, dates, figures) to creative thinking (i.e., interpreting poetry, creative writing, artwork) so it has time to take a mental breather and change styles.

Tip 3. Congratulate yourself each time you complete an assignment so you associate pleasure and satisfaction with studying. This may sound silly, but educators say giving ourselves mental pats on the back ("Nice job on that essay"; "Good for you for persevering through those complex case studies") can turn drudge work into a gratifying experience we don't dread quite so much. Psychologists say we get a shot of confidence every time we successfully complete something, so don't miss these opportunities to boost your self-esteem.

Tip 4. Facilitate a clean transition by saying "break, break." When truckers communicate via CB radio, they often signal the end of their statement and/or a change in topic by saying "break, break." That's their way of indicating "I'm through with this idea" so their words don't run together and cause confusion. I suggest you get in the habit of saying "break, break" to yourself every time you complete an assignment so what you've read or worked on doesn't run together and get confused. Saying "break, break" can become your ritualistic way of switching from one train of thought to another.

A forty-year-old who had gone back to night school to get his degree snorted after hearing these ideas and said, "I used to think I was disciplined when I kept at it for hours on end. Sometimes I was so tired I could hardly keep my eyes open. I realize now I was learning very little when I was that exhausted. I've learned it's better for me to break my homework up and do half at night and half the next morning before I leave for work. I don't much like getting up earlier in the morning, but I know I retain more of what I study."

Maya Angelou said, "If we step away for a time, we are not, as many may think and some will accuse, being irresponsible, but rather we are preparing ourselves to more ably perform our duties and discharge our obligations." Take Angelou's wise words to heart. You are not being lazy when you take *planned* time-outs, you are increasing the likelihood that you'll learn optimally.

S.T.U.D.Y. = Use Learning Aids

I had the worst study habits in the history of college, until
I found out what I was doing wrong—highlighting with a
black magic marker.
—Jeff Altman

We can study smart, or we can study long and hard. Pascal said, "When we read too fast or too slowly, we understand nothing." These learning aids can help us read, take notes, and learn from lectures so we understand more.

READING

Tip 1. Identify our purpose and parameters. Before beginning, state in one sentence what we're going to read, why, and for how long. "I will read this section on helping employees cope with change so I can learn at least three ways to facilitate a smooth move to our new headquarters. I will spend the next thirty minutes reading these two chapters."

Tip 2. Skim the assignment *before* doing the real reading. Note titles, headings, and subheads and review summaries so we understand what the material is about. If we don't do this, our mind is reading without context. This is equivalent to reading a road map before starting a trip. Our mind is clear about our destination and directions and will be better able to ConZentrate because we're in familiar territory.

Tip 3. Read the most important parts instead of trying to read everything. Samuel Goldwyn said it best: "I read part of it all the way through." Pay special attention to the first and final sentence of every paragraph. They often identify and restate the main idea. By focusing on lead and closing paragraphs and on chapter summaries, we can pull out the most relevant points even if we don't have enough time to read all about it.

Tip 4. Review what we've read to test comprehension. Can we answer the questions at the end of the chapter? Would we be able to explain this material to someone else? Can we close the book and summarize what we've just learned? If not, we need to reread the material until we can. Woody Allen quipped, "I took a speed-reading class and read *War and Peace* in one hour. It's about Russia." Uhhmm, sounds like Woody might want to go back and study this a little more thoroughly next time.

NOTE-TAKING

Tip 1. Be selective. Instead of randomly or religiously recording every think, use the three I's to determine whether information is worth writing down. Is it interesting? Is it important? Will it be included on the test? Nondiscriminately marking every idea that seems the least bit important is counterproductive because our mind can't remember all that. The quality of our notes has little to do with length; the quality depends on whether we captured the core ideas.

Tip 2. Mentally and physically highlight material. The simple act of highlighting doesn't enter information in our brain in a way in which it can be recalled unless we dialogue with it. Instead of making mindless notations, ask, "How does this relate to what I need to learn?"

Tip 3. Record the main ideas exactly only if we need to regurgitate them verbatim later. Some professors are "sticklers" for accuracy and will grade us down unless we get every phrase just right. If that's the case, copy vital data word for word so we can reproduce it perfectly when required. Otherwise, it's to our benefit to summarize what we read and hear in *our own words*. Why? Paraphrasing packages what we've just read and heard in a personally meaningful way so it becomes ours.

Tip 4. Develop and use your own style of shorthand. Abbreviating frequently used words (*w/o* for without, *esp* for especially) saves time and lets you focus on key concepts. Creating your own graphic symbols engages the right brain so you're thinking optimally. For example, you can use an arrow, >, for "leads to"; an exclamation point, !, or star, *, to indicate important points; a question mark, ?, for material you don't understand; and so forth.

Tip 5. Number your points and write legibly. It doesn't do any good to take copious notes if we can't make sense of them afterwards. Discipline yourself to write so clearly someone else could read your notes if necessary. Numbering each idea puts information into bite-sized mental chunks that make them easier to digest. Leave space between ideas so they're visually accessible and so you can elaborate on your notes later.

LECTURES

Tip 1. Mentally prepare. Scan what was covered in the previous session to "re-mind" your mind about the topic. If you walk in cold, it may take a while to mentally warm up to the subject, which might cause you to miss valuable information.

Tip 2. Sit up front. Sitting in the back of the room literally and figuratively distances us from the teacher and makes it difficult to stay focused. If the instructor is dynamic, sitting nearby gives us a chance to get caught up in her enthusiasm. Furthermore, professors direct a majority of their attention to active participants. Learning is a two-way street. If we look interested, speakers look in our direction more frequently, which makes it seem they're talking just to us. Feeling included (instead of ignored) gives us even more incentive to pay close attention.

Tip 3. Listen for buzz words and pet phrases. Teachers often showcase material they think is important. If the instructor ConZentrates on one particular concept, we'd be smart to do the same. It's also worth asking instructors: "Of the information we've covered, what should we focus on?" While instructors usually won't tell you exactly which points will be on the test, they will often give general guidance about which points it would be smart to pay special attention to.

Tip 4. Ask questions. Murphy's Law says the one concept we don't understand is the one that will be asked about on the quiz. Believe it or not, it's not our teachers' responsibility to make sure we learn the material, it's *ours*. If we don't get what the teacher is telling us, we should speak up until we're sure we do.

An Internet list of punny definitions said, "A professor is a person who talks in someone else's sleep." If you're unfortunate enough to get a lecturer who's passionless about his/her topic, provide your own. How can you do that? By following up on the lecture tips above and by acting on Christopher Morley's insight: "No man is lonely while eating spaghetti; it takes too much attention." In other words, we better pay attention when eating spaghetti or we'll end up wearing it.

What does this mean for you? If your teacher isn't very interesting, *force* yourself to focus by sitting up straight, leaning forward, lifting your eyebrows, and taking notes. As discussed earlier (page 234), giving the teacher L can help you stay alert and pay attention even when you would rather not.

S.T.U.D.Y. = Duplicate Test Situation

> The ability to concentrate and use your time well
> is everything.
> —Lee Iacocca

In our section on ConZonetration, we discussed the idea that how well we play depends on how well we practiced. The same concept holds true for taking tests. From now on, instead of just cranking out assignments, always do homework with a mind toward "What form will the test take? How can I input this data into my brain in a way I'll be able to retain and regurgitate it as needed on the big day?"

Tip 1. Prepare in the same style as the test. If this will be an oral essay test, ask someone to ask you open-ended questions so you can practice thinking and speaking on your feet (seat?). If this will be a multiple choice test, have a study buddy quiz you with multiple options, to which you have to pick the best response. If this will be a timed test, clock yourself working the problems at the end of each chapter so you have experience answering questions under pressure.

Tip 2. Wake up early on the big day and test yourself with as many senses as possible. A rule of thumb is, the more senses we use to imprint information, the more likely we are to remember it. If we see ideas in a book, write them in our notes, say them out loud, and hear ourselves repeating them, we are exponentially increasing the odds we'll be able to regurgitate that information when needed.

Scan your text to review what will be covered on the test and then go for a vigorous walk. Practice answering anticipated questions while pumping your arms and legs. You'll be driving oxygen to your brain and enhancing recall in this energized state. Recite dates and data from memory. Look over your notes to find key facts and then say them while looking up and away.

Tip 3. Focus on thoughts that create test assurance, not test anxiety. We can talk ourselves into poise or we can talk ourselves into panic. Repeat to yourself, "I know this material, I know this material. I've studied and I'm sure I'll do well on this test." Instead of freezing up with fear by focusing on our worst fears—"What if I flunk? I'll have to go to summer school"—focus on our hoped-for result so we can walk in with confidence.

Tip 4. Read the instructions first. We don't want to find out in the last few minutes that we were supposed to check *every* correct answer, not just the one best answer. Scanning the test first can help us allocate our T.I.M.E. wisely so we can ConZentrate on and complete the most important parts. We don't want to get to the last page only to discover a complex essay question waiting for us that will take more time than we have left.

Tip 5. Clarify if there are penalties for guessing. To guess or not to guess? That is the question. If three points will be given for every correct answer and one point will be subtracted for every wrong answer, you may want to leave some questions blank unless you're 60 percent or more sure of your response. Our initial hunches are *usually* accurate. If you have time to recheck your work, change your original answers *only* if (a) your first thought was a wild guess and you've remembered the right response; (b) a problem on another part of the test lends new insight as to a better answer; (c) you find a miscalculation in figures; and (d) you reread a question and realize you misinterpreted it the first time around.

Tip 6. Compartmentalize other concerns. If you've got something on your mind that you can't stop thinking about, vow to address it *after* the test is over. Say, "I will ask Roger what he *really* meant when he said he wants more space when I see him at dinner tonight. For the next twenty minutes, I am going to give my full attention to answering these questions." If this worrisome issue has broken your ConZentration and your mind is drawing a blank, collect your thoughts by reviewing the remainder of the test and answering something you know for certain. This can help you regain confidence by getting your mind back to the business at hand.

An English professor at Leeward Community College teaches these tips to her students the first week of class. Lani says, "I have eighteen-year-olds fresh out of high school and adults of all ages taking my courses. What they all have in common is that hardly any of them have ever been taught how to study. It's amazing to me that students can make it all the way to college without ever having been instructed on how to take a test. We cram their minds full of information and never tell them how to get it back out so they can make the grade."

From now on, make sure you're inputting mental data in a way you can get it out when you need it. Author Harvey Mackay says, "Don't equate activity with efficiency." Don't equate studying with learning *unless* you use these tips.

S.T.U.D.Y. = Yearn to Learn

> The illiterate of the year 2000 will not be the individual who cannot read and write, but the one who cannot learn, unlearn, and relearn.
> **—futurist Alvin Toffler**

At the 1998 Maui Writers Conference, I met businesswoman Patricia Wade, who was working on a manuscript called "Yearn to Learn." Her premise is that our personal and professional future depends on our willingness to learn. Unfortunately, many of us agree with Winston Churchill, who confessed, "I am always ready to learn, although I do not always like being taught."

We can do ourselves a favor by reframing any resistance we might have about learning. We may believe studying is hard work and should be avoided at all costs. We may have spent twenty years in school earning a doctorate and have vowed never to go back again. Perhaps we're renowned for our intellect and don't relish the awkwardness that comes from being an amateur.

If any of these are the case for you, or if you subscribe to the can't-teach-old-dogs-new-tricks philosophy, the following **Yearn to Learn Quotes** may inspire you to revise any limiting beliefs. Hopefully, they'll convince you of the value of adopting what the Japanese call *shashin*, beginner's brain, and persuade you to put ego aside so you can approach learning with an open mind.

Quote 1. "Anyone who stops learning is old, whether at twenty or eighty. Anyone who keeps learning stays young."—Henry Ford

Quote 2. "The little I know I owe to my ignorance."—Samuel Butler

Quote 3. "Research shows that adults are better learners than children, if they have the patience to be beginners."—Marilyn Ferguson

Quote 4. "Know-it-alls know everything except how little they know."—Anonymous

Quote 5. "It is not true that we have only one life to live; if we can read, we can live as many kinds of lives as we wish." —S. I. Hayakawa

Abigail Adams said, "Learning is not attained by chance; it must be sought for with ardor and attended to with diligence." From now on, vow not to leave learning to chance. How are you going to S.T.U.D.Y. more diligently so you stay mentally young?

Action Plan 25. S.T.U.D.Y. Do Right

If ignorance is bliss, why aren't more people happy?

—office poster

Ignorance is not bliss. Learning is bliss. What are you going to do to improve your S.T.U.D.Y. habits? Are you going to schedule topics according to your energy level and the conduciveness of the surroundings? Are you going to take time-outs to improve your comprehension and retention? Are you going to duplicate test situations so you know the score? Vow to incorporate these ideas into your daily life so you can become a happy lifelong learner.

Confusion	ConZentration
Dive right into homework	*Determine the best way to do homework*
"I don't know how I'm supposed to study with that racket going on, but I don't have any choice."	"I'm going upstairs and shut the door so I can have some peace and quiet. I'll gather everything I need first."
Start studying what's easiest	*Schedule topics using difficulty, energy, environment*
"I'm going to put off those algebra problems as long as possible. I wish I didn't have to do them at all."	"Well, I'm alert and I've got some privacy, so I better work on algebra while I'm at my best."
Take hours to finish	*Take breaks every hour 'til finished*
"I can hardly see straight, much less think straight, and I haven't even started my English paper."	"Okay, I finished my vocabulary words. I'll take a shower to freshen up and then write my English paper."
Use little assistance	*Use learning aids*
"I'm forgetting this as fast as I'm reading it. I'm going to flunk that test for sure."	"At the end of every page, I'll look away from the book and summarize the key points of what I just read."

Confusion	ConZentration
Do what told to do	*Duplicate test setting*
"Mrs. Aikens said the quiz would be on chapters 7 through 9. I read those, so I'm ready for the test."	"Mrs. Aikens likes us to know definitions, so I'm going to ask Mom to quiz me on the meaning of the words."
Yearn to quit	*Yearn to learn*
"I can't wait to graduate. I'm never going into another classroom for the rest of my life."	"I like improving myself. I don't want ever to stagnate. I want to keep learning and growing."

WAY 26

◉

Memories Are Made of This

I have a photographic memory.
I just haven't developed it yet.

—Henny Youngman

Do you have a hard time remembering thinks? Are you afraid of becoming more forgetful in your old age?

A teacher friend was sharing some Fun Fu! responses her students have given, intentionally and unintentionally, over the years. One of her favorites was the time she asked a second grader why he hadn't turned in his homework assignment. He looked at her innocently and said, "I must have had ambrosia."

The good news is, we can develop a better memory. Memory is a skill that can be learned and a habit that can be honed. No matter our age or intellect, we can remember more if we put our mind to it. If you suffer from "ambrosia" or from "milk of amnesia," the collection of ideas in this chapter can help. These five techniques won't produce total recall, but they can *improve* recall.

Memory Technique 1. Develop Better R.E.C.A.L.L.

To expect a man to retain everything is like expecting him to carry about in his body everything he has ever eaten.
—Arthur Schopenhauer

Schopenhauer's point is well taken. We won't be able to remember everything we want to remember, but these R.E.C.A.L.L. steps can help us remember more.

R = Repetition is the mother of memory. We can't expect our mind to remember things it's heard or seen only once. The more times we imprint data, the more likely we are to remember it. Why? When our mind receives information numerous times, especially when it's recalled again and again over time, it concludes: "This must be important. I'll store it in long-term memory."

E = Emotional context. Simply said, the more emotional impact we attach to an idea, event, or individual, the more our mind *wants* to remember it. Laughing and smiling engages our right *and* left brain so we're fully focused instead of mentally listless. Many older Americans remember exactly where they were when John F. Kennedy was assassinated (I know, I'm dating this myself) because that moment made such a powerful emotional impact on them. You can purposely imprint sensory triggers to recall specific information. Educational specialists recommend you pump yourself up for a test by playing the celebratory title song from the movie *Rocky* while studying. When it's time to take the test, tap back into that joyous mood and the data you imprinted in that excited state will easily come back to you.

C = ConZentrate. For this moment, make whatever you want to remember the most important think in your world. Temporarily put everything else out of your mind so you can give this your full attention. If we're preoccupied, our mind isn't paying sufficient attention to permanently imprint the data. Lady Bird Johnson said, "Become so wrapped up in something that you forget to be afraid." The application of her idea to memory is to become so wrapped up in what you want to remember that you forget everything else but that one think.

A = Acrostics.   You probably noticed a long time ago that I'm partial to acrostics. Why? They are a way to connect and make sense out of what might otherwise be unrelated items. Need to stop by the market and don't want to forget you need mayonnaise, apples, and milk? Just say to yourself, "MAM, MAM, MAM." Imprint those letters and when you walk into the store, you'll remember you need M (mayonnaise), A (apples), and M (milk). Actually, we don't have to use acrostics; *any* structure or system that gives us a way to relate and remember random items helps.

You may have heard the suggestion that you tie a string on your finger or a rubber band on your wrist to remind yourself of something you need to do. My son tried this with mixed results. He wanted to remember to tell his science teacher that he could help out with the reef walk the following week. He dutifully tied the string on his wrist so he'd remember. The next day at school, he saw Ms. Gaston, eagerly ran up to her . . . and forgot what he was supposed to tell her. Oh, well.

This demonstrates why our memory aids need to be meaningful. Arbitrarily arrange an acrostic so it spells something associated with what you want to remember. The acrostics throughout this book are deliberately designed to spell out the steps needed to perform the different ConZentration skills. For example, we can create a fun **H.O.U.S.E.** that's a haven instead of a hassle by **holding** the Phone, establishing **order** with rituals and routines, using **uncommon** Courtesy so we get along with our loved ones, filling our home with pleasing **sounds** that create harmony, and providing a private **escape** so we have somewhere to retreat and recuperate.

L = Link something new to something old. Robert Frost said, "All thought is a feat of association: having what's in front of you bring up something in your mind that you almost didn't know you knew." It makes sense that our mind more readily remembers familiar information. When we associate something new with something we already know, the mind quickly grasps it. From now on, expedite assimilation and retention by linking what we *want* to remember with something we already easily remember. When we encounter something new, ask, "What does this remind me of?" My optometrist practices a clever variation of this idea. At my annual eye exam, she discovered I was wearing my contacts backwards. She easily solved this problem by making the *left* contact *blue* (both words have four letters) and the *right* contact *white* (both words have five letters and they rhyme as well). Now, no matter how exhausted or preoccupied I am, I remember exactly which contact belongs in which eye—thanks to her memory aid.

L = Look for details. The fuzzier our impression, the fuzzier the memory. The more specifically and comprehensively we imprint information, the more likely we'll be able to recall it. This is why it helps to notice the color of a person's eyes when trying to remember his or her name, and why noticing that our red rental car is parked under the Section A sign can help us remember where to find it when we return to the parking lot. Retention is directly proportionate to the intensity of our intention and attention. It makes sense. The more care we take in noticing details, the more hooks we have on which to hang our memory.

Memory Technique 2. You C.A.N. Remember Names

> I can't remember your name, but don't tell me.
> —Alexander Woollcott

Contrary to Woollcott's tongue-in-cheek remark, tell yourself you C.A.N. remember people's names. Be that rare person who cares enough to imprint, remember, and use people's names. You've probably heard the oft-repeated observation that a person's name is the sweetest sound in the world to him or her. A decision to get good at remembering names not only makes a positive first impression, it is a way to let people know they are genuinely important to us, and it's a great way to practice ConZentration and memory skills on a daily basis. Remember, you **C.A.N.** remember names—if you make an effort to do so.

C = Commit. Many people think they're terrible at remembering names. This type of "failure-forecasting" mindset means they walk into a room, take one look around at all the people, and think to themselves, "I'll *never* be able to remember all these names." The mind chirps, "Okay," and is let off the hook. Remembering doesn't just happen. We need to give our mind what's called a determining tendency, a conscious order to commit this person's name to memory. Ask yourself, "How do I feel about people who have mastered this skill?" Impressed? "How do I feel when someone cares enough to remember my name?" Flattered? From now on, set yourself up for success by thinking, "I *will* remember this person's name. He/she is my chosen project. Everything else for now is irrelevant." Increasing your intention will increase your retention.

A = Attention on the face. No glancing over someone's shoulder to see who just entered the room. No nodding to an acquaintance passing by. Look the person in the eye to preclude preoccupation. If we don't look at the person's face, we won't be able to link it with a name. Keeping our eyes on his or hers will cause us to lose sight of our surroundings so it's easier to stay focused. Would you like to know a *tangible* way to ConZentrate on their face? Shake hands. Shaking hands cements name retention because it causes us to physically lean forward, which singles out this individual as the object of our attention. This is especially important in noisy, crowded spaces. A handshake creates a tangible bridge so the two of you feel connected.

N = Numerous repetitions. As soon as the person says his or her name, repeat it out loud. This benefits us in several ways. We want to make sure we've heard the name correctly—for example, it's Phil, not Bill; Katie, not Kathy. Also, by *hearing* the name, *saying* it out loud, and repeating it to ourselves every time we *look* at his or her face, we are using several senses to log that information into our memory bank. Obviously, if we can *write* down the name (perhaps on a business card with a word or two about our conversation to jog our memory of the person), we'll enhance recall even more.

After you meet people, silently say their name whenever you glance back at their face. Throughout a meeting or social function, look around the room at intervals and review the names of the people you've been introduced to. This repeated imprinting and recalling should cause their name to pop into your mind next time you see them, even if it's days or weeks later.

I'll always remember a prominent social figure who said, "Sam, I meet hundreds of people a week. I sometimes go to three or four functions a day. I've realized I'll never be able to remember everyone's name. With this system, I C.A.N. remember more of them!" Keep her wise remark in mind, and you too C.A.N. improve your memory of people's names.

Memory Technique 3. Reduce Data Smog

> In the practical use of our intellect, forgetting is as important as remembering.
> —William James

One woman said, "I've got information overload. Any suggestions on how to weed out what's important and what I can let go?" She's right. Many of us are bombarded with newspapers, computer printouts, e-mails, faxes, letters, manuals, and websites, and the list goes on. We've got mental fog because we've got so much data smog. It's impossible to think we could or should remember all this, so we're not even going to try. From now on, ask yourself these questions to determine what you need to focus on and what you can safely forget:

1. "What will happen if I don't remember this?" If it won't make any difference, mentally move on.
2. "How soon do I need to use this information?" If it's in the near future, it warrants our attention now.
3. "Does anything else depend on me remembering this?" If this item is necessary to help you achieve something crucial, give it your complete attention so you can retain it. If it's not, mentally walk on by.
4. "Can I access this easily if I need to find it?" If so, simply note where it can be located and then turn your attention to other things. Samuel Johnson said, "Knowledge is two kinds: we know a subject ourselves, or we know where we can find information about it." No need to overload our mind with knowledge that can be kept elsewhere.

Memory Technique 4. Jot That Thought

The King says, "The horror of that moment, I shall never, never forget!" "You will, though," the Queen replies, "if you don't make a memorandum of it."
—Lewis Carroll

I learned the importance of making memos to myself while I was on a walk with *National Geographic* photographer Dewitt Jones. There we were, brainstorming while taking a "walk/talk" along Wailea's user-friendly beach path. Dewitt kept stopping every two minutes to scribble something in his small notebook. When I asked what he was doing, Dewitt said, "Sam, if we don't record our epiphanies, we'll forget them." How right he was.

The muse has a mind and schedule of its own . . . and it doesn't keep office hours. If the angel of eloquence decides to rewards us with a pithy phrase, brilliant idea, or perfect insight, we better keep our part of the bargain by taking a few seconds to write it down. If we don't, it's gone, never to be recalled. From now on, **jot the thought while it's hot!**

Also remember to record mental messages ("Be sure to stop by the vet's on the way home and pick up that flea medicine") on our master list so we are free to forget them and can give full focus to our true priority of the moment.

Some techies may think I'm hopelessly outdated and will scoff at my suggestion to carry a notepad with us so we can ink it when we think it. They prefer to carry their Palm Pilot or electronic notepad with them so they can key in their thoughts. My response to that? Whatever works! Comedian Alicia Brandt said, "I have e-mail, a pager, a cell phone, and a fax line. I've got an answering machine, three phone lines at home, one in my purse, and a phone in my car. The only excuse I have if I don't return your call is I just don't like you." As Brandt pointed out, there is such a wide variety of resources available to us, the only excuse we have for forgetting something is if we don't want to remember it in the first place.

I was watching my son's end-of-the-season basketball game and chatting with a fellow mom. Tiffany invited us to dinner the following Friday and I asked for directions. They were rather complicated, and since this was a new home for Tiffany, she couldn't remember several street names. She promised to call later that evening with the specifics. Then, without saying a word, she picked up her cell phone and started dialing. I was taken aback and wondered why and whom she was calling since I was right there. She spoke into the phone: "Tiffany, call Sam with directions for Friday night." She smiled and said, "I called to remind myself not to forget to call you." We both broke up laughing.

Tiffany says she often does this. A quick call home to remind her to bring a special paper to work the next day. A quick call to her job answering machine to say, "Don't forget to ask Ann about the budget hearing." As mentioned, whatever works. It might be worth a trip to your local office supply warehouse this weekend to see what they have in the way of digital Day-Timers that can help you keep track of appointments, agreements, and deadlines. Might as well jot your thoughts and memos to yourself electronically.

266 | SAM HORN

Memory Technique 5. Make Some Rhyme or Reason (or Rap)

Memory is the library of the mind.
—Francis Fauvel-Gourand

Would you like to know how to catalog information so you can check it out from your mental library any time you want? Put info in a rhythmic rap or rhyme. This is how children learn their ABCs and simple nursery rhymes. Remember? "ABCD, EFG, HIJK, LMNOP . . . " and so on. Think of "Jack and Jill went up a hill to fetch a pail of waa-ter. Jack fell down and broke his crown . . . and Jill came tumbling af-ter." Hear how it works? The rhyming and rhythm engage our brain and make thinks easier to recall.

Now try this with a phone number. Instead of trying to remember the seven-digit phone number 455-1138, use a singsong voice to say "four-five-five, eleven thirty-eight." Say it again: "four-five-five, eleven thirty-eight." If you say it a few times, you'll find you'll be able to remember it even after you close this book. Repeating sequences of numbers (driver's license, social security, or frequent flyer) in a snappy rhythm can help you recollect them. You can even help very young children remember their address if you put it in a playful chant for them.

◎

Action Plan 26. Memories Are Made of This

There are three things I always forget: names, faces, and—I can't remember the third.

—coffee mug slogan

Maybe you've seen the poster that says, "We have to arrange in advance for pleasant memories." We have to arrange in advance for *all* memories. As one seminar participant said at the end of our section on memory, "So, you're reminding us not to forget to use the R.E.C.A.L.L. steps?" Exactly.

Confusion	ConZentration
Remember nothing "I'll never be able to remember everyone's name. There's fifty people here."	*Repeat what want to remember* "That was Jill. This is Roman. There's Martha and Stuart. And . . . I've got it . . . Barbara!"
Embarrassed because can't remember "I just met the guy five minutes ago, and I can't remember his name. I'll avoid him."	*Emotional context so can remember* "Ralph looks a little bit like Uncle Ralph. That will help me place him."
Can't recall "No one could remember all these people. That's asking too much."	*ConZentrate on what want to recall* "I will give each person my complete attention to help me remember."
Angry because we forget "I just wasted a trip to the store. Cindy's going to kill me if I come without those items she wanted."	*Acrostics so we don't forget* "Cindy wanted me to get MMAD—mayonnaise, milk, aspirin, and Diet Pepsi. Hey, this system works!"
Lose our way and place "What were the names of those streets again? I have no idea where I am."	*Link so we have a way to place* "Laurie said to turn by the deli. There it is, and now I take a right by the bookstore."
Look for excuses "She said her name so quickly, I didn't hear it. It's not my fault if I can't remember it."	*Look for details* "You said your name is Delilah? How is that spelled? Am I pronouncing it correctly?"

PART 10

Good Thinking

I'm undecided, and that's final.

—coffee mug slogan

WAY 27

◉

Make Up Your Mind

A vibration is a motion that cannot make up its mind
which way it wants to go.

—Internet entry of kids' crazy definitions

t's hard to figure out which way to go when we've got too many
options. Futurist Alvin Toffler calls this overchoice. We might
think it's a good thing to have lots of alternatives, but our mind
often becomes so confused by the plethora of choices, it doesn't
know which to pick. And when it doesn't know what to do, it often
doesn't do anything.

The good news is there are six steps we can take to turn confusion into clarity. These criteria can help us make up our mind even
when we can't think straight.

What's Your Decision?

Give me ambiguity, or give me something else.
—T-shirt saying

"If I had to sum up in one word what makes a good manager,"
concluded Lee Iacocca, "I'd say decisiveness." Well, maybe yes,
maybe no.

Indecisiveness is the death of ConZentration. Think about it.
Confusion is the antithesis of ConZentration (which is why I

juxtaposed these two qualities in the Action Plans at the end of each chapter).

Turn this chapter into your own private problem-solving lab. What is a decision you need to make? Are you thinking of switching jobs? Are you considering buying a home? Are you wondering whether to move to a different city?

You may be thinking, "I'm not facing any big decisions right now. Do these ideas work for everyday decisions, too?" You bet. You may merely be trying to make up your mind whether to get season tickets to your city's pro hockey team or use that money to add a patio to your home. Perhaps you're considering asking someone out for a date. It could be as simple as deciding whether to buy a new outfit.

Napoleon said, "Nothing is more difficult, and therefore more precious, than to be able to decide." Whatever quandary you're facing, momentous or minute, these six steps can make it easier to D.E.C.I.D.E. what is the best course of action so you can use your precious T.I.M.E. to ConZentrate on being productive.

D.E.C.I.D.E. = Define the Problem

A problem well stated is a problem half solved.
—Charles Kettering

Please understand that the word "problem" doesn't have to mean something's wrong. A problem can just be the difference between what we have and what we want. The first step is to succinctly state what needs to be resolved, improved, or acted upon. In his classic tale *Alice in Wonderland*, Lewis Carroll describes Alice coming to a fork in the road and seeing the Cheshire cat in a tree. "Which road do I take?" she asks. His response is a question: "Where do you want to go?" "I don't know," Alice answers. "Then," says the cat, "it doesn't matter."

Ask yourself, "What is the matter? What is *not* the way I want it to be?" Imagine the dilemma you're facing is that your boss has asked you to work overtime to finish a project, and you've promised to watch your grandson's soccer game, which starts at five P.M. The problem is, you want to keep your commitment to your grandchild, but if you don't stay to complete this assignment, your boss could get mad and accuse you of not being committed to your job.

D.E.C.I.D.E. = Explore Options

All our resolves and decisions are made in a mood or frame of mind which is certain to change.
—Marcel Proust

Evaluate the logical and logistical pros and cons of each option. Could you come in early the next day to handle the task your boss wants you to do tonight? Is this just one of many games your grandson will be in this season? Could you see him play next week? Factor in any relevant history of the situation. Have you broken previous promises to see your grandson play and so feel it's important to keep this commitment, no matter what? Do you frequently work overtime, so it's fair and reasonable for you to explain you can't do so this time?

Take into account, as Proust pointed out, the fact that circumstances might change. How will you feel about this decision if, two weeks from now, it's an entirely different scenario? A friend once accepted a job in a large corporation because she was excited about the opportunity to work side by side with the visionary who directed this division. She went against everything she held dear (she hated bureaucracies and liked to work independently) so she could learn from this respected leader. Two weeks after she took the job, he was hired away by another firm. She wouldn't have been so quick to lock herself into a contract with this organization if she'd taken that eventuality into account.

To the degree possible, anticipate potential changes and be sure enough of your decision so you won't regret it if things don't work out as planned.

D.E.C.I.D.E. = Compare Alternatives to Your Values

I had a great idea this morning, but I didn't like it.
—Samuel Goldwyn

I think I know what Goldwyn meant. This idea looked or sounded good initially, but after he thought it through, he knew it wouldn't work and wasn't for him. It's smart to give thinks a second thought so we don't make snap decisions that come back to bite us.

Sigmund Freud recommended we compare our logical, left-brain options against our emotional, right-brain gut feelings to see how they stack up. Freud said, "In vital matters, such as the choice of a mate or a profession, the decision should come from the unconscious, from somewhere within ourselves. In the important decisions of personal life, we should be governed, I think, by the deep inner needs of our nature."

Once you deduce how you *really* feel about the prescribed course of action (you know what "deduce" is, right? Da lowest card in da deck), you may realize it looks good on paper, but it is not congruent with your principles and values.

Back to the grandson's soccer game. Perhaps you know your grandson is going through a fragile time and canceling out would devastate him. You check in with your values and reconfirm your belief that *nothing* is more important than family. It may be worth turning down your boss so you can honor your commitment to (literally and figuratively) be there for your grandson. Roy Disney said, "It is not hard to make decisions when you know what your values are." Let's just say it's easier to make decisions when we reclarify what our values are.

D.E.C.I.D.E. = Invite Feedback

> The best way to have a good idea is to have lots of ideas.
> —Linus Pauling

The best way to reach a good decision is to have lots of input. Oliver Wendell Holmes said, "Many ideas grow better when they are transplanted into another mind than the one where they sprang up."

Two heads are better than none. Sometimes the best way to get clarity when our mind is muddled is to ask outsiders for their perspective. As Holmes said, other people often see thinks with fresh perspective, bringing new experience to the table. We can make a more well-rounded decision by looking at the situation from all angles.

Of course, this can be carried too far. Motion picture director Billy Wilder said, "Trust your instincts. Your mistakes might as well be your own instead of someone else's." I'm not suggesting we abdicate our authority to others; I *am* suggesting we ask for advice and consider it carefully. Henny Youngman once said, tongue firmly planted in cheek, "The closest some people come to a brainstorm is a light drizzle." If your idea well is dry, fill it by asking others to contribute innovative options. They may come up with a solution that wouldn't have occurred to you.

Be sure to follow the dos and don'ts of brainstorming to maximize its value. Cartoon figure Dilbert says, "The first rule of brainstorming is to openly mock the opinions of others." As my teenaged son would say, "Not!" The first rule of brainstorming isn't to knock other people's opinions, it's to piggyback off them. Encourage your friends to think outside the box. In the initial idea-generating phase, make sure no one judges, censors, or negates suggestions. After everyone has finished contributing, then it's okay to come back and evaluate which options are feasible and which aren't.

"Great discoveries and improvements invariably involve the cooperation of many minds," noted Dr. Jonas Salk. Brainstorming is a way to ConZentrate many minds on your dilemma. The resulting decision will be an improvement on one reached alone.

D.E.C.I.**D**.E. = Distance Yourself

> One sees great things from the valley, only small things from the peak.
> —G. K. Chesterton

The first time I read that quote, it puzzled me. What did it mean? Then I thought, "Ah, when we're in the middle of things, the obstacles seem huge. We lose perspective. Only when we distance ourselves from the situation can we see it more clearly, can we literally and figuratively put in perspective."

Give yourself time to reflect. Avoid being caught off guard and agreeing to something on the spur of the moment. Ask for the time before giving a yes or no so you can think this through. If possible, go for a walk to air this out. The cross-patterning of walking right, left, right, left, accesses and synchronizes both sides of your brain and stimulates creative thinking so you're more apt to arrive at a workable solution. George Trevelyan said, "I have two doctors, my left leg and my right. When body and mind are out of gear I know that I shall have only to call in my doctors and I shall be well again."

D.E.C.I.D.E. = Elect the Boldest Option

People "died" all the time when they made the wrong kinds of decisions—you could see it in their eyes; the fire had gone out. When you made a decision against life . . . the door clicked and you were safe inside—safe and dead.
—Anne Morrow Lindbergh

If there's really no way to predict which is the best option or if there are too many uncontrollable variables, take British general W. J. Slim's advice: "When you cannot make up your mind which of two evenly balanced courses of action you should take—choose the bolder."

But whatever you do, **act.** Opportunities can disappear if we take too much time deliberating. If our final decision is congruent with our values, we may get flak for it or there may be fallout for not toeing the party line, but we can accept that because we know, in our gut, we made the best possible choice.

Baseball manager Casey Stengel was contemplating retirement at one stage and reporters kept pestering him with questions about it, hoping for a scoop. Finally he announced he'd made up his mind. The reporters eagerly asked, "Which way?" He trumped them with his answer: "Both ways!"

Most of the time, we don't have the luxury of making our mind up both ways. If you're wallowing in ambiguity, get out paper and pencil, divide the sheet into three columns—pros, cons, and values—and write down the advantages and disadvantages of every available option. If you have time, contact a couple of valued friends to get their input as to which they feel would be a wise choice. Give yourself a goal line for making your decision, and then act. As Andrew Jackson advised, "Take time to deliberate; but when the time for action arrives, stop thinking and go in." If you've deliberated, it's time to make your decision and go in.

Action Plan 27. Make Up Your Mind

Indecision is the key to flexibility.

—T-shirt saying

Baseball player Bobby Mercer described the classic "paralysis by analysis" syndrome: "You decide you'll wait for your pitch. Then as the ball starts toward the plate, you think about your stance. And then you think about your swing. And then you realize the ball went past you for a strike that was your pitch." Don't overthink the decision-making process and miss the pitch of a lifetime. Use these **D.E.C.I.D.E.** steps to make up your mind so you don't waste valuable T.I.M.E. wallowing in "What should I do?" Batter's up.

Confusion	ConZentration
Can't decide	*Can D.E.C.I.D.E.*
"Joe's asked me to marry him, and I'm not sure what to say."	"I told Joe I wanted to have some time to think this over."
Don't know what to do	*Define the problem*
"What am I going to tell him? It'll break his heart if I turn him down."	"I've got to figure out if this is who I want to spend the rest of my life with."
Only one answer	*Explore options*
"He wants a yes or no by Monday."	"I wonder if it would be smart to take more time to get to know each other."

Confusion

Go with what looks good on paper
"Well, we have a lot in common and he's a very nice man, but . . . "

In this alone
"I'm torn. I like him, but I don't know if I love him."

Too close to the situation to have perspective
"It's the end of the weekend and I still am not clear what my answer is."

Elect option that's most logical
"Well, he's not everything I wanted, but he's a good person. I'm going to accept his proposal."

ConZentration

Compare alternatives to values
"Do I love him? Is he my soulmate, the one meant for me?"

Invite feedback so in it together
"I'm going to visit Mom this weekend and get her opinion."

Distance ourselves so we can get perspective
"I'm going up into the mountains for a hike. That'll help me gain perspective."

Elect option we can live with
"I'm just not ready. I'll let Joe know I'd love to keep spending time with him, but I don't want to get married right now."

WAY 28

◉

Mental F.I.T.N.E.S.S.

A sound mind in a sound body is a short but full description
of a happy state in this world.

—John Locke

Do you agree with Locke's belief about the relationship between
a sound body and mind, or do you agree with Thomas Edison,
who said, "The chief function of the body is to carry the brain
around"?

Cardiologist Paul Dudley White has conducted revealing research
into the mind-body connection. He said, "Mental and spiritual fitness, both dependent on a good brain, are greatly enhanced by optimal physical fitness. Body, mind, and soul are inextricably woven
together, and whatever helps or hurts any one of these three sides of
the whole [wo]man helps or hurts the other two."

This chapter suggests steps we can take to optimize physical and
mental F.I.T.N.E.S.S. so we can think smart.

F.I.T.N.E.S.S. = Food for Thought

I come from a family where gravy is considered a beverage.
—Erma Bombeck

There are foods that help us ConZentrate, and foods that make it
almost impossible for us to ConZentrate. Erma Bombeck (bless her

soul) must have been related to comedian Bob Zany, who said, "I had a cholesterol test: They found bacon." Uh-oh. It doesn't take a rocket scientist to know that gravy and bacon weigh heavy on the stomach *and* on the mind. If you come from a family who thinks a balanced meal is a french fry in each hand and fresh food means you just opened the can, it's time to feed your body and brain nutrients that *clear* thinks up instead of clog thinks up.

Have you seen the T-shirt that says, "Eat nutritiously. Exercise daily. Die anyway"? It's true we'll die eventually, but eating balanced, nutritious meals will help us think and perform better until the day we say adieu. Of course, it's not just the *quality* of food we eat, it's the *quantity*.

I've found a wonderful way to ConZentrate every time we eat so it becomes a mindful rather than mindless activity. It's called **"Savor, don't shovel."** Paying attention to what we eat and *how* we eat not only helps us appreciate this often-overlooked blessing; it is a way to focus fully on our priority of the moment. Such a deal. Here's how it works.

Step 1. Invest in a unique eating utensil I call a spork (half spoon, half fork). I searched antique shops for an interesting spoon and then arranged for a jeweler to shape it so it has tines to pick up food (i.e., salad and fish) *and* a bowl so you can scoop up food (i.e., soup and cereal).

Step 2. Carry this spork with you wherever you go and use it at every meal. I keep it in my purse and use it whether I'm eating at home, at restaurants, or on a plane. The spork becomes a tangible, visible reminder to eat one bite at a time. Instead of falling into a feeding frenzy and mindlessly stuffing our face, we s-l-o-w down and focus on eating each morsel mindfully. Instead of shoveling food in as fast as we can, we put the spork down after each bite so we experience the act of eating fully.

Step 3. Repeat the mantra "savor" or "taste" as you roll each bit of food around your mouth and enjoy its incredibly tart, sweet flavors and smooth, crunchy textures. Forget what you've been told all those years—it's not just okay to play with your food, it's the way to go. Chew each morsel thoroughly. Engage your mind and *think* about the delightful pleasure and sustenance of each and every bite.

Psychologists say we shovel food in because we're bored, angry, and/or starved for love. We're trying to stuff our feelings and fill our void with something, anything. They say we self-medicate, as it's called today, because it's an immediate, tangible way to make ourselves feel better. *Savoring* food is also an immediate, tangible way to make ourselves feel better. Filling our mind with appreciation for what we're eating helps us feel full and satisfied. The experience fills the emptiness, so we no longer feel a mindless compulsion to consume.

A student asked rather incredulously, "You actually pull your spork out of your purse and use it at restaurants? Don't people think you're weird?" I told her my mom once relieved my fears about how others felt by sharing this piece of timeless advice with me: "We wouldn't worry what other people thought of us if we realized how infrequently they did." I told her, "A lot of people are curious. They want to know what it is and why I'm using it. Once I explain, they usually want to know where they can get one of their own."

F.I.T.N.E.S.S. = Intellectual Activity

> If I had to live my life again, I would make a rule to read some poetry and listen to some music at least once a week; for perhaps the parts of my brain now atrophied would thus have been kept active through use.
> —Charles Darwin

It's said, "Age doesn't make you boring, boring makes you boring." In other words, age doesn't make us lose our mind; not using our mind is what makes us lose our mind.

This isn't just my opinion. In her excellent book *Roads Home: Seven Pathways to Midlife Wisdom*, fellow speaker/author Dr. Kathryn D. Cramer explains there are basically two types of intelligence: crystallized intelligence (our mental software, which determines how well we reason and solve practical problems) and fluid intelligence (our mental hardware—the mechanics of how our mind works, including such things as memory capacity).

The good news is *both* types of intelligence can be improved by engaging in mental challenges that cause our brain to tackle complex problems, deal with ambiguity, and recall bits of information. Dr. Cramer said, "Most people expect intellectual performance to be on a steady incline until the stage of middle adulthood; they presume some degree of decline after that. The fact is, those of us over forty can actually expand our intellect as we age, because it depends more on how the mind is used than anything else."

In other words, the adage "You're as old as you think" is true. Anthropologist Ashley Montagu was once asked, "What advice do you have for elderly people who are faced with the challenges of aging?" With a twinkle in his eye, the seventy-year-old Montagu said, "You must die young, as late as possible." How do we do this? We stay mentally fit by engaging in intellectually demanding activities such as learning a new language or building something with complicated directions.

A retired stockbroker signed up for my class because he was desperate to discover how he could reverse his quickly disappearing ability to concentrate. "I spent half an hour looking for my glasses last week and finally found them on top of my head. I used to pride myself on being mentally sharp. Now I forget what people tell me and can't seem to stay focused on anything for more than ten minutes at a time."

I asked Bill what mentally challenging tasks he had in his life. After thinking about it for a moment, he admitted with a trace of embarrassment, "Not many." I suggested he engage in at least one mentally demanding task each day. It could be reading literature or completing a crossword puzzle. Anything that taxed his brain would retrain it to think smart.

Bill subsequently discovered a chess game room on the Net. He told me, "I just go to Netscape's home page, log on to Games, click Chess, enter my screen name and password, and I'm on. I play several times a week against some very good players. It took only a couple of weeks to get my brain back. At first, I didn't see the board the way I used to. Just yesterday I checkmated a guy who beat me in twenty moves the first time I played him. Best of all, it's fun and I can play whenever I want without having to leave my living room."

Chess champion Bobby Fischer agrees. "Chess appears to be as cerebral and sedentary as a human pursuit can get," Fischer said in a *Life* magazine interview. "But when grandmasters battle, it's physical. Intelligent performance requires energy. And with every year that goes by, I have greater appreciation of the importance of exercise to my performance."

What can you do to improve your physical and mental stamina? Senator Theodore F. Green said, "Most people say that as you get old, you have to give up things. I think you get old *because* you give up things." Vow today to take up things that make you think. Do the following mental calisthenics while you're sitting in traffic to keep your intellect active. Choose one letter of the alphabet (for example, S) and name twenty words that begin with that letter as quickly as you can, numbering them as you go ("one, sun; two, sonar; three, supermarket; four, submarine . . . ").

Erik Erikson, one of the most influential developmental psychologists of our time, proposed that we pass through seven developmental stages through our lives. Stage 7 is our older years, when we either stagnate or become what he calls generative. Generativity is the deep instinct to care, find tangible ways to give back, and improve the quality of life for yourself and others.

Peter De Vries said, "Every novel needs a beginning, a muddle, and an end." If you're feeling mentally muddled, understand you can turn around a midlife malaise by engaging in mentally challenging tasks and by using your brain in ways that make a positive difference for others. A sixty-five-year-young woman named Gladys told me she planned to accomplish both of these by reading out loud to patients in her local hospital. "I've volunteered there two days a week for the last several years. Some of the long-term patients lie in bed for hours every day with nothing to do, and no one comes to visit them. Hopefully, they'll enjoy being read to, and it will help me stay in good mental shape."

F.I.T.N.E.S.S. = Talk Nice

I take care of me. I am the only one I've got.
—Groucho Marx

Our fitness depends on how we *treat* our body and how we *talk* to our body. In her insightful book *Your Body Believes Every Word You Say*, Barbara Hoberman Levine makes a compelling case that what we say (knowingly or not) has a direct impact on our mental and physical health. When we innocently say, "My back's killing me," "I can't stomach that guy," "She broke my heart," or "Everyone's picking on me," our body may manufacture the very malady we're unintentionally introducing to our consciousness. We end up with an aching back, ulcers, heart problems, or skin disease and wonder why.

That's why it's so important to monitor our language and make our self-talk constructive rather than destructive. Examine what's wrong with your life, brain, and body and then reword how you talk about it so your body doesn't innocently reflect what you're unintentionally ordering it to do. Even though we may use phrases without being aware of their origin and impact, they still have the power to manifest conditions that are unconsciously troubling us.

If we tell ourselves we can't stand the way our boss treats us, and we're flat on our back and can't get out of bed, we may need to understand it's time to stand up for ourselves and ask for fair treatment instead of suffering in silence. Instead of calling your neighbor a pain in the neck because he borrows tools and doesn't return them, and then waking up the next day with a crick in *your* neck, tell your neighbor he can borrow that shovel he requested just as soon as he returns all the other tools he's borrowed. Look for unintentionally negative meanings in what you say—"I don't have a leg to stand on," "I'd give my right arm to have that decision back"— and take steps to rephrase those messages so your body isn't compelled to act out unintended messages.

F.I.T.N.E.S.S. = No, to Mind-Altering Drugs

> If you drink, don't drive, don't even putt.
> **—Dean Martin**

If you drink, don't expect to think. Maybe you've seen the T-shirt that says, "I'm not so think as you drunk I am." Anyone who's had a few knows the ability to think clearly goes out the window as soon as we imbibe one or two. It almost goes without saying (almost!)

that if we want to think optimally, we need to lay off the booze and any other substance that will dull our senses. Anyone who needs to perform responsibly (for example, surgeons, commercial pilots) are required by law not to have any alcohol or mind-altering drugs within a certain number of hours of being on duty, so they don't impair their mental process.

If you are taking over-the-counter medication or prescription drugs and have been experiencing difficulty ConZentrating, read the label. Inattentiveness, irritability, drowsiness, and dizziness are side effects of many types of medication. It's worth asking your doctor if there are any substitutes you can try that will not cause you to jump out of your skin or doze off on the job.

F.I.T.N.E.S.S. = Exercise

> The only exercise program that has ever worked for me is occasionally getting up in the morning and jogging my memory to remind myself exactly how much I hate to exercise.
> —Dennis Miller

Do you, as comedian Paul Cisura confessed, "go to a sports bar when you feel athletic"? Whether we like it or not, our level of physical activity directly impacts our mental acumen. In 1980, the U.S. Bureau of Statistics reported over 70,000 (!) studies confirming a direct positive relationship between physical exercise and mental performance.

Ralph Waldo Emerson said, "Activity is contagious." So is exercise. The more active we are, the more active we want to be. The less active we are, the more lethargic we become. Anyone who has embarked upon a fitness program invariably says, "I feel so much better." An increase of energy is the first benefit; weight loss and improved muscle tone follow.

Most of us know the advantages of exercise, yet millions of us still don't find time to do it. For some people, it's not that they don't have time to exercise, they have an aversion to physical exertion. Perhaps they share Joan Rivers's opinion: "I don't exercise. If God wanted me to bend over, he would have put diamonds on the floor." You may agree with Ellen DeGeneres, who claims she prefers "buns of cinnamon rather than buns of steel." So the question is, what is something you could and would do that gives you the benefits of exercise without the hassle?

In one word, walking. Walking is the no-excuse exercise. It doesn't cost anything and can be done almost anywhere, anytime, and by anyone. In my research, I've come across literally hundreds of quotes and anecdotes praising the joys of walking and linking it to improved thinking. Friedrich Nietzsche went so far as to say, "A sedentary life is the real sin. Only those thoughts that come by walking have any value." George F. Will said, "Walking is the most civilized and civilizing exercise because it is the one most conducive to thinking." And Søren Kierkegaard said, "I have walked myself into my best thoughts, and I know of no thought so burdensome that one cannot walk away from it."

Wow. It's encouraging to know there's something that's within our control to do that will make us feel grateful to be alive and healthy. The good news is, there's probably someone out there who wants to walk as much as we do, and they're waiting for someone to give them the incentive to get out there and hit the sidewalk, path, trail, or track. Call up a neighbor, ask a friend, or persuade a family member to start walking at a *set* time three to five days a week. Walking at a set time is key. Remember earlier we talked about the necessity of making healthy behavior a nonthinking ritual? Vow to walk even if you are tired, have a lot on your mind, or have had a bad day. Just go.

"Never have I thought so much," claimed Jean-Jacques Rosseau, "never have I realized my own existence so much, never have I been so much alive than when walking." You will never, not once, regret getting outside, pumping your arms, clearing your head, and getting back in touch with the sheer miracle of being gloriously active and alive.

F.I.T.N.E.S.S. = Sleep

Give us to go blithely on our business this day, bring us to our resting beds weary and content and undishonored, and grant us in the end the gift of sleep.
—Robert Louis Stevenson

What if we're not gifted with sleep at the end of the day? What if we're not blessed with what Euripides called "the divine oblivion of my sufferings"? What if we go to bed restless and upset? Sleep researchers say most of us fall to sleep within five to fourteen minutes. On the other hand, insomniacs may sleep for only five to fourteen minutes at a time. Some can't fall to sleep (initial insomnia), others wake up frequently in agitation (intermittent insomnia), and others wake up prematurely, unrefreshed, weary, and unable to fall back to sleep.

The National Sleep Foundation in Washington, D.C., says we need seven to eight hours of sleep a night to function optimally, but reports that many of us are operating on much less than that. After a while, we pay a price: dull perception, diminished attentiveness, memory lapses, poorer task performance, impaired judgment, and increased hostility. An April 4, 1999, *San Francisco Examiner* article said the upshot of this mass sleep deprivation is that many Americans are "yawning their way through life." The article suggested we follow the example of Amazon.com's chief executive, Jeff Bezos. Bezos makes time in his demanding schedule for eight hours of sleep each night because, he says, "I'm more alert, I think more clearly, and I just feel so much better all day long."

Are you thinking, "I don't have any trouble going to sleep, I have trouble going to bed"? Perhaps you'd love to get more z's but have so much to do, it's midnight before you can slip into bed and into dreamland. Or you may have a new baby at home that hasn't yet learned how to sleep through the night. The following **Go to Sleep** tips can help you get a good night's sleep so your mind gets the rest *it* needs so you can function the next day the way *you* need.

Tip 1. Go to bed earlier. A single parent said, "I got into the habit of watching the late show when I went to bed because it was the only time of day I had to myself. I finish up some chores after I put the kids down, and if I just went straight to bed after that, it seemed my days were full of nothing but one responsibility after another. That hour of leisure was the only time I indulged and did something just for me. This was taking a toll, though, because I was getting more and more tired. Your workshop made me realize I needed sleep more than I needed an hour of TV." Have you fallen into a similar routine? Why not experiment with an earlier bedtime this week? Rediscover the joy of waking up refreshed and raring to go instead of dog tired.

Tip 2. Go to bed and get out of bed at the same time every day. Inconsistent sleep patterns confuse the mind. The mind doesn't know when or if it's going to get some rest, and how long a rest it will get. This causes anxiety, which is the opposite of the serene state of mind that is central to sleep. As explained before in this book, establishing a set time for desired behaviors and ritualistically repeating that pattern puts the mind on automatic pilot. Our brain knows what's going to happen and when, so it relaxes.

Tip 3. Listen to soothing music. We've discussed the ability of music to establish mood. If we want to lull ourselves to sleep, play lullabies. The *Goldberg Variations* by J. S. Bach were actually composed to soothe the mind of a patron who was an insomniac. The radio, with its chatter and frequent commercials, will probably keep you awake. It's better to opt for tapes or CDs of nature sounds, piano sonatas, and love songs that are pleasing to the ear and mind.

Tip 4. Drink chamomile tea or warm milk. Having a cup of either of these natural sedatives can soothe the spirit and become a Pavlovian trigger. Milk has tryptophan, an essential amino acid for a metabolic process that helps produce serotonin, the so-called sleep juice. A warm bath can also relax muscular tension and quiet a racing mind. Sleeping pills are not an answer. Doctors agree they often cause more problems than they solve.

Tip 5. Don't try to go to sleep. Sleep is a quiescent state, and the act of trying to sleep is an excited state. Furthermore, the more we tell ourselves "I've got to get a good night's sleep," the more pressure we place on ourselves and the more tense we feel; our fear becomes a self-fulfilling prophecy. We'll end up staring at the ceiling watching the minutes (hours?) tick by while we exhort ourselves to get to sleep.

Tip 6. Meditate. Shakespeare called sleep the "balm of hurt minds." You can balm yourself to sleep by practicing the Five-Minute F.O.C.U.S. exercise or one of the meditations covered in Way 22. You can actually learn to put yourself to sleep by duplicating the normal sleep breathing pattern of four counts in and four counts out. I can personally vouch for the four-count breathing pattern. I've used it dozens of times on media tours to fall asleep in minutes almost anywhere (yes, even in the middle seat on an airplane). Transcendental meditation has successfully allowed thousands of people to slow their metabolism sufficiently to get a good night's rest. Plant and presume the desired behavior by silently repeating this affirmation to yourself: "I go to sleep easily any time I want. I am safe and secure. I wake up relaxed and refreshed." Any of these exercises can quietly occupy the mind and turn panic into peacefulness.

Tip 7. Use the Scarlett O'Hara philosophy. If you have serious concerns that are keeping you up, vow to think about them tomorrow. Mary Crowley said, "Every evening I turn worries over to God. He's going to be up all night anyway." Assign your worries to a specified time the next day or you'll be the one up all night.

F.I.T.N.E.S.S. = Support

You've got to find the force inside you.
—Joseph Campbell

What if there is no force inside you right now? Maybe you don't have enough energy, willpower, or discipline to fuel your genuine desire to do the right think. Seek a support group of like-minded individuals. If you can get yourself to that first meeting, you'll be able to borrow and benefit from the collective energy you'll find there.

Lily Tomlin said, "Remember, we're all in this . . . alone." The good news is, we don't have to be. Seek out someone to share and support your commitment to eat and exercise properly. If you have problems with substance abuse, a twelve-step program or a professional counselor can guide you in your resolve to turn around bad habits.

In an ideal world, we could pull this off by ourselves. We'd sit ourselves down, give ourselves a good talking-to, and lead a healthier life through sheer willpower, logic, and discipline. In real life, our good intentions may fall by the wayside if we don't have someone to shore us up when we're feeling down. That's why I suggest you team up with a buddy to hold yourself accountable. Chances are there's somebody who wants to better himself just as much as you do, and they'd love to have someone initiate a mutually beneficial relationship that helps both of you get going. Collaborating with someone on your mental F.I.T.N.E.S.S. program will not only help you fulfill your good intentions, it will make it more fun. So, who ya gonna call?

Action Plan 28. Mental F.I.T.N.E.S.S.

A man too busy to take care of his health is like a mechanic too busy to take care of his tools.

—Spanish proverb

Vow today to start taking care of your physical and mental health. Have some protein at lunch instead of that pasta and see if it doesn't help you stay alert during the afternoon. Catch and correct yourself if you inadvertently say something that could send the wrong message to your brain and body. If you've gotten in a habit of having a cocktail with dinner, pass on it tonight. Instead, go for a walk/talk around the block with your partner. Enjoy the night air and each other's company. And then turn off the TV and go to bed early. Get a good night's sleep and see how much better you feel in the morning. By taking better care of your body, you'll be taking better care of your brain, and you will reap a renewed and much-welcomed mental alertness.

Confusion	ConZentration
Mental flabbiness "I'm afraid I'm getting senile. I'm forgetting everything these days."	*Mental F.I.T.N.E.S.S.* "I'm going to sign up for that bridge tournament."
Fool for food "Let's go to the buffet at the hotel. All we can eat for eight ninety-nine."	*Food for thought* "Let's stop by the market and pick up some fresh strawberries."
Intellectually apathetic "All I feel like doing is watching TV."	*Intellectually active* "Let's ask some friends to join us for a book club."
Talk any way we want "You about gave me a stroke. Don't ever surprise me like that again."	*Talk nice to and about body* "Please let me know if you come in my room and I don't see you."
No limits on drugs and booze "Hey, it's pitcher night. Sure, let's go ahead and order one."	*No to drugs and booze* "No thanks on the pitcher. My limit is one beer."
Exercise? Got to be kidding "I'm too tired to go for a walk. I just want to take it easy."	*Exercise? Got to be walking* "Sure, let's take Hot Dog to the park and let him run."
Uptight about sleep "I've got to talk with Mark about coming in late tomorrow. I'm dreading this. Oh, no. It's midnight."	*Sleep right* "I'll get up at six and make some notes about my meeting with Mark. For now, breathe in calm and . . . "
In this alone "I really intended to work out with those weights, but I just can't motivate myself."	*Support* "I'm going to ask Matt and Brian if they want to come over twice a week and work out with me."

PART 11

It's All in Your Head

I've been on an emotional roller coaster lately. The other day my mood ring exploded.

—comedian Janine DiTullio

WAY 29

◎

Worried? R.E.S.T. Assured

Worry is a form of fear and all forms of fear produce fatigue.

—Bertrand Russell

Worry (which comes from a Greek word that means "to divide the mind") is also a form of ConZentration, a harmful form because it drains and divides our mental energy. In simple terms, worrying is projecting a pessimistic future. Unfortunately, playing horror movies in our head creates a type of triple jeopardy. **Worrying:**

1. **Produces the fight-or-flight response.** Nothing has actually happened, but our body acts as if it had. Projecting a scary "What if . . . ?" about the future produces physical and psychological stress in the present. Our muscles tense, our heart races, and our system is flooded with adrenaline so we can escape or defend ourselves from this (imaginary!) foe.

2. **Makes a mental hell of the moment.** Imagining a negative outcome creates a negative now. The dreaded results aren't (yet) real, but the damage caused by worrying about them certainly is because we're experiencing this feared situation as if it were actually happening. As Seneca said, "Our fears are more numerous than our dangers, and we suffer more in our imagination than in reality."

3. **Sets up a self-fulfilling prophecy.** Picturing worst-case scenarios actually increases the likelihood of a noxious outcome because that's what we're ConZentrating on. Failure-forecasting produces the very think we've feared.

In my research, I have discovered dozens of quotes about the consequences of worrying and giving in to our fears. Seneca said, "What madness is it in expecting evil before it arrives?" Krishnamurti reminded us that when "our eyes are blinded with our worries, we cannot see the beauty of the sunset." Michel de Montaigne noted, "He who fears he shall suffer already suffers what he fears." Erma Bombeck once quipped she listed worrying as her occupation on her driver's license.

Why do we do this to ourselves when we know worrying jeopardizes our mental and physical health and all but eliminates the possibility of a positive performance? More important, how do we stop doing this to ourselves? How can we, as Ram Dass suggests, "turn our melodrama into a mellow drama"?

We can reverse this self-punishing process by reminding ourselves that *we* create our dramas. We can scare ourselves silly by playing mental movies of terrifying coming attractions or we can play previews of shows we'd really like to see. Which is a better use of our T.I.M.E.? From now on, fear not. Use the following ideas to R.E.S.T. assured.

R.E.S.T. = Resolve to Do, Not Stew

I've been absolutely terrified every moment of my life and I've never let it keep me from doing a single thing I wanted to do.
—**Georgia O'Keeffe**

Georgia O'Keeffe understood that fear doesn't have to preclude acting. Dr. Karl Menninger said, "Fears are educated into us, and can, if we wish, be educated out." I agree that fears are educated into us. The good news is, they can, if we *act*, be cast out. We can teach ourselves to take action when we're afraid instead of passively awaiting whatever dreaded fate might befall us. We can choose to expect the best and do our best to bring that about, instead of sitting idly by drowning in our doubts and fears.

I enjoy interviewing people about ConZentration, asking them to think of a time they concentrated well and to share what tips they've learned over the years to help themselves focus. While talking with some fellow soccer moms about this issue of worrying, I asked what they do to make sure worry doesn't rule and ruin their lives.

One woman said, "Last year only two girls showed up at Jennie's eighth birthday party. My daughter was devastated. She had sent out ten invitations, so we had eleven places set at the table, eleven party favors, eleven balloons. I found out afterwards two of her classmates had birthday parties that day, and several were in a dance recital that night, which is why most of her friends couldn't make it. We didn't know that at the time, though, and Jennie was heartbroken.

"This year, when I asked Jennie what she wanted to do for her party, she said she didn't want to have one because she was afraid no one would show up. I explained we could prevent that from happening by planning things a little better this year. First, we called around and made sure there weren't any conflicting events on her birthday weekend. Then we sent out invitations several weeks in advance so her friends could save the date, and finally we put an RSVP on the invitation and called parents to ask if their child was coming to the party. This year, everyone we invited was there, and Jennie had a super time."

This is a great example of how this woman educated her daughter to *act* on her fears instead of *allowing* what she feared to happen. What are you worried about? You can sit and *stew* about that situation, or you can choose to *do* something about that situation. What's it going to be? As W. Clement Stone said, "When thinking won't cure fear, action will."

R.E.S.T. = Erase Anxieties

Tain't worthwhile to wear a day all out before it comes.
—Sarah Orne Jewett

Forget the day. Worry wears us all out *before* the day comes. Imagine you're going to interview for a new job. As the big day approaches, you find yourself thinking, "What if they ask me something I don't know? What if they ask why I quit my previous job? What if they insist on talking to my previous boss?" Focusing on your fears will cause you to be a nervous wreck by the time you walk in for your appointment—which will not improve your chances of landing that position.

Furthermore, once we start focusing on fears, our worry often escalates and becomes exaggerated. Our mind runs away with us and blows things further out of proportion. "If I don't get this job, I won't be able to pay the mortgage this month. If I'm not hired, I won't be able to pay my bills and they'll cut off the electricity and the water. We may have to sell the house, and then we'll be out on the streets!"

A friend has a pillow that has "Worry is like a rocking chair. It gives us something to do, but it doesn't get us anywhere" embroidered on it. Instead of mentally pacing back and forth and letting anxieties get the best of you, take tangible steps to erase your anxieties by preparing for and preventing what you're afraid of.

Call the company and ask for an annual report so you can research the organization's history and recent accomplishments. Prepare substantive, extemporaneous answers so you won't be tongue-tied when the moment comes. Rehearse a succinct, interesting response to the often-asked question "So, tell me about yourself." Organize your thoughts so you can give three reasons you're the best person for the job. Be ready to explain why this business should hire you when they have fifty applicants interested in the position. Instead of spending precious preparation T.I.M.E. worrying about being caught off guard, spend it doing mental homework so you won't be.

R.E.S.T. = Self-Create Calm

I've suffered a great many catastrophes.
Most of them never happened.
—Mark Twain

Been there, done that, huh? It's time to turn our self-created catastrophes into self-created calm. I learned this one the hard way. Not too long ago, my dentist whispered those two dreaded words in my ear: "root canal." Yikes! I had two weeks until my feared visit to the endodontist—two weeks to wait, two weeks to worry. My mind kept conjuring up nightmarish images of needles, pain, and extractions. I experienced the trauma of a hundred root canals and hadn't even set foot in the doctor's office.

The actual day came, and thanks to a sensitive and skilled endodontist, I was in and out of the chair in under an hour, with minimal discomfort. Too late I remembered Mark Twain's wise words. Oops. I had multiplied my misery by imagining worst-case scenarios, none of which materialized. As Ralph Waldo Emerson said, "What torments of grief you endured, from evils that never arrived."

We have a choice of how we spend our thought time preceding an event. We can spend it worrying and working ourselves into a state of apprehension, or we can spend it imagining the event turning out well, which reaps a calm anticipation of good.

My sister and business partner Cheri Grimm was diagnosed with breast cancer several years ago; her physician recommended surgery. It would have been easy to spend the days leading up to the operation dwelling on how scared she was. Instead Cheri chose to fill herself with the faith that she would come out of the surgery with a clean bill of health. Any time her mind started dwelling on what could go wrong, she immediately filled it with an image of the doctor telling her afterwards they had gotten it all and that she wouldn't need radiation or chemotherapy. Who knows what role her calm conviction played, but Cheri did emerge with a clean bill of health, and the days preceding her hospital stay were as positive as she could make them instead of being filled with fear.

R.E.S.T. = Trust

Don't worry; please, please. How many times do I have to say it? There is no way not to be who you are and where.
—**Zen master Ikkyu**

This advice is enormously comforting. It instantly reminds us how futile worry is. Worry serves no *good* purpose. Any time we worry, we're mentally getting ahead of ourselves and forgetting to be grateful and accepting of where we are and what we're doing right now. Remember Shakespeare's often-repeated line "To be, or not to be?" When we're worrying, we're not "being." We're filling our heads with alarming predictions instead of experiencing current circumstances with contentment. Worry is the opposite of Zen.

A single mom was a self-described world-class worry wart who constantly imagined disaster befalling her twin daughters. Claire admitted she was overprotective, but didn't know how to turn her mind off. She said, "I can't help myself. I worry about their grades, I worry about crime and drugs at their college, I worry about how I'm going to pay their tuition, I worry when they come home late from a date. If they're not back on time, I panic. I picture them in a ditch somewhere, or lying in some hospital emergency room, or (worse yet) in the backseat of their date's car."

Claire's concerned daughters finally sat her down and told her, "Do you realize worrying is a way of saying you don't trust us? Worrying yourself sick doesn't mean you love us more. All it does is make you anxious and us guilty. Have a little faith, Mom. From now on, trust that we'll be okay and that we'll use good judgment."

Claire realized the girls were right. Worrying was a way of mentally clinging to them. It was time *she* grew up and mentally let them go so they could live their own lives. She understood the way to turn her mind off was to choose to trust that things would go well instead of choosing to live in constant fear that something might go wrong. It was a basic mental shift in how to view the world. Did she want to continue to pessimistically see it as a place where bad things happen, or did she want to optimistically see it as a place where good things happen?

The poet Ovid said, "Happy is the man who has broken the chains which hurt the mind, and given up worrying once and for all." Worry does indeed set up a negative chain reaction. From here on out, vow to set up a positive chain reaction by **R**esolving to do, not stew; **E**rase anxieties; **S**elf-create calm; and **T**rust that thinks will turn out well.

Action Plan 29. Worried? R.E.S.T. Assured

If you keep saying things are going to be bad, you have a good chance of being a prophet.

—Isaac Bashevis Singer

Doesn't it make sense to be a prophet of good rather than a prophet of doom? What are you worried about? What's something coming up you're not looking forward to? You have the power to make up your mind one way or the other. Are you going to dwell on everything that could go wrong or are you going to close your eyes, relax your body, and root yourself in who you are and where you are—without wanting or needing to be anyone or anywhere else?

Could you keep the faith instead of focusing on your fears? I once saw a poster that said, "Fear is faith that it won't work out." Instead of sitting and stewing, could you stand up and start doing? From now on, vow to spend your T.I.M.E. figuring out how things *can* work out instead of focusing on why they won't.

Confusion	ConZentration
React and stew "What if I don't get elected? It will be so embarrassing if I lose and Linda gets more votes than me."	*Resolve to do* "I really want to get elected PTA president. I have so many ideas that could help the school."
Obsess about anxieties "What if she wins and asks me to be her vice-president? I could never work with her. We're complete opposites."	*Erase anxieties* "I'm going to tell the other parents some of my plans so they'll support my campaign and vote for me."
Self-created catastrophes "I'm sorry I ever let them nominate me. I can't stand this tension. I'm going to leave the room while they count the ballots."	*Self-created calm* "I'm proud my peers respect me enough to nominate me. I trust that I'll be elected and this will work out for the best."

Confusion	ConZentration
Doubt	*Trust*
"Uh-oh. Mary Alice just looked over at me with a grimace. Oh, no. Linda's going to win."	"I'm going to walk over and greet that new couple. They look like they could use some welcoming."

WAY 30

◉

Sad? B.E.A.T. the Blues

The only way to break the cycle of brooding thoughts is to
act responsibly on one's behalf.

**—Richard Burton, seventeenth-century scholar
who wrote *Anatomy of Melancholy***

Burton was right. To break a "brood mood," we've got to act fast.
The quicker we do something to dispel our depression (instead
of just dwelling on it), the less power those destructive thoughts
have to dominate our mind. Malaise is a result of mental malinger-
ing—our mind is dwelling on melancholy thoughts, and as a result,
we feel dispirited. From now on, if you're feeling down and out, lift
your spirits by becoming more up-B.E.A.T.

B.E.A.T. = Be Specific About What's Really Bothering You

He who cannot describe the problem will never find the
solution to that problem.
—Confucius

It's tough to know how to feel better if we don't know what's making us feel bad. Try to pinpoint exactly why you're feeling down-
hearted. Are you disappointed because that special someone didn't

call as you'd hoped? Are you sad because it's the anniversary of your mother's death? Are you experiencing a vague dissatisfaction because your life is off track? Your black mood will persist until you identify the source of your blues.

Sometimes the cause of our mental malaise is apparent; other times it's not. A woman in a seminar approached me afterward and said, "I don't know why I'm feeling so depressed. I never feel like doing anything, but I don't have any reason to be unhappy. I'm married to a wonderful man, I have two happy, healthy kids, I live in a big house in a great neighborhood. I have everything I want."

If we don't know why we're feeling down, it's time to start digging. We can often unearth the buried reasons for our lack of energy by free-associating to certain loaded phrases. *Artist's Way* author Julia Cameron believes, "When we are not current with ourselves, the world around us becomes lackluster." Cameron suggests we answer each of these questions several times, being sure to give our first, uncensored response each time so we can work down through any layers of denial.

1. "If I let myself admit it, I feel . . . "
2. "If I let myself admit it, I think . . . "
3. "If I let myself know it, I suspect . . . "
4. "If I let myself enjoy it, I like . . . "
5. "If I let myself have permission, I would . . . "

The workshop participant had a mind-opening experience when she answered these questions. Despite her voiced assertions that she had a perfect life, answering these questions allowed her to admit that she felt she wasn't doing anything with her life. When she let herself think it, she realized she felt like she was "losing the best years of her life, and no one, not her husband or her kids, noticed or cared." When she gave herself permission to voice these unpretty thoughts, she understood these suppressed resentments had dampened her vitality. Now that she'd identified the source of her blocked circuits, she was in a position to unjam them.

B.E.A.T. = Examine Your "Whether Forecast"

Life appears to me too short to be spent in nursing animosity
or registering wrongs.
—Charlotte Brontë

Brontë's right. It's to our benefit to evaluate our "whether" forecasts
to determine if we're exaggerating circumstances.

When we're down in the dumps, we're often "under the
whether." "No one cares whether I live or die." "It doesn't matter
whether I show up to work. No one notices anyway." Exaggerated
"whethers" overstate the case and are at least partially responsible
for creating our funk.

Identify any bleak projections and pronouncements you're making and simply ask yourself, "Is this true?" "Is it true that no one
cares whether I live or die?" "Is it true that no one notices whether
I come to work?" Well, no, it's probably not true. Then ask yourself,
"What is true?" "Well, what is true is I just broke up with my
boyfriend." "What is true is I just worked overtime for the last week
to help finish a project and no one thought to thank me for all the
extra work." Is it true? "What is true?" questions can help us put
things in perspective so we respond appropriately to life's events
instead of awfulizing them.

B.E.A.T. = Activate Your Energy by Moving out of Your House

Action is the antidote to despair.
—Joan Baez

No, I don't mean *that* kind of moving out of your house. I mean getting up and going outside. Staying inside keeps us in an insulated,
introverted frame of mind. We continue to think dark thoughts
because we're not seeing the light of day. We're not receiving any
fresh stimuli, so we stay focused on our misery.

Unfortunately, this sets up a destructive spiral. The more morose
we feel, the more we want to retreat. The more alone we are with
our dark thoughts, the more depressed we become, which makes us

want to withdraw even further, and down, down, down the despair spiral we descend. When we don't feel like going outside and being around people is exactly when we need to go outside and be around people.

The way to reverse how we feel is to reverse what we're doing. You've probably heard the popular saying "If you keep doing what you're doing, you'll keep getting what you're getting." It's sometimes hard to talk ourselves out of lethargy, because our head is already full of self-recriminations. Trying to persuade our mind to quit this self-absorbed funk can sometimes backfire because emotional states don't respond to logic. Admonishing ourselves can sometimes drive us deeper into depression because now we not only feel awful—we feel awful for feeling awful because we don't feel we have the right to feel awful. (Whew!)

Such was the case of an elderly salesclerk I met in a boutique. She had seen one of my TV programs and confessed she'd been having a hard time ever since her beloved husband had died seven years ago. She said tremulously, "I still miss him. Everyone tells me it will get better with time, but it doesn't. I think about him every day." She had taken this part-time job, not because she needed the money, but because she knew she had to get out of the house.

We talked about other ways she could move on. Movement improves mood. As we discussed in Way 28, "Mental F.I.T.N.E.S.S.," there's a direct correlation between physical activity and frame of mind. As Carl Jung observed, "If you are unhappy, you are too high up in your mind." Simply said, the more active we are, the happier we are. The less active we are, the less happy we are. This woman recognized that missing her husband would continue to be her primary focus unless she filled the vacuum in her life with other activities and people.

I asked if there was something she would enjoy doing that would force her to continue to get out of the house and be around other people. She thought about it for a minute and then said, "The bookstore across the street has a reading group once a week." She agreed to go the following Tuesday night. There's a wonderful end to this story. The last time I stopped by the boutique she reported she had started going to the book club meetings, that she had met someone there who told her about volunteering at the Maui Arts and Cultural Center, and that she was now ushering at concerts, plays, and other performances at least once a week. "I've met a whole new group of friends. I wake up in the morning with something to look forward to, instead of wondering how I'm going to get through the day."

Good for her. If for some reason you're feeling sad, could you follow her example? Give yourself a chance at a new life by activating your energy and moving out of the house. Remember it this way: if you're down, get yourself out.

B.E.A.T. = Treat Someone Kindly

> We cannot cure the world of sorrows, but we can
> choose to live in joy.
> —Joseph Campbell

Cynics may scoff at Campbell's philosophy and call it idealistic, but he has a point. While we will never be able to eliminate all sources of sadness from our life, we can choose to *give* joy instead of focusing on our lack of joy.

One of the quickest ways to make yourself feel good is to make someone else feel good. Many psychologists believe depression is a result of self-absorption. We get locked into listing what's wrong with our lives. Instead of dwelling on our disappointments and disillusionments, we might better dwell on how we can serve others.

Burton suggested we break our cycle of depression by acting responsibly on our behalf. We can also transcend depression by acting charitably on someone else's behalf. As soon as we do, our introverted antipathy turns into outward empathy. Instead of feeling sorry for ourselves, we feel sorry for someone else. Making an effort to alleviate someone else's pain alleviates our own. As Mark Twain said, "The best way to cheer yourself is to try to cheer somebody else up."

Frank Schneller is my favorite example of someone who B.E.A.T. his blues. Early in my speaking career, I was lucky enough to come to the attention of Frank, the education chair for a major national association. At that time I didn't have many big-name clients, but Frank took a chance on a new speaker and scheduled me for their huge (8,000 attendees) convention in Honolulu. His mentoring helped launch my speaking career, for which I'll always be grateful.

At a recent convention for a related group, the meeting planner told me that Frank, an avid shell collector, had retired to his beloved Florida, and that, unfortunately, he was battling cancer. I got back in touch with Frank to let him know what a difference he'd made in my life. It came as no surprise that this perpetually positive man was handling this adversity with his always present grace.

He briefly described the devastating chemo and radiation treatments and then immediately switched the conversation to how lucky he was because he had the support and love of many friends, family members, and fellow cancer survivors.

He said, "I went through a blue period during my treatments. It was easy to brood, and sit home alone and feel sorry for myself, but that just made me feel worse. I looked at the jars of shells I'd collected over the years, and decided to give other people an opportunity to enjoy them. I packaged them up in thirty baggies, took them to the beach, and gave them away to children. There wasn't a shell on the beach (it was summertime) and these kids couldn't believe I was giving them such beautiful shells. Their excitement and appreciation put me in such a good mood, I'm going to give away sixty baggies this year!"

He continued, "I also started volunteering at Children's Hospital. Believe me, it put things in perspective very quickly." He said modestly, "I know a few magic tricks. I don't know how much good it does, but when I say hi, they're usually not smiling, and when I say bye, they usually are."

I complimented Frank on his lack of self-pity, and he said, "Sam, it's simple. If I don't moan and groan, I get more phone calls. If I droned on and on about how miserable I was, people would stop calling. They've got their own problems, they don't want to hear about mine."

What a practical philosophy. Are you depressed? Like Frank, are you going through some tough times and it's oh-so-tempting to sit home and withdraw further into yourself? Wouldn't it make thinks better to get out of the house and do something nice for someone nice? Break the chain of brooding thoughts by acting on your behalf *and* on other people's behalf.

Note: If your depression persists, please consult a medical doctor. You may be suffering from clinical depression, which can be diagnosed and treated with medication and therapy.

Action Plan 30. Sad? B.E.A.T. the Blues

I am in that temper that if I were under water I would scarcely kick to come to the top.

—John Keats

Ouch! That's a bad mood. From now on, kick start yourself out of sadness by pinpointing the problem, examining your whether forecast, activating your energy, and treating someone else with the kindness you wish others would show to you.

Confusion	ConZentration
Be vague about what's wrong "I don't know why, I just can't keep my mind on anything."	*Be specific about what's wrong* "If I let myself admit it, I know I picked the wrong major."
Wrong "whether" "The only thing that matters is whether I become a doctor like my dad."	*Examine your "whether" forecast* "Whether or not I get my medical degree, my parents will still love me."
Apathetic, no energy "I don't feel like going anywhere. I'm going to call and cancel out."	*Activate your energy* "I'm going to get out of the apartment and go see the school counselor."
Drown in self-pity "No one cares how I feel. No one even notices how depressed I am."	*Treat someone nice* "I'm going to call the counselor and thank her for her good advice."

WAY 31

◉

Mad? Be a C.O.O.L. Head, Not a Hot Head

Anger is fuel. It is meant to be acted on, not acted out.

—Julia Cameron

Anger is a legitimate response to something or someone that's unfair, unkind, or inappropriate. As long as we express our anger constructively, it is an important component to getting our needs and rights honored.

Unfortunately, though, some people haven't been taught how to express anger constructively. Some people act out their anger indiscriminately, but far more deny it ("I'm *not* angry!"), pretend it doesn't exist ("It doesn't bother me"), dismiss it ("There's no reason to get upset"), and/or stuff it ("I want to scream my head off, but that wouldn't be ladylike"). As a result, their outrage backs up in their brain and seethes until it dominates their thoughts and destroys their peace of mind.

Bette Midler said, "I don't hold grudges. I have a brain that retains nothing." Wise woman. It's been said that holding on to resentment is like eating poison and then waiting for the other person to keel over. Holding in anger causes similar self-inflicted damage. From now on, we want to express our anger in helpful, not harmful, ways instead of holding it in where it does no one any good. Here are four ways to **keep your C.O.O.L.** even if others are losing theirs.

C.O.O.L. = Control Your Reaction

> Be silent in one moment of anger and you will save
> a thousand days of sorrow.
> **—Chinese proverb**

Notice I didn't say control your thoughts. As discussed, we can't control what thoughts come into our head; we can only control how long they stay there. We may not choose the spiteful retorts that spring into our mind; we can choose whether to blurt them out. At the moment of anger, we can choose to hold our tongue instead of giving that person a tongue-lashing and saying something we regret. So bite back that mean-spirited put-down and choose to take the mental high road. Our goal is to resolve, not retaliate.

C.O.O.L. = Objectively State Your Perception of What Happened and How It Made You Feel

> No man can think clearly when his fists are clenched.
> **—George Jean Nathan**

No man can think clearly when his mind is clenched. The way to express our anger instead of suppress it is to tell this person what they said or did and how it impacted us. I know, this smacks of pop psychology lingo, but therapists call this the "When you———(did this), I felt———(this)" and claim it is one of the clearest ways to communicate that someone's violated our rights or sensibilities without blaming. For example, "When you pointed out my bald spot at the dinner party tonight, I felt humiliated." "When you said the turkey was so dry you could hardly swallow it, I felt like the six hours I spent trying to cook a nice Thanksgiving dinner were wasted."

The point of this is not to make the other person feel bad, it's to honestly communicate how their behavior has affected us in an effort to coexist more sensitively. Instead of feeling stepped on and doing nothing about it, our goal is to speak up and let the other person know that we think what they did or said was not kind, fair, or appropriate. A popular Tongue Fu'ism is "There are no victims without volunteers." Volunteer how their actions affected you instead of suffering and simmering in silence and volunteering to be a passive victim.

C.O.O.L. = One Think at a Time

Don't go to bed mad. Stay up and fight.
—Phyllis Diller

Resist the urge to bring up baggage or you'll be up all night fighting. Keep to one issue. Avoid adding on other slights and insults. We know we're in danger if we're tempted to say, "And furthermore . . . " or "And that's not all. Last week you . . . " ConZentrate on what happened right now instead of letting your mind jump back to previous wounds.

C.O.O.L. = Look for Solutions, Not Fault

Our task is not to fix the blame for the past, it's to fix the course for the future.
—John F. Kennedy

Our goal in expressing anger is not to find fault, it's to find a resolution. Instead of focusing and/or dwelling on how people hurt us, we're going to suggest or request how they can behave more sensitively or appropriately from now on. As Julia Cameron pointed out, we voice anger in an attempt to correct things, not criticize them. We're letting people know they've violated our boundaries and taking steps to improve the situation instead of whining because it's not what we want.

Have you been going along to get along? Were you taught, or did you believe, that arguing was to be avoided at all costs? At what cost? Have you repressed righteous anger for so long that your ability to think clearly and cleanly is suppressed? Resolve right now to keep a cool head next time someone or something makes you mad. ConZentrate on constructively expressing your anger and see if it doesn't clear your head of seeing red.

A workshop participant approached me after a seminar and thanked me for this section on anger. He said, "Five years ago, I lent my brother twenty thousand dollars to start up a business and it failed. He promised to pay me back, but backed out of his agreement. We got in a real shouting match when his business went bankrupt, and I haven't spoken to him since. That quote from Kennedy really made me think. I realize we could go the rest of our lives not speaking to each each other, and I don't want that. The truth of the matter is, I can afford the money, and I'd rather have my brother back than hang on to this grudge."

Goethe said, "We are shaped and fashioned by what we love." We are also shaped and fashioned by what we hate. This man fortunately decided to let go of his need to be right and chose to ConZentrate on reaching a peaceful resolution with his brother instead of staying focused on the painful past.

Action Plan 31. Mad? Be a C.O.O.L. Head, Not a Hot Head

If you can keep your head when all about you are losing theirs, it's just possible you haven't grasped the situation.

—Jean Kerr

Or maybe you've grasped the situation and realized that losing your head serves no good purpose. As Buddha said, "Holding on to anger is like grasping a hot coal with the intent of throwing it at someone else—but you are the one who gets burned."

Has someone been making you mad? Have you been giving yourself a headache by holding in your anger? How are you going to keep a C.O.O.L. head? Are you going to fix the problem instead of fix blame? Are you going to stick to the subject instead of bringing up slights from the past? Vow to act on instead of act out your anger. Resolve to constructively confront that person or situation so that anger doesn't jam your mental circuits and keep you from ConZentrating on more important matters.

Confusion

React, say what's on the tip of our tongue
"You're a jerk. Dating you is the worst mistake I've ever made. I wish I never met you."

Criticize the person so he feels bad
"It was so rude of you to go off with your buddies and leave me by myself at that party. How selfish can you get?"

Everything at once
"This is like last month when we went to your office Christmas party, and you ended up palling around with your coworkers while I stood in a corner twiddling my thumbs."

Lash into them
"Didn't your mama teach you better manners than that? Can't you ever think of anyone other than yourself?"

ConZentration

Control our reaction, hold our tongue
"Okay, wait a minute. I don't want to say something I don't mean and can't take back."

Objectively communicate how his behavior made us feel
"When you went outside to play football with your friends, I felt abandoned because I didn't know anyone there."

One think at a time
"When you left without telling me where you'd gone, I felt like you wanted to be with your friends more than you wanted to be with me."

List what you'd like in the future
"In the future, can you let me know before you take off somewhere? If I don't know anyone there, I may want to come with you, okay?"

WAY 32

◉

Keeping It Together When Your World's Falling Apart

This is the mark of a really admirable man;
steadfastness in the face of trouble.

—Ludwig van Beethoven

Are you thinking, "What if it's more serious than just being sad or mad? What if I'm facing troubles that are making it almost impossible for me to stay focused?"

I talked with a friend who flew to the Mainland last month to take care of her seriously ill mother-in-law. Her caretaking included daily sponge baths and diapering, giving enemas, cleaning a condo that had been let go for months, cutting up credit cards and closing charge accounts (much to the horror of several free-loading sister-and-brother-in-laws), and having the thoroughly unpleasant task of taking away this woman's car keys (and independence?) after sixty plus years of safe driving.

Another woman found out her sixteen-year-old son has been using drugs . . . in their house, no less. Another's twenty-year marriage is on the rocks after her husband decided to meet his Internet girlfriend . . . and move her out to Maui. Another is experiencing deep ennui because her husband wants her to stay home and she is yearning to do something with her life. Still another has suffered two years of divorce hell (including a nasty custody battle). A male friend is facing prostate cancer, and a woman who is forty-two and single is facing the thoroughly depressing fact that she'll probably never have the children and family she's always yearned for. The list goes on and on.

Major stress seems to be the norm for most people these days. As one interviewee said, "I'm not trying to be happy or anything, Sam. I'm just trying to make it through the day without falling apart."

Throw Me a Mental Lifesaver

> When I have trouble writing, I step outside my studio into the garden and pull weeds until my mind clears.
> —Irving Stone

When we have trouble coping, what can we do to clear our mind? How can we ConZentrate when our mind is overcome or preoccupied with personal tragedy? Most of us don't have the option of crawling in a hole and hiding until things get better. That may be what we feel like doing, but we've got to force ourselves to function. We've got to go to work, keep our commitments, be responsible, and show up. Yet the awfulness of what we're going through can be debilitating. It's hard to keep our mind on what we're *supposed* to be doing when all it can think about is the trauma we're experiencing.

These next thirteen suggestions can help us function when all we really want to do is creep under the covers and make the world go away. These are *healthy* mental escape hatches. It can be tempting to anesthetize psychic pain by drowning our sorrows in booze, food, sleep, TV, or drugs. Those harmful outlets are temporary ways to get our mind off our troubles, but of course they create a whole new set of problems in the process. Our goal is to engage in *healthy* mental release valves that help us keep it together when our world's turned upside down.

You've heard of lifesavers? These activities are *mental* lifesavers. They help us stay sane when our mind is threatening to shut down. If you're going through some trials and tribulations, try these on for size. Hopefully, these thirteen mental lifesavers will help you cope, ConZentrate, and carry on in a world gone crazy.

Mental Lifesaver 1. When You Don't Know What to Do, Do What You Know

Order is the shape upon which beauty depends.
—Pearl S. Buck

...ape upon which sanity depends. I debated whether ...ther personal information in this book. It could be more ... ...r wanted to know about my private life. I decided to do it, ...at it would make this a more honest book, and that sharing what I've been going through might help you relate to this material and make it more personally meaningful for you.

The ironic aspect of this book on ConZentration is that I've been writing it during the *least* concentrated time of my entire forty-eight-year life. That woman in the previous section who was going through a difficult divorce is me. Suffice it to say, there have been days during the past couple of years when I was writing about serenity, peace of mind, and focus, and needed to hear every word I was composing at the computer because I was in the middle of some unpleasant scenario that was making it hard to function.

So what did I learn first-hand from the most trying experience of my life? That when what's happening is so convoluted we don't know what to do, the only thing we can do is to do what we know.

I believe this is ConZentration at its best. When life has become uncertain, we need to, first, find something simple and pure and immerse ourselves in it. It does no good to focus on all the hullabaloo surrounding us. It's far better to lose ourselves in an activity that's simple and good instead of losing ourselves in the swirl of psychic pain that's often part and parcel of traumatic experiences. It's a way to bring some sense of order into a world that's out of order.

One particularly bad day I was almost incapacitated with a "This can't be happening" disbelief. The surrealness of the situation I was in stupefied me. I sat there and spiraled down and down into a mind-numbed paralysis. Then I looked at my sons and realized I had to get out of this funk because it didn't help me, didn't help them, and didn't change what was happening. Somewhere, out of my consciousness, rose a voice that said these simple and lifesaving words:

"When you don't know what to do, do what you know." So what did I know? I knew that playing ball with my sons in a swimming pool was pure innocent fun, so that's what we did.

Tom, Andrew, and I changed into our swimsuits, took out a brightly colored beach ball, and went to the pool. For the next hour, we were *carefree*. For that brief, blissful amount of time, we lost ourselves in laughing, playing—being together, healthy, and completely in the moment. It was one of the most healing things I've ever done in my life. The memory of that clear, clean experience—completely devoid of the ugliness that had surrounded us—helped carry me through the unpleasant days and weeks that followed.

And in the months that followed, whenever I found myself on the verge of sinking back into that mental despair, I either thought back to that experience and reminded myself what was important, or identified and immersed myself in "one true thing," as Anna Quindlen so eloquently described it in her book of that title.

What could that one true thing be for you? For an attorney friend, it's baking. Sara occasionally gets discouraged by the outrageous and/or cruel human behavior she encounters in her court cases. When it all gets to be too much, she heads into the kitchen to lose herself in several hours of chocolate-chip-cookie-aroma therapy. She's discovered for herself the truth of something Helen Keller said: "Smell is a potent wizard that transports us across thousands of miles and all the years we have lived." Sara says, "Fixing favorite recipes is a way to bring back happier, more innocent times when everything was right with the world. The mouthwatering smell of my grandmother's famous cookies is a way to revisit good memories. I usually don't even eat what I bake; I give it away. It's the process that's cathartic and therapeutic."

Another friend loses herself in making music. She said, "Playing piano is my outlet. If something's bothering me, I 'take it out' on my music. I rip into Rachmaninoff if I'm frustrated and vent my rage pounding out forte passages, and then calm myself down by playing a little Chopin. I can experience an entire range of emotions playing one piece of music by Mozart. By the end, I've played out the junk in my system and am ready to re-greet the world."

What is a healthy activity you could temporarily lose yourself in so you can return refreshed and ready to go? What is your one true thing that can bring back some sweetness into a world gone sour?

Mental Lifesaver 2. Pour Out Your Soul to Sympathetic Ears

> A person with whom I may be sincere. Before him
> I may think out loud.
> —Ralph Waldo Emerson

Friends are people with whom we can be sad; before them we can say out loud what's in our hearts and minds. We're taught to be strong. We grow up being told to keep a stiff upper lip and to tough out tough times. Unfortunately, trying to deal with a trauma by ourselves seals the mental anguish in our head, where it accumulates because it's not being given an opportunity to get out. Going it alone turns our mind into a mental pressure cooker. All the hurt, sadness, anger, and stress build and build until the mind finally has no alternative but to blow a gasket and explode—often in inappropriate ways and at inappropriate times.

Pouring out our soul purges our psychic pain. Getting our frustrations and sorrows *off* our chest gets them *out* of our chest, where they would otherwise cause heartache. Think back to a time you told all to a friend. Remember how relieved you felt afterwards? You may have even let out a heartfelt sigh and said, "I feel so much better!" Your friend didn't offer advice; she simply let you talk it out. That's what pouring out our soul does. It talks our troubles right out of our system. We feel like we're a new person, because we are! We are now free to carry on because we are no longer carrying inside us all those collected insults and injuries.

Mental Lifesaver 3. Go to the Dogs

> Dogs are the god of frolic.
> —Henry Ward Beecher

I have a pet theory. (Ahem.) It's almost impossible to be in a bad mood around a puppy, kitten, or loving pet. Playing Frisbee with

Fido or stroking Fifi, who's contentedly purring in our lap, takes us out of ourselves and immerses us in a comforting, tactile frame of mind in which we're no longer thinking about whatever cataclysmic event has befallen us. We're, at least momentarily, in that pleasant place with an animal that knows only love, play, and good things.

This isn't just my theory. Some progressive hospitals and rest homes have introduced pet visitations for their patients. A friend sneaked their Yorkshire terrier into a hospital room to cheer her daughter up the day before surgery. "You should have seen Amy's face light up when I brought Toto into the room. For those few moments she forgot where she was and what was going to happen the next day. She just snuggled and held Toto and had at least a few happy moments."

Mental Lifesaver 4. Run Away

Running is sport, amusement, and a telephoneless, bossless escape into freedom from everyday pressures.
—Jim Fixx

Several people I talked with said that when it all gets to be too much, they put on their athletic shoes and take off. It's their way of *temporarily* losing their mind and running away from their problems. One friend said, "After the first mile, my body and mind switch over to automatic pilot. I'm in a sensory place where I'm not even thinking about what I'm doing." She's also not thinking about her trials and travails. Running, basketball, swimming, tennis—*any* kind of strenuous physical workout does just that. It's an opportunity to *work out* our frustrations. Aerobic exercise allows us to escape into a physical haven that's in sharp contrast to the mental hell we've been living in.

Mental Lifesaver 5. Laugh Your Head Off

If you can laugh at it, you can live with it.
—Erma Bombeck

Thank heaven for my attorney's sense of humor. What a saving grace it's been these last couple of years. When Sara would call with bad news, she would inevitably turn it around and somehow have me laughing at the ludicrousness of it all. I remember one time she commented, "You must really be down in the dumps. I can tell because you're not laughing at any of my jokes." She was right. Cracking jokes is a great way to put thinks in perspective. Sara believes, "When things get really awful, the only thing you can do is laugh at it. It's better than crying." Wise woman.

If you're thinking, "You've got to be kidding. What I'm going through is no laughing matter," I understand that life-and-death situations can seem much too serious to take lightly. More and more though, medical professionals are understanding and recommending the healing power of humor. In his groundbreaking book, *Anatomy of an Illness,* Norman Cousins introduced the idea that laughing can be good medicine. Cousins brought his favorite videos and joke books into the hospital and found that laughing produced endorphins that eased his physical and psychic pain.

I read an Internet joke on-line recently that said, "He who laughs last thinks slowest." I think he who laughs last thinks quickest. Be quick to see the humor in stressful situations. It will remove their power to make you miserable.

One of my favorite stories about a quick thinker happened on a packed plane. A five-year-old boy wearing cowboy boots and a cowboy hat was running up and down the aisle pretending to shoot passengers with his straw. Everyone was getting rather exasperated and kept waiting for the tike's mother to get him under control. The mother had an infant on her lap, though, and it was all she could do to keep up with the baby's demands. She had obviously given up on the little sharpshooter.

Finally, the senior flight attendant came over, got down on the little boy's level, put her hands on his shoulders, looked him in the eye, and asked, "Would you like to play outside?"

The little cowboy's eyes got *this* big (picture deer in headlights), and then he scurried back to his seat and sat there quietly for the rest of the trip. What a classic example of someone handling a challenging situation with a chuckle instead of a curse. The flight attendant could have come down on that boy like a ton of bricks. Instead, with a little forethought, she handled that hassle with humor instead of harsh words or a heavy hand.

Mental Lifesaver 6. Get to Work

If my doctor told me I had only six months to live,
I'd type a little faster.
—Isaac Asimov

Now *there's* a man who loves his work. My sister Cheri and I were discussing this topic of how to keep going when all we want to do is give up. Cheri said, "Losing Dad was especially tough because we had just been elected president and vice president of the chamber. We had spent hours talking about the upcoming year and had planned some fund-raising events we were really looking forward to." Cheri continued, "I don't get relief from doing fun things. When Dad died, I was overcome with grief. Work became my lifeboat and kept me from sinking into a depression. I'm good at what I do and feel like I'm contributing, so it kept me going."

Cheri's right in that losing ourselves in our work, especially when we have the satisfaction of knowing that our work makes a difference, can be solace for the soul. It's important that we not take this distraction too far, though, and become a workaholic. Dedicating ourselves wholeheartedly and whole-mindedly to our work to forget our problems can be healthy in the short term, but becomes unhealthy avoidance if it's done over the long haul.

Mental Lifesaver 7. Compartmentalize

I see the different things competing for my attention as drawers
in my mind. I never have more than one drawer open at a time.
—Napoleon Bonaparte

You may be thinking, "What if I'm so mentally paralyzed by what's happening, my mind refuses to cooperate?" If your mental reserves are so depleted by your ordeal that your brain refuses to function, you may need to compartmentalize this trauma (mentally push it aside) so you can fulfill your responsibilities for the moment.

See the different things competing for your attention as drawers in your mind. If you are at work and all you can think about is your loved one in the hospital, make your mind a trade. Say, "I will call them at such and such a time, and for the next hour I will give one hundred percent attention to these proposals," or "I am going to take an hour off at lunch to go visit her, and I need to keep my head glued to the screen so I can finish these letters by eleven-thirty A.M."

Notice we are telling the mind what it *can* do, not what it can't. As mentioned before, the mind will take bribes, but it will rebel if it is told *not* to think about something. The more we tell ourselves not to think about something that is bothering us, the more power it has to bother us. Instead, make the mind a deal it can't refuse and it will focus on what it needs to do now, as long as it knows it will get to do what it wants later. Stash the topic you can't think about now in its own mental drawer or compartment and bring it out at a more suitable time.

Mental Lifesaver 8. Write, Right Now

> I have forced myself to begin writing when I've been utterly exhausted, when I've felt my soul as thin as a playing card . . . and somehow the activity of writing changes everything.
> **—Joyce Carol Oates**

If your soul is feeling as thin as a playing card, pull out a notebook and start writing. Journaling your every thought (no matter how unpleasant) is an excellent way to get toxic thoughts out of your brain. Don't try to be eloquent. This isn't meant to be Hemingway. It's simply an opportunity to get what's inside, outside.

Don't worry if you whine. You're supposed to. This may be the only place you can say exactly how you feel—without worrying whether it's selfish, kind, or fair. We all need an *outlet* where we can *let out* the noxious stuff that's sullying our soul. It may not be nice to have these feelings about this person, but we do. It may be petty, not pretty, to think these thoughts, but we do. If we deny unattractive or unwelcome emotions, if we stuff them down and try our best to ignore them, they don't go away. They simply accumulate until they take over our thinking and we can't think of anything else. Get those thoughts off your mind by purging them on paper. Expressing what we think and feel through our fingertips clears the crud from our system and frees space for more constructive thoughts.

Do you have something on your mind that's bothering you right now? Or do you feel lousy and aren't certain why? Erica Jong said, "How can I know what I think unless I see what I write?" Grab a piece of paper and a pen or pencil. I mean it. Get up from where you're sitting, get something to write with and something to write on, and write out, right now, *exactly* what you're feeling. No editing or censoring. No one is going to see this except you. Tangibly express your fears, scattered thoughts, and concerns.

Now, don't you feel better? Next time you say to yourself, "I just can't get_____(fill in the blank) off my mind," pull out your paper or journal (which you keep with you for occasions just like this) and write down what you're thinking and how you're feeling. Are you saying, "But I don't have time"? Would you rather take a few minutes to purge that mental gunk that's blocking your ConZentration, or would you rather spend the next few hours preoccupied with these unwanted images and ideas crowding your mind?

Mental Lifesaver 9. Identify Something You Care About More than Yourself

Without some goal and some effort to reach it,
no man can live.
—Fyodor Dostoyevsky

Without someone to love and some commitment to care for them, it can be tough to live. This idea also comes from my sister. Cheri said, "If I'm overwhelmed, the bills are mounting up, deadlines are piling up, and I'm tempted to give up, I imagine what would happen to Christie [her daughter] if I did. The picture of that is so unacceptable, whatever I'm going through becomes secondary. Sliding into a depression is no longer an option." What is your raison d'être—your reason to live? If you are so mentally exhausted you don't think you can go on, picture that loved one, reassert that overriding commitment, remind yourself of the consequences of giving in. This can give you the strength to go on.

Mental Lifesaver 10. Bring Beauty into Your Life

I don't think of all the misery, but of the beauty that still remains . . . Go outside, to the field, enjoy nature and the sunshine, go out and try to recapture happiness in yourself and in God. Think of all the beauty that's still left in and around you and be happy.
—Anne Frank

Anne Frank was one courageous young woman, wasn't she? Whatever we're going through, it can help to imagine Anne Frank writing these powerful, life-affirming words expressing her choice to believe in beauty in spite of her incredibly bleak circumstances.

As I write this, a single exquisite rose sits by my computer. Every once in a while, I glance up and marvel at its astounding perfection. In the midst of dreadful experiences, it's easy to lapse into all-or-nothing thinking. A phenomenon of physical pain is that our world shrinks and all we can think about is that pain in our body. Pain is so immediate, it's hard to focus on anything else. Any woman who's experienced a long labor can attest to this. Nothing else exists in the midst of those overpowering, all-consuming contractions.

The same phenomenon happens with psychological pain. Misery takes over our mind and the rest of the world recedes from our consciousness. We're aware of nothing else in view of the awfulness we're experiencing. The problem with focusing telescopically on our problems is it becomes our whole world. We lose sight that there's anything right with the world because we're focused only on what's wrong.

That's why it's so important to intentionally introduce beauty into our surroundings—to remind us that good still exists. As Buddha said, "If we could see the miracle of a single flower clearly, our whole life would change." Seeing the beauty of a single flower brings us out of ourselves. It serves as a visual reminder that while we may be encased in a "world of hurt," there are still wonders in the world.

Mental Lifesaver 11. Learn the Lesson

All experience is education for the soul.
—Zen saying

It's been said that self-pity is our worst enemy. Self-pity perpetuates our problems because feeling sorry for ourselves reinforces a sense of powerlessness. The more we focus on the terrible things that are happening to us, the more we see ourselves as an undeserving victim of events. *National Geographic* photographer and friend Dewitt Jones calls me a "happy-chondriac" because my there-must-be-a-pony-in-here-somewhere philosophy makes me determined to find purpose in every painful experience.

This isn't being a Pollyanna. It's simply to our advantage to search for value in whatever is going on. I agree with the Zen saying: "All experience is education for the soul." If we don't believe we're here to learn, if we're not convinced that everything that occurs is an opportunity to grow a little wiser, a little closer to our Higher Self . . . then when bad things happen, all we do is suffer. We rant, wail, bemoan our fate, and wonder "Why me?" We stage a one-person pity party.

Instead of wailing "Why me?" or "Woe is me," say, "Go is me." It's far better to understand that everything happens for a reason, and it's up to us to go find that reason. If we do and if we absorb the insight and improve how we operate as a result, then *everything* that happens serves a purpose.

As Kahlil Gibran said, "In every winter's heart there is a quivering spring, and behind the veil of each night there is a smiling dawn." I know. You may be thinking incredulously, "Having a heart attack serves us? Losing a loved one can be good?" I'm not saying these traumatic events are pleasant occurrences we wish upon ourselves or others. I'm saying that *if* they happen, we have a choice of how to respond. Cursing them, resenting the gods, has no constructive value. It doesn't change anything and it causes us to become bitter and angry. Approaching these events with an "Okay, this is what's taking place; what can I do about it? What can I learn from it?" attitude means that every single thing that happens to us or around us can move us closer to enlightenment—*if* we accept those experiences as part of our path instead of seeing them as meaningless pain.

Mental Lifesaver 12. Be Well-Read

I've given up reading books. I find it takes my mind off myself.
—Oscar Levant

That's the point! Some people who have experienced devastating losses find that losing themselves in a book is the only way to take their mind off their troubling circumstances. For those precious few moments, they are absorbed in another world and can forget the one that is causing them so much distress. If you've had enough grief for one day (or for a lifetime), pick up a book by a favorite author and find comfort in their prose.

We can also be well-read by studying self-help books such as Rabbi Harold S. Kushner's classic *When Bad Things Happen to Good People*. A walking partner whose young adult son had committed suicide found solace by reading one spiritual book after another. She said, "I think I would have gone crazy otherwise. Those books kept me centered. Reading the wisdom passed down through the ages kept me from falling to pieces. If I hadn't read those books, I would have spent all my time wondering if I could have done more and hating myself for not seeing the danger signals sooner. I copied some of the most meaningful passages and posted them all around my house on mirrors, doors, the refrigerator, the computer, everywhere. I would have drowned in grief and self-recrimination if I hadn't."

This woman had intuitively understood a truism about mental health that Fulton J. Sheen believed: "Each of us makes his own weather, determines the color of the skies in the emotional universe which he inhabits." Reading life-affirming, courage-enhancing books is a tangible way to stay focused on proactive thoughts. Some of my favorites are *Simple Abundance* by Sarah Ban Breathnach, *Gift from the Sea* by Anne Morrow Lindbergh, *Don't Sweat the Small Stuff* by Richard Carlson, *The Vein of Gold* by Julia Cameron, and (this may seem self-serving, but what the heck) *Fu! for Thought*, a collection of my favorite Tongue Fu'isms and "Common Zense," the companion quote calendar to this book.

Winston Churchill said, "Quotations, when engraved upon the memory, give you good thoughts." By engraving inspirational thoughts in our minds, we can call upon them when we're down in the dumps. I recite Meister Eckhart's simple yet profoundly insightful quote "If the only prayer we ever said was 'Thank you,' it would be enough" every morning as soon as I wake up. It helps put me in the right frame of mind.

Ask a friend to recommend a book or a quote they've found meaningful and then keep it in sight, in mind. Dorothy Parker, she of the acerbic wit, said, "I might repeat to myself, slowly and soothingly, a list of quotations beautiful from minds profound—if I could remember any of the damn things." You don't have to remember the profound and soothing quotes you find *if* you write them down and post them at strategic places throughout your home where you can read them at will. Their constant positive presence can have the power to lift us up and reconnect us to our belief that life is a blessing, not a burden.

Why are quotations so powerful in times of grief? I think it's because we couldn't have said it better ourselves. Grief is often inarticulable. We can't describe or express the emotions flooding our brain and drowning our soul, but then, if we're lucky, we come across a quote by someone gifted with eloquence—and they found the perfect words for us. We read their prose and sigh, "Yes. That's how I feel," and suddenly we're not so alone with our sorrow. Sometimes these poets with a pen articulate what we *want* to feel and their life-affirming words move us in that direction.

That was the case on September 4, 1997, at the Maui Writers Conference. Almost a thousand people had gathered from around the world to hear the likes of journalist Carl Bernstein, movie director Ron Howard, and novelist David Guterson. All of a sudden there was a pall cast over our opening-night reception as the stunning news of Lady Di's untimely death swept through the crowd. At a time like that, all one feels is horror and a feeling of helplessness. There's nothing one can do about the situation.

Ah, but there is. As emcee, it was my job to inform the group of the tragedy. I knew this occasion demanded perspective, so I searched through my quote books hoping to find just the right thing to say that could lessen the negative impact of this sad news. I found just that in the timeless words of Mary Jean Iron:

Normal day, let me be aware of the treasure you are.
Let me not pass you by in quest of some rare and perfect
   tomorrow.
Let me hold you while I may, for it may not always be so.
One day I shall dig my nails into the earth . . . or raise my
   hands to the sky
and want, more than all the world, your return.

Her marvelous insight reminded us, in the middle of our shock, not to lose sight of what a gift it is to be alive. We couldn't undo the damage that had been done to Lady Di and her family . . . we could be motivated by her death to appreciate and take advantage of the treasure of this normal day we had been blessed to see.

Mental Lifesaver 13. Have Faith

People talk about finding God—as if he could get lost.
—Internet line

If you're lost, maybe it's time to find God. What is your religion or faith? Could you reinvolve yourself so you have outside help in helping you cope with whatever crisis you're facing?

A friend was blindsided when his wife unexpectedly announced she was moving out. At first he thought it was a temporary midlife crisis, but was devastated to find out she'd been desperately unhappy for years and could no longer stand to be in the same house with him. He said it destroyed everything he thought he knew. He didn't trust anything or anyone anymore, and said self-examining didn't help because he couldn't be sure his conclusions were valid. After all, he had thought he knew his wife, and realized, too late, he didn't have a clue of how she really felt.

So what did he do when his world turned upside down? He started going to church. A lifelong agnostic, he said it's the only place where things makes sense. He was fortunate to find a local chapel with a caring minister and compassionate parishioners, and has placed his faith in a power higher than himself. "It helps enormously to believe there's a plan in all this. I may not understand the plan," he admitted ruefully, "but at least now I believe there *is* one. Before, it all seemed so senseless. Singing hymns every Sunday, really listening to the sermon, surrounding myself with good people, and believing in something bigger than myself has helped me deal with this. I wouldn't have been able to handle it otherwise."

Henry David Thoreau said, "It is only by forgetting yourself that you draw near to God." It works the other way around, too. Drawing nearer to our God can help us forget our problems, or at the very least can put them in proper perspective.

Action Plan 32. Keeping It Together When Your World's Falling Apart

Everything can be taken from a man but one thing: the last of human freedoms—to choose one's attitude in any given set of circumstances.

—German psychiatrist, author, and concentration camp survivor Dr. Viktor Frankl

So, what trauma are you dealing with? What crisis is threatening to shut your mind down? What is one of these suggestions you're going to do *today* to help yourself function? What step are you going to take to keep your mind going instead of giving in to the temptation to give up?

Many of our greatest philosophers agree with Frankl because they say the same think, in slightly different ways. French aviator and writer Antoine de Saint-Exupéry said, "The meaning of things lies not in the things themselves but in our attitudes toward them." Helen Keller, a role model of an individual who handled adversity graciously and accomplished great things with her life despite her hardships, said, "When one door of happiness closes, another opens, but often we look so long at the closed door that we don't see the one which has been opened for us."

What doors have closed for you recently? Is your mind so preoccupied with what you've lost or with what was done to you that you're not seeing what else is available? Open your eyes and mind by engaging in one of these healthy mental lifesavers. See if it doesn't have the power to free your mind from its preoccupation with pain and focus it on more positive possibilities.

Confusion

Don't know what to do
"Everything's turned upside down, and I have no idea how to turn it around."

Be strong and keep a stiff upper lip
"I have to hold it together and handle this myself. People don't want to hear my troubles."

Can't forget our problems
"I'm so mad at her I can hardly see straight. I'll never forgive her for what she did to me."

Mental hell
"My mind just keeps going over and over what happened. Why wasn't I more alert? I should have seen this coming."

So awful you could cry
"This can't be happening to me. Stuff like this only happens in soap operas."

Lost and can't work
"How am I supposed to ConZentrate in the midst of this insanity?"

Mentally incapacitated
"How am I supposed to keep my mind on these invoices when Judy is in the hospital?"

ConZentration

Do what you know
"I'm going out to the garden to pull some weeds and plant some herbs."

Pour out our soul to sympathetic ears
"I've got to get this out of my system. I'm going to ask Denise if we can get together so I can talk this out."

Can forget our problems with pets
"Come on, Rover. Let's take your ball and head to the park. I've got to get my mind off this."

Physical haven
"I'm headed to the gym. I need to just not think for a while. It'll help to work out and sweat this out."

So awful you might as well laugh
"So, what's the latest installment of *How the Stomach Turns*?"

Lose ourselves in our work
"I'm going to ConZentrate on finishing this paperwork so I can stay sane."

Mental compartments
"I will check in with Judy at ten A.M. For the next hour I will keep my mind on getting these invoices out."

Confusion

ConZentration

Don't have an outlet right now
"I can't tell anyone how I feel. I'm embarrassed to be having such hateful thoughts."

Write now to let it out
"I'm going to purge these hateful thoughts on paper so I can get them off my mind."

Many reasons to give up
"This is more than can be asked of any person. It's too much to bear, and it's never going to get better."

A meaningful reason to go on
"What would happen to my sons if I gave in to my grief? I will be strong and go on for them."

Life is bleak and full of pain
"It's horrible that something so unfair, so undeserved like this could happen. I don't want to live in a world where such awful things take place."

Life is full of beauty
"I will gaze at my rose whenever I am overwhelmed with what's wrong to remind myself there are still things right with the world."

Feel sorry for ourselves
"Why me? I didn't do anything bad. I don't deserve this."

Feel there's a purpose to everything
"What can I learn from this? I know there's value if I can just find it."

Spend all our time wondering what we could or should have done
"I can't figure out what I did wrong. This doesn't make any sense."

Spend time reading what we can do to gain insight and improve
"I'm going to buy some self-help books to make sense out of this."

Lost faith
"I don't trust anyone or anything anymore."

Have faith
"I trust things will work out. I believe there's a plan and a purpose for everything."

PART 12

Keep This in Mind

Thomas Carlyle once asked a
friend what his aim in life was.
The young man replied that he
had none. Carlyle fired back,
"Get one, then, and get it quick."

WAY 33

◉

Are You Having the T.I.M.E. of Your Life?

BASEBALL PITCHER TOM SEAVER: What time is it?

YOGI BERRA: You mean now?

That Yogi. As usual, his malapropism has deeper meaning than at first glance. The only time any of us have is right now. That's one of the main points of ConZentration: Instead of wasting energy by bemoaning the past or worrying about the future, we want to focus on making the most of this moment. How do we do that? By spending our T.I.M.E. wisely.

You've heard the expression "Time will tell." In truth, time *won't* tell us how to best spend it. We've got to make that decision ourselves, dozens of times each day, when choosing to whom and what we give our Thoughts, Interest, Moments, and Energy.

This book has focused on *how* to ConZentrate in dozens of different situations. It's equally important to ask ourselves, "What am I ConZentrating *on?*" If we're spending our T.I.M.E. on the right things, we're leading a life that will lead to results. If we're spending our T.I.M.E. on the wrong things, we're leading a life that will lead to regrets.

The purpose of this chapter is to ask ourselves, "How am I spending my T.I.M.E.?" Am I ConZentrating on my true priorities? What *are* my true priorities? If I'm not focusing on what's really important, how can I? What is my aim in life? And how can I have the courage of my ConZentration convictions so I pay attention to what *I* want instead of what everyone else wants?

"How Am I Spending My T.I.M.E.?"

Time is the coin of your life. It is the only coin you have, and only you can determine how it will be spent. Be careful lest you let other people spend it for you.
—Carl Sandburg

I realize there's no such thing as a normal week. But we need to track how we're actually spending our T.I.M.E. before we can assess whether we're spending it on the right things. Commit to keeping a time log of how you spend every waking hour for the next seven days. This can be an incredibly insightful exercise. Yes, I know you're busy; however, the few extra moments you invest documenting your T.I.M.E. usage can help you make decisions that will positively impact the rest of your life. It helps to do this from a Monday to a Sunday so you're gaining insight into how you spend time at work, at home, on workdays, on weekends, and so forth.

Am I ConZentrating on My True Priorities?
What *Are* My True Priorities?

I wish there were ten of me, and we could each be doing what we wanted.
—filmmaker George Lucas

Do you, like George Lucas, wish there were ten of you so you could attend to all the priorities you need or want to do? There's only one of us, though, so we need to pick our top priorities and then, to the best of our ability, focus on them.

We do this by reviewing our T.I.M.E. log to see if we're spending the majority of our T.I.M.E. on priorities congruent and consistent with our aim in life. Which begs the question "What is your aim in life?" Have you clarified a mission that directs your days and gives meaning to your existence? Can you say in one sentence what you're trying to achieve with your life?

If you already can, great; skip to the next part. If you can't, reach deep down in your gut and pull out your raison d'être—your reason for being. You may want to write down everything that's important to you, and then shape those priorities into one succinct sentence that captures the essence of what you live for. You'll know you've got it when your mission statement resonates within you and feels just right.

Promise yourself, at your next meal, to take out a notepad and commit ten to twenty minutes to producing this. One man who followed up on this suggestion incredulously reported back that he realized he spent more time figuring out which video he wanted to watch the previous Friday night than he had figuring out what he wanted to do with his life! "I went to lunch by myself the next day and sat there thinking about this. I realized I had lived the first forty years of my life making it up as I went along. I had no plan and had never asked myself what I was trying to achieve past getting a job, getting married, having kids, and doing the best I could. No wonder I was having a midlife crisis. I am going to invest some time thinking what I could do to make the second half of my life more meaningful, instead of leaving things to chance."

Craft your own aim in life or adopt an eloquent quote that articulates what you want to accomplish with your time on earth. You're welcome to use my mission statement—**My purpose is to make a positive difference for as many people as possible while maintaining a happy, healthy lifestyle with friends and family**—if it rings true with you. I spent an hour crafting this years ago and fine-tuned it until I wouldn't change a word. It's as right on now as when I first arrived at it way back when. This life philosophy, typed in bold letters and surrounded by a rainbow border I drew myself, is posted above my desk where I see it dozens of times throughout the day.

Now pick the three most important things in your life. Your health? Partner? Car? Children? Job? Extended family? Friends? Recreation? Church or religion? Home? Money? Hobby? Personal growth? Community? Politics? Sex? Food? Education?

Look back over your time log. What three things do you spend the most T.I.M.E. on? Are they the three most important things in your life? Or, like many people, is how you *actually* spend your time not even close to how you would *ideally* spend your T.I.M.E.?

A man named Scott said, "This exercise was a real eye-opener for me. I picked as my three most important things my family, my health, and my faith. Guess what I spend the most time on? My job, my job, my job. Everything really important to me has been squeezed out of my life. I work sixty hours every week and commute two hours a day. I never have time to relax with my family. I stopped exercising a long time ago and rarely go to church because I simply have too much to do on my only day off. I know I'm leading a life that will lead to regrets, but I don't know what to do about it. I can't quit my job—we need the money."

If I'm Not Focusing on What's Important to Me, How Can I?

> If you board the wrong train, it is no use running along the corridor in the other direction.
> —Dietrich Bonhoeffer

What if, like Scott, your time log and priority analysis show you're on the wrong track? What if you've been running as fast as you can, but realize you're going in the wrong direction? You've heard the saying "We don't want to get to the top of the ladder and realize we're against the wrong wall"? Are you climbing ladders on the wrong walls?

If that's the case, it's time to take yourself off tracks you know in your heart are going the wrong way, and switch to ones that are going the same direction as your heart. A friend recently ended a marriage that was not right for her and moved from Hawaii to the Mainland to join a seminary. She did this even though her Christian friends told her she was committing a sin by divorcing this good man, even though it meant leaving the successful business she had built, even though she's in her late forties, and even though she didn't know a soul in her new city. It took guts for this lady to start all over again from scratch, and she admits it's been scary and lonesome. She also knows in her gut that this is the right thing to do and reports she feels "truly, truly alive" and is experiencing joys she never would have known had she stayed in her safe, secure life.

Maybe you're not in a position to make drastic, wholescale changes to your life. Perhaps you're in a golden handcuffs situation, or have obligations to others that preclude you from living a life of your own. You know you're not spending T.I.M.E. the way you want, but feel you don't have the right, freedom, luxury, or where-withal to ConZentrate on what you really care about. Au contraire.

If you identify one thing in your life you really care about and start partaking in or pursuing that one priority, it can compensate for the other 90 percent of your life that is a compromise. This is great news. You can feel good about yourself and your life if you clarify and then ConZentrate on one truly meaningful person or project. The problem, of course, is how to identify that one thing.

Have you ever played word-association games in which someone asks a question or says a phrase and you respond with the first thing that pops into your mind? It's important not to second-guess your answer, because that censors your from-the-gut response. Your first thought is usually the most honest, and that is what you want. The following exercise can help uncover what you really care about—as long as you write down the first response (and any others that come to mind) regardless of appropriateness. Have a pen or pencil in your hand so you're ready to write as soon as you read the instructions.

INSTRUCTIONS

Write in Square 1 your first response to this question: "What are you doing in your life that you want to?" Are you taking country dance lessons, living near the ocean, taking computer classes, dating someone you like? In other words, what are you doing in your life that's satisfying?

Write in Square 2 your first response to this question: "What are you *not* doing in your life that you want to?" Are you not spending enough time with your family, not exercising, not going back to school to get your degree, not traveling? In other words, what do you wish you were doing that you're not?

Write in Square 3 your first response to this question: "What are you doing in your life that you *don't* want to?" Are you overeating, commuting two hours every day, fighting with your partner? Are you working for someone you dislike, living in a cramped apartment, spending too much time on the Net? In other words, what is happening in your life that you wish wasn't?

Write in Square 4 your first response to this question: "What are you *not* doing in your life that you *don't* want to?" Yes, this is a double negative. It's an important question, though, because it identifies those things you'd rather not do that you are currently keeping out of your life. Perhaps you don't want to do drugs or smoke and you're not; you don't want to live in a crime-ridden neighborhood and you're not; you don't want to work sixty hours a week and you're not.

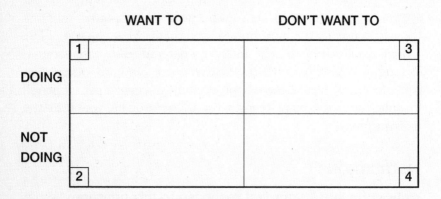

Take a few extra minutes to go back and fill in additional responses as they occur to you until you can't think of anything else you want to say. Initial responses that come out quickest are often the most enlightening, but others can offer additional insight.

When you're finished, look at the answers in Squares 1 and 4. These are the things you're doing that are keeping your life on the right track. Continue them. They are what's right with your life, or they represent behaviors that would get you off track if you indulged in them.

Now, circle the answers in Squares 2 and 3. These are the true priorities in your life that for some reason are being neglected. They represent what's wrong with your life, what's pulling you off track. You need to make T.I.M.E. for at least one of these activities so your life is more of what you want it to be.

Understand it's not selfish for you to ConZentrate on one priority that's congruent with your purpose—it's smart. It's not rude for you to say no to T.I.M.E.-consuming commitments that are not in alignment with your aim in life—it's right. It's not insensitive to change tracks when you know in your heart, mind, and soul you're going in the wrong direction—it's imperative that you do.

How Can I Have the Courage of My ConZentration Convictions?

Few is the number who think with their own minds and feel with their own hearts.
—**Albert Einstein**

Please review your time log again. How much of your time is spent serving other people and fulfilling obligations? How much time is spent doing things you have (versus want) to do? If you're like most people, you may spend anywhere from 60 to 90 percent of your time putting other people's priorities before your own.

Wouldn't you agree it's fair to identify one thing *you* really care about, and for you to get actively involved in doing or pursuing that? As Oscar Wilde said, "Selfishness is not living as one wishes to live, it is always asking others to live as one wishes to live."

What is one thing you'd love to do *just for yourself*? Look over your answers in Squares 2 and 3. What is something not currently in your life you wish was? What is something you used to enjoy, but haven't had time for lately? What is something you've always wanted to try, but other people said it was silly and you let them talk you out of it?

You owe it to yourself to bring that one thing that calls to you into your life. Maybe you used to be a great dancer who loved moving joyfully and creatively. Perhaps you used to enjoy trying new recipes, but have had to satisfy yourself with takeout for the last few months because you've been so busy. You might have dropped your social life because you're a single parent and all your attention has been focused on your kids.

Your future is a phone call away. Promise yourself that you will pick up the phone *today* and call some individual or organization to reactivate this interest. Call the dance studio and sign yourself up for an eight-week class. Set aside Saturday nights as gourmet night and experiment with a new recipe each week. Let your kids know you are a person in your own right with your own needs and that you are going out with your friends on Friday night.

Don't wait. Do it right now. Once you set the wheels in motion, once you get involved in this activity that makes your soul sing, you'll thank yourself for getting your life back on track.

One man said, "I grew up playing just about every sport our school offered. Being an athlete was my identity and I derived a lot of pleasure from being physically fit. Then I got married, had three children. My wife died in an automobile accident when the kids were eleven, fourteen, and sixteen. I couldn't take care of them myself and work fifty hours a week, so I moved back home to Minnesota so my mom and dad could help raise my three sons. I ended up working two jobs to put the kids through college . . . and got fat. They're all out on their own now . . . but I'm still fat."

He continued: "When I did that word-association exercise, everything I wrote down in Squares 2 and 3 had to do with weight. What I was doing that I didn't want was eat everything in sight. What I wasn't doing that I wanted was exercise and meet women— neither of which I was doing because I'm so overweight. You read us a quote by John Foster Dulles: 'The mark of a successful organization isn't whether it has problems, it's whether it has the *same* problems it had last year.' Well, I've had this problem for ten years now, and I figured it was time for me to do something about it."

He went on: "Our local shopping mall has a walking club that meets three days a week. This was perfect for me because it's free, it's inside (we have long, cold winters), it's in the morning, so I can get in my walk and still get to work on time, it's not too strenuous, so I can get back into shape without killing myself, and I'm *meeting women!* We walk around the inside of the mall ten times, which is about a three-mile walk. That takes about fifty-five minutes, and we talk the whole way. I'd known about this group for years but had never done anything about it. The afternoon of your workshop, I called to get information and showed up that following Monday ready to go. It's been the best thing I've done for myself in years."

What action could you take that would be the best thing you've done for yourself in years? There's a saying in the South, " 'Mean to' don't pick no cotton." Don't just mean to make that phone call. Put this book down, get up from your chair, and make it right now. Or if you're reading this in bed or someplace that doesn't have a phone nearby, write yourself a note of whom you intend to call and place it on your mirror or in your calendar, so you'll call first thing the next day.

As St. John Perse said, "The only menace is inertia." Move yourself out of inertia by taking action on one activity that's more congruent with your purpose by the end of this week. Call that gym and show up for that tae bo workout, place that personals ad in the local paper, set aside Sunday for some R&R with someone you love. You'll immediately feel an increase in your energy and your mind will say, "Now this is more like it!"

Think for Yourself

> It is necessary to the happiness of man that he be mentally
> faithful to himself.
> **—Thomas Paine**

"You make this sound so simple and straightforward," said one woman. "It's not that easy. I've got a lot of people counting on me. I can't just tell them, 'Sorry, I'm off to do my own thing.' "

Please understand I'm not suggesting we abandon *all* our responsibilities and think only of what we want. It's just that many of us live with the opposite extreme. We put everyone else's priorities first and end up with a life that is not our own. I'm simply proposing we balance our life's activities more evenly . . . that we start honoring *our* needs at least as much as we honor others', and that we spend at least *some* of our T.I.M.E. on activities that are impor-tant to us.

The woman came back with, "What am I supposed to do when what I want conflicts with what others want?"

We remember we have the right to be our own person and to **think for ourselves**. In my research, I have found numerous quotes that describe the importance of being true to ourselves. William James said, "Seek out the particular mental attitude which makes you feel most deeply and vitally alive, along with which comes the inner voice which says, 'This is the real me,' and when you have found that attitude, follow it." Robert Louis Stevenson said, "To know what you prefer, instead of humbly saying 'Amen' to what the world tells you you ought to prefer, is to keep your soul alive." Seneca said, "What does reason demand of a man? A very easy thing—to live in accord with his own nature." And of course, William Shakespeare said, "This above all: to thine own self be true."

What is your own self? Philosopher Jean Houston describes a concept called entelechy, which is from a Greek word meaning "the dynamic, purposeful unfolding of what we are." "Entelechy is that which propels us to actualize our essence," Houston explains. "It is the entelechy of an acorn to be an oak tree; the entelechy of a baby to be a grown-up human being."

What did you want to be when you grew up? What is it you feel you were born to do? What are you gifted at? What unique ability do you have? Are you actively involved in that, or have you let oth-ers talk you out of it? Have you been pressured, coerced, or intimi-dated into giving up your passion? Thomas Wolfe said, "If a man has a talent and cannot use it, he has failed. If he has a talent and uses only half of it, he has partly failed. If he has a talent and learns somehow to use the whole of it, he has gloriously succeeded, and won a satisfaction and a triumph few men ever know."

A seminar participant told me he came from a long line of doc-tors. His father, grandfather, and great-grandfather had all been physicians. Guess what he was supposed to become? From the time he first set foot in school, he was expected to follow in his forefa-thers' footsteps. The problem was, he didn't want to go into medi-cine. He loved to act. He'd been involved in his high school and college drama clubs, and it was all he ever wanted to do.

This was *not* what his parents had in mind for him. They patiently explained he could do theater as a hobby, but there was no future in it. Acting simply was not a noble or practical career choice.

The time finally came when he had to decide whether to please his parents or please himself. He needed to answer the age-old question "Whose life is it anyway?" He chose to become an actor, even though it disappointed his parents, who denounced it as a frivolous lifestyle they wouldn't support. "It wasn't easy going against their wishes," he said. "At first I felt I had let them down. And in those beginning years when I went from one audition to the next and worked as a cook to pay the bills, they wasted no opportunity to tell me, 'I told you so.'

"Ironically, I ended up being a chef, not an actor. I apprenticed under a renowned chef and found I had a talent for it. I now make a very good living (in a job that I love), working in one of our city's fine restaurants. I've never once regretted not going into medicine. It just wasn't me."

Are you leading a life that isn't you? What is one thing you really care about that you could bring into your life? What is your love, gift, vision, talent, or dream? Even if the significant people in your life don't care for this particular priority, you owe it to yourself to balance your existence so you're serving your needs and spending T.I.M.E. on one thing you love and do well. It may be frightening to speak and act on your truth, but it would be more frightening not to.

◎

Action Plan 33. Are You Having the T.I.M.E. of Your Life?

The road to happiness lies in two simple principles: find what interests you and that you can do well, and put your whole soul into it—every bit of energy and ambition and natural ability you have.

—John D. Rockefeller III

Are you ConZentrating on what interests you? Are you taking advantage of your natural abilities and doing what makes your soul sing? Or have you been too busy and overwhelmed with obligations to do what you do well? Remember what Anne Morrow Lindbergh observed: "Too many demands, too much to do; competent, busy, hurrying people—it just isn't living at all."

Vow to make T.I.M.E. *this week* for at least one activity that makes you happy and that is congruent with your raison d'être. Philosophers are of two minds about the future. Charles F. Kettering said, "My interest is in the future because I am going to spend the rest of my life there." Albert Einstein said, "I never think of the future. It comes soon enough." I believe the best approach is a combination of both. Spend your T.I.M.E. on the right thinks, ConZentrate on your true priorities, and your future will take care of itself.

Confusion	ConZentration
Don't know how spending T.I.M.E. "Time log? You've got to be kidding. I'm too busy as it is. Forget it."	*Know how spending T.I.M.E.* "I'd rather spend a couple of hours finding out how I'm actually filling my days and nights."
Unclear about raison d'être "I'm just trying to hang in there until I can retire. Then I'll have the time and money to do what I want."	*Clear about raison d'être* "I want to live a life that matters, and leave a legacy of integrity for my children and community."
Doing what don't want "Why did I ever agree to head up this fundraising committee? It's taking up all my time."	*Doing what want* "I'm going to recruit some other volunteers so this committee isn't taking up all my free time."
Not doing what want "I really want to start my own business. I'm tired of working for other people."	*Not doing what don't want* "Well, I'm not going to go in debt. It took me five years to pay off those credit card bills as it is."
ConZentrate on others' priorities "Ted asked me to join our company bowling team. I'll have to turn him down because I've got to take the kids to hockey practice on Thursdays."	*ConZentrate on one true priority* "I'm going to tell Ted yes, and then arrange with one of the other parents to get the kids to and from hockey on Thursdays."

WAY 34

◉

Common Zense

In every childhood, there is a moment when a door opens and lets the future in.

—Graham Greene

I hope this book opens the door to a better future for you. The following C.O.N.Z.E.N.T.R.A.T.I.O.N. acrostic can help us make wise choices about how to put our mind to work for us at work, home, in relationships, school, sports, and hobbies.

"There's only one corner of the universe you can be certain of improving," observed Aldous Huxley, "and that's your own self." These suggestions (what one student cleverly referred to as the Cliffs Notes of ConZentration) summarize specific steps we can take to improve our ability to focus anytime, anywhere.

C = Create a fun H.O.U.S.E. Make home your castle, not your hassle. As Joni Mitchell expressed it, "My special place. I put things back together there. It all falls right in place—in my special space." Honor the ConZentration Catch-22 principle and simplify, simplify. S.T.U.F.F those possessions so you're not weighed down by having to take care of acquisitions that create mental and physical clutter. Establish your own private Utah so home is a place to rest your head, not hang it.

O = Organize your office. Victor Hugo suggested, "He who every morning plans the transaction of the day and follows out that plan, carries a thread that will guide him through the maze of the most busy life. But where no plan is laid, where the disposal of time is surrendered merely to the chance of incidence, chaos will soon reign." Use ergonomics so your surroundings support rather than sabotage your work efforts. Keep a master list and a to-do-today list to keep chaos at bay, and practice Tactful Termination and Diplomatic Deflection to avoid ConZentration Interruptus.

N = No worrying. Winston Churchill advised, "Let our advance worrying become advance thinking and planning." Worrying is mentally burning our bridges before we come to them. We want to build bridges to our desired (versus dreaded) performance by rehearsing what we *want* to happen, not what we don't. We can R.E.S.T. assured if we make an effort to B.E.A.T. the blues, keep our C.O.O.L., and throw ourselves mental lifesavers so we can keep it all together when our world's falling apart.

Z = Zen consciousness. On his seventieth birthday, Fred Rogers, host of TV's *Mister Rogers' Neighborhood*, was asked by a reporter how he felt. He said, "I've never made much of a fuss over big things, like birthdays or milestones. I'd much rather focus on the little moments, the quiet times, the simple things of life. When people ask, 'What's next?' I always say, '*This* is next.'" Wise man. This *is* next. Vow to focus on the little moments and the simple things of life and you can be here and now. Know that rushing and hurrying are mutually exclusive with contentment. Joseph Campbell said, "Eternity has nothing to do with the hereafter . . . this is it . . . if you don't get it here, you won't get it anywhere." Calm to your senses and *see* your surroundings so you experience life as Katherine Mansfield described it: "It was one of those days so clear, so silent, so still, you almost feel the earth itself has stopped in astonishment as its own beauty."

E = Energize yourself. Overcome "vigor mortis" and motivate yourself to pay attention—even when you would rather not—

with the Godfather Approach, Face the Music Philosophy, and with reasonable G.O.A.L. lines that encourage, not discourage, you. Lucille Ball once quipped that she got up at the crack of noon. A friend has her own variation of that quip. She claims her husband gets up at the "crank" of dawn. Get up and get going—whether you feel like it or not—with the Five-Minute Rule and by trying a little A.R.D.O.R.

N = No mental flabbiness. Joe DiMaggio said, "If I knew I was going to live this long, I would have taken better care of myself." Instead of waiting until it's too late, honor and appreciate your health by taking care of your brain and body now with the F.I.T.N.E.S.S. steps. Stay intellectually active, get some z's, give your mind nutritious food for thought, and talk nice.

T = T.I.M.E. of your life. "The days come and go," noted Ralph Waldo Emerson. "If we do not use the gifts they bring, they carry them silently away." Vow to ConZentrate on at least one of your true priorities *now*, not someday. Resolve to unwrap and take full advantage of your talents and the gift of today by focusing on people and projects that are in alignment with your true values, so every day is T.I.M.E. well spent.

R = Replace, reframe, remove troublesome thoughts with images and ideas that contribute to versus compromise your productivity and peace of mind. Ursula K. LeGuin reminds us, "To oppose something is to maintain it." ConZentrate on proactive, not reactive, thoughts. Instead of opposing harmful images and ideas by trying not to dwell on them, fill your mind with hoped-for outcomes.

A = ADDitude. Use systems so you can turn an alert, active mind into an asset. Baseball player Lenny Dykstra once boasted, "I'm in the best shape of my life, and that includes my brain." Resolve to shape, not shame, your behavior by choosing to work *through* frustration. Take steps to stay O.N. T.A.S.K. If you have an "If it's not one think, it's another" brain, remind yourself of what you need to do with checklists and "same time, same place" rituals. Mind your manners so you can be suitably sociable.

T = Train your brain.   Use Focus Pocus, Hold That Thought, and the Five-Minute F.O.C.U.S. exercise to learn how to ConZentrate on Command. There is a Tibetan saying: "If you want to know your future, look at what you are doing in this moment." If you want to know your future, look at what you're *thinking* this moment. Teach your mind to mind so it pays attention to what you want, when you want, for as long as you want.

I = Immerse yourself in the flow.   Ralph Waldo Emerson said, "A man should learn to watch that gleam of light which flashes across his mind from within." Lose yourself in timeless Con-Zonetration by picturing exactly how you want to play and by developing a W.I.N.N.E.R.'s mentality. Use ritualized routines to trigger the trance-like state where you're playing out of your head. Learn to honor the gleam of light from within so you access and sustain peak performance.

0 = On purpose.   "The secret of success," thought Benjamin Dis-raeli, "is constancy to purpose." Throughout the day reclarify your purpose and check to see if you're focusing on the right thinks. Practice mental triage in your professional and personal life to make sure you're getting the biggest bang for your ConZentration buck. Focus on the 20 percent, the vital few, so you pay attention to the highest-payoff priorities at work and at home.

N= New Learning.   Henry Miller said, "If faced with an open mind, every moment is a golden one for him who has the vision to recognize it as such." Adopt a beginner's brain and seek new knowledge. "Dare to be naive," as Buckminster Fuller sug-gested. Use the S.T.U.D.Y. techniques to become a lifelong learner and commit to expanding your mental capacity by using the brain you've been blessed with.

How about one last quote from the great Yogi Berra? Yogi was once asked if first baseman Don Mattingly had exceeded his expectations that season. Berra, an ever-flowing fount of malapropisms, said, "I'd say he's done more than that."

I hope this book has more than exceeded your expectations. I hope it's given you the motivation and information you need to manage your mind and make the most of your T.I.M.E. And I hope that putting these ideas into practice helps you exceed your own expectations in terms of improved effectiveness and quality of life.

Action Plan 34. Common Zense

Let us, then, be up and doing . . .

—Henry Wadsworth Longfellow

"Every exit is an entry somewhere else," noted Tom Stoppard. I exit with the wish that ConZentration serves as your entrance to a more productive and satisfying life. George Washington said, "Labor to keep alive in your breast that little spark of celestial fire, conscience." I hope you labor to keep alive in your mind the sparks of cerebral fire, ConZentration, and that your improved ability to focus and maintain attention—no matter what—will serve you all your days.

Postscript

◉

Have you developed your own ways to focus and mantain attention—no matter what? Did one of these ideas improve your effectiveness and you'd like to share your story with others so they can benefit too? Is there a ConZentration conundrum I forgot to address?

As you can tell, I like to illustrate points with real-life anecdotes so you can see how to use these ideas in your day-to-day situations. I'd love to include your tip or testimonial in my upcoming books and seminars. I know you're busy, so I've made it easy to get in touch. You are welcome to e-mail your questions or comments to info@samhorn.com. My sister, Cheri (who runs my business Action Seminars), or I will get back to you quickly with a reply and a thank-you.

Did you like the quotes in this book? You can order the companion calendar "Common Zense" (complete with 365 thought-provoking quotes), along with my other books and tapes at our website: www.samhorn.com/books/tonguefu.

Are you interested in training your employees in these ConZentration techniques? Would you like a fun and fascinating keynote for your next conference? I'd love to have a chance to present ConZentration or Tongue Fu! to your group. Call 805-528-4351 for rates, availability, a demo video, and a complete media packet. I would gladly tailor my talk so we cover practical ideas your participants can put into practice immediately at work and at home.

Sam Horn, Action Seminars
Attn. Cheri Grimm
P.O. Box 6810
Los Osos, CA 93412

Phone 805-528-4351
Fax: 805-528-2581
E-mail: info@samhorn.com
Website: www.samhorn.com/books/tonguefu